Child and Adolescent Suicidal Behavior

The Guilford Practical Intervention in the Schools Series

Kenneth W. Merrell, Series Editor

This series presents the most reader-friendly resources available in key areas of evidence-based practice in school settings. Practitioners will find trustworthy guides on effective behavioral, mental health, and academic interventions, and assessment and measurement approaches. Covering all aspects of planning, implementing, and evaluating high-quality services for students, books in the series are carefully crafted for everyday utility. Features include ready-to-use reproducibles, lay-flat binding to facilitate photocopying, appealing visual elements, and an oversized format.

Recent Volumes

Child and Adolescent Suicidal Behavior

School-Based Prevention, Assessment, and Intervention

DAVID N. MILLER

Foreword by Alan L. Berman

THE GUILFORD PRESS
New York   London

© 2011 The Guilford Press
A Division of Guilford Publications, Inc.
72 Spring Street, New York, NY 10012
www.guilford.com

Printed in Canada

This book is printed on acid-free paper.

Last digit is print number: 9   8   7   6   5   4   3   2   1

The authors have checked with sources believed to be reliable in their efforts to provide information that is complete and generally in accord with the standards of practice that are accepted at the time of publication. However, in view of the possibility of human error or changes in behavioral, mental health, or medical sciences, neither the authors, nor the editor and publisher, nor any other party who has been involved in the preparation or publication of this work warrants that the information contained herein is in every respect accurate or complete, and they are not responsible for any errors or omissions or the results obtained from the use of such information. Readers are encouraged to confirm the information contained in this book with other sources.

Library of Congress Cataloging-in-Publication Data

Miller, David Neil, 1963–
    Child and adolescent suicidal behavior : school-based prevention, assessment, and intervention / David N. Miller.
        p. cm.–(The Guilford practical interventions in the schools series)
    Includes bibliographical references and index.
    ISBN 978-1-60623-996-4 (pbk.)
    1. Students—Suicidal behavior.   2. Teenagers—Suicidal behavior.   3. Suicide— Prevention.   4. Educational counseling.   5. School psychology.   I. Title.
    HV6545.8.M55   2011
    371.7′13—dc22
                                                                    2010024960

Mixed Sources
Product group from well-managed forests, and other controlled sources
www.fsc.org Cert no. SW-COC-002358
© 1996 Forest Stewardship Council
FSC

To my dad, Donald A. Miller—devoted husband, loving father, diehard Yankee fan, and lifelong resident of Johnson City, New York—with gratitude, affection, and love. A member of the 299th Engineer Combat Battalion during World War II, at age 20 he believed he would die in the Ardennes forests of Europe fighting the Nazis in the Battle of the Bulge—the single largest and deadliest battle in U.S. history. But he survived both the battle and the war, and in 2009 celebrated his 85th birthday surrounded by family and friends. A man of exceptional character and uncommon decency, there is no one for whom I have greater respect or admiration. I am proud to be his son.

—D. N. M.

About the Author

David N. Miller, PhD, is Associate Professor of School Psychology at the University at Albany, State University of New York, where he has served as Director of the School Psychology Program. He is a certified school psychologist and has extensive experience working with children and adolescents exhibiting suicidal behavior, as well as other emotional and behavioral problems, in both public and alternative school settings. Dr. Miller is senior author of the book *Identifying, Assessing, and Treating Self-Injury at School*; is the author of several journal articles and book chapters; and serves on the editorial advisory boards of several professional journals. His primary research and clinical interest is suicidal behavior and related internalizing problems in children and adolescents, particularly issues in school-based suicide prevention.

Foreword

Foreword. An odd word, it seems to me. My dictionary defines it as "prefatory remarks." Just why does a book need prefatory remarks? You bought this book, or perhaps you are reading this in consideration of buying this book, not because of what I am about to write, but because the book's content speaks to you in some meaningful way. I understand that a foreword is meant as an introduction of the author and his work to you, his intended audience. So, my role in writing these remarks is to serve as sort of an emcee at a dinner meeting at which David N. Miller is about to give a keynote address—in this case, a rather long and significant one that you will be able to archive on your bookshelf and take down to review, study, and learn from whenever you are hungry for the fabulous brain food that it is.

Let me be honest with you. David asked me to write this foreword. That's as it should be (and this, indeed, is the way these things are done). David is a friend and a colleague whom I admire greatly—you don't ask someone who doesn't know and respect you to introduce you. Being asked to do this unquestionably is an honor, mostly because it aligns me with him and with this most significant piece of scholarship, meaning my name will be in this book for as long as it sits on your bookshelf! Moreover, it is an honor because he asked me to write this, not any of his other friends and colleagues. So, at the very least, he believes that my (vs. someone else's) writing the foreword to his book adds value to this work. How did I get to matter this much?

I have to believe it is because I have paid my dues as a suicidologist for almost 40 years and as a research clinician with a focus on adolescent suicide for 30 of those years—so, as you might surmise, I am older than David. No less, I am senior author of a text on adolescent suicide that David repeatedly references in this volume (thanks, David). But therein lies the rub. Is this not a potential conflict for me? By introducing and praising this book, am I not giving weight to a publication that competes with my own? My meager annual royalties are at stake here, right?

Not in the least.

I could not be more welcoming of this volume and what it adds to the other resources already available. Five years have passed since I and my coauthors published the second edition of our work and, in that time, hundreds, perhaps thousands, of new research studies have been published, prevention efforts piloted and catalogued as evidence-based or best practices, and clinical interventions tested in real-world settings. I welcome and laud this addition to the field and, even more so, because it is addressed to school-based professionals who are best situated to save lives of children at risk.

If we want to prevent the tragic premature loss of life caused by youth suicide and the traumatic impact these events have on those directly affected, we have to better detect those at risk before they turn self-destructive thoughts into acts. Moreover, if we can better identify them, we have to foster their alliance with caregivers and supports that will help reduce their risk and, we hope, redirect their lives toward meaning and purpose. This can best be accomplished by finding them and, for the most part, this means at school or in front of a television or computer screen. The latter opportunities do not allow for direct visual observation and immediate human interaction, so it simply makes great sense to offer school personnel the understanding and tools needed to reach these goals.

David N. Miller is an accomplished school psychologist who has written a must-have book for school personnel on a subject lived with and confronted daily by them. School-based mental health professionals, administrators, teachers, and staff need all the help, direction, and practical advice they can get about how to deal with the potential for a school-based suicide, suicide attempt, or threat, and the reality that they will have to deal with the consequences of these events in their schools. If your school has not yet had to deal with the impact of a suicide of one of its students, you have my guarantee that it will, and after the event is not the time to prepare for just such an occurrence. If your school has not yet crafted a school-based prevention program, you most definitely need to, and you should do this with an understanding of what is known that is likely to be effective. If your school wants to minimize the likelihood that a lawsuit is initiated against you and others at your school because you buried your collective heads in the sands of denial, believing that suicide would not happen in your school, when it surely will, this volume is essential reading to accomplish that purpose. If your school has already addressed the prospect of youth suicide in one or another way, this book will help you refine your policies and procedures with the help of a skilled consultant. Dr. Miller knows his subject and he knows his audience. Without a doubt, he has delivered a rich and needed tool for you and your colleagues.

As emcee for this effort, I urge you to digest and savor what you are about to read. David has done a terrific job translating what is known into what needs to be implemented, and he has given you, the reader, an essential guide to use the tools to do that.

I could not be more proud or honored to have been asked to make this introduction. Ladies and gentlemen . . .

ALAN L. BERMAN, PhD, ABPP
Executive Director, American Association of Suicidology
President, International Association for Suicide Prevention

Preface

There is no tragedy in life like the death of a child.
—Dwight D. Eisenhower

Surviving the death of a dear one is to endure great pain. Surviving a *suicidal* death is to compound that pain with such embarrassments as public ridicule and private humiliation, and often exaggerated feelings of guilt and anger.
—Iris Bolton

Suicide is a whispered word, inappropriate for polite company. Family and friends often pretend they do not hear the word's dread sound even when it is uttered. For suicide is a taboo subject that stigmatizes not only the victim but the survivors as well.
—Earl A. Grollman

The quote above by Dwight Eisenhower, Supreme Commander of the Allied forces in Europe during World War II and later the 34th President of the United States, reminds us that there are few if any more tragic events in life than the death of a child. Eisenhower and his wife were well acquainted with such tragedy; their first-born son died from scarlet fever at age 3. Every year for nearly half a century thereafter, until his own death in 1969, Eisenhower would send his wife a bouquet of flowers on the anniversary of their son's birth—a somber reminder of their irreplaceable loss (Ambrose, 1990).

Like Eisenhower, countless others throughout history have had to endure the death of a son, daughter, family member, or friend. Although an individual's death at any age arouses emotions such as sadness and grief, when children or adolescents die it is particularly tragic because of the brevity of their lives and the frequent suddenness of their deaths. The emotional devastation experienced by the family and friends of the deceased is often accompanied by anguished thoughts of lost possibilities and wasted potential; a life is extinguished before it has the chance to fully bloom.

The premature ending of a young life is made even more difficult when a child or an adolescent dies by suicide. Suicide is generally regarded as the most shocking cause of death among young people, as well as the most inexplicable. Because it is not well understood, youth suicide often results in misguided fears, myths, and misunderstandings. Iris Bolton, a counselor whose teenage son died by suicide, has described how the heartbreak and anguish experienced by surviving family members of a suicide victim are often exacerbated by other highly aversive, intense, and conflicting emotions, including guilt (which often occurs if people perceive themselves as being somehow responsible for not preventing the suicide) and anger (at themselves, at others, and even at the suicide victim, which then reinforces feelings of guilt).

Parents of a child or an adolescent who dies by suicide are often especially overwhelmed with grief and despair (Linn-Gust, 2010). Although no single person or event is to "blame" for suicide, these parents are frequently haunted and guilt-ridden by a sense of having failed their child at a critical time, of being insensitive to the extent of their child's pain, or of overlooking important clues of suicidal behavior (Jamison, 1999). Joiner (2010) has also noted that people are often "stunned by many things following their loss, including the profound change in their address books—once trusted friends fall out of the book after ignoring a loved one's suicide, or after saying hurtful and appallingly glib things like 'It was God's will'" (p. 3).

The emotional suffering experienced by surviving family members and friends is certainly understandable, but what are we to make of Bolton's contention in the quote above that the death of a loved one by suicide also causes feelings of "embarrassment," including "public ridicule" and "private humiliation"? The reason clearly seems to be that although suicide often arouses public sympathy, it also arouses public stigma. According to Joiner (2010), whose theory of why people die by suicide is discussed in Chapter 1 of this book, "stigma combines fear with disgust, contempt, and lack of compassion, all of which flow from ignorance" (p. 272).

The stigma associated with suicide needs to change if effective suicide prevention on a national and international level is to occur. Changing the *fear* associated with suicide, however, is not something that needs changing. As Joiner (2010) has pointed out, "suicide is very fearsome and intimidating, and it is right and natural that it should remain so" (p. 272). The fear of suicide, and death generally, clearly prevents some people from attempting suicide and therefore serves a positive function for society. The *stigma* associated with suicide, however, is another matter. Having occurred for centuries (Minois, 1999), the stigmatization of suicide is certainly not a new development (Alvarez, 1971; Colt, 2006). In fact, suicide may well be the most stigmatized of all human behaviors (Joiner, 2010), as well as one of the last major societal taboos (Grollman, 1988).

Why are people who die by suicide so highly stigmatized? The answer to this question is complex, but in part reflects evidence that individuals who are believed by others to play a greater role in their condition are stigmatized to a greater degree than people who are perceived as being victims of circumstances beyond their control (Joiner, Van Orden, Witte, & Rudd, 2009). For example, the extent to which individuals believe that people who are alcoholics or who are overweight are responsible for their condition predicts more hostile attitudes toward those groups (Joiner et al., 2009). Suicide, like alcoholism and obesity, has been linked to both environmental and genetic causes, indicating that personal "choice" in such matters is clearly limited. Despite this fact, it appears that for many people suicide represents "an extreme case of personal responsibility" (Joiner et al., 2009, p. 168), in the sense that it is widely perceived as being a decision fully within an individual's control. Unfortunately, the inaccuracy of this perception has not reduced its pervasiveness. Consequently, suicide remains a problem "in which too many of us still tend to blame the victims" (Satcher, 1998, p. 326).

The stigma associated with suicide affects not only victims and their families but also entire communities. For example, former U.S. Surgeon General David Satcher (1998) described a rash of youth suicides that occurred during the late 1990s in a small town in an upper Midwestern state. The town, which had a population of about 3,000 at the time, experienced 11 suicides in a 3-year period—a rate of about 13 times what would normally be expected. All 11 suicide victims were between the ages of 13 and 23, and 8 of them were teenagers. The victims' obituaries often used the euphemism "died at home" and made little or no mention of suicide. Furthermore, a parent of one of the suicide victims reported that she had to dispel "gasping" behind her back about what was "wrong at home" that presumably led to her son's suicide.

When concerned citizens tried to hold open discussions about the rash of youth suicides at the local high school, they met resistance from parents who erroneously believed that talking about suicide would only romanticize or encourage it among other students—a belief that is not only inaccurate but also one that clearly undermined prevention efforts. The broader community effect produced by the stigmatization of suicide became further evident when it was revealed that if an individual from the town was suicidal and called 911 for assistance, he or she would be placed in a jail cell until an assessment could be conducted by a mental health professional, who often had to travel over 200 miles to complete the evaluation.

The community reaction to suicide in this case was not an unusual or isolated one, and as Satcher (1998) states, "could just as easily have been found in countless places around the country" (p. 326). In fact, the stigma associated with suicide is so prevalent that it has led many families of youth suicide victims to make appeals to physicians to indicate that their son's or daughter's death was due to some other cause (e.g., an accident) on the victim's death certificate (Nuland, 1993), the implication being that *any* cause of death would be preferable to suicide. Joiner (2010) even refers to a chief medical examiner who stated that he never records a youth's death as a suicide, even if the evidence clearly indicates that is the case, because he does not want to "stigmatize" the parents.

Joiner (2010) also recounted an anecdote that occurred in Oklahoma in 2007 involving the family of a young woman who had died from a gunshot wound to the head. It was not clear whether the wound was self-inflicted, but the woman's family was determined to prove that it was not the result of suicide and to have an insurance company pay death benefits. A judge decided that the insurance company did not adequately demonstrate that the cause of death was suicide, and ordered the company to pay the family. The family's lawyer was quoted as saying that "it wasn't about the money" but was rather "about clearing the daughter's name of the stigma of having committed suicide" (quoted in Joiner, 2010, p. 49). What is perhaps most interesting about this quote is the lawyer's apparent belief that it was more important to clear the daughter (and, by association, the family) from the "stigma" of suicide than it was to catch her presumed killer (Joiner, 2010).

Because of the stigma associated with it, suicide is clearly a topic that causes a great deal of discomfort for many if not most people. According to Satcher (1998), who made suicide awareness a major public health priority of his administration, suicide is a topic we as a society "do not like to talk about" (p. 326). The writer Andrew Solomon (2001), whose mother died by suicide and who has experienced his own bouts of suicidal depression, made a similar observation when he described suicide as "a vast public health crisis that makes us so uncomfortable that we divert our eyes from it" (p. 248). Unfortunately, as with most other problems in life, diverting our attention from the problem of suicide will not make it go away.

The idea of having frank and candid conversations about suicide is distressing to many people, and the topic of youth suicide seems to make people particularly uneasy. Because openly discussing and confronting the issue of youth suicidal behavior makes many people highly uncomfortable and therefore avoidant, we are not as effective as we could be in preventing it. Fortunately, this situation can be rectified, and school personnel can be an important part of the solution to this problem. This book is designed to assist school personnel in that process.

PURPOSE AND OUTLINE OF THE BOOK

The purpose of this book is to provide school personnel, including school-based mental health professionals (e.g., school psychologists, counselors, and social workers) as well as other school-based practitioners (e.g., administrators, teachers, nurses, support staff), with useful and practical information regarding suicidal behavior in children and adolescents and its effective school-based prevention, assessment, and intervention. Chapter 1 provides a broad overview of youth suicidal behavior, defining what is meant by this term and placing it in an appropriate context. Topics covered in this chapter include a review of the demographic data on youth suicidal behavior, as well as information regarding age, gender, ethnicity, geography, and other variables that may influence it. Also discussed in this chapter are when, where, and how youth suicide most often occurs. Some possible reasons why young people die by suicide are also provided, with a particular emphasis on the interpersonal–psychological theory of suicidal behavior, which has growing empirical support as well as direct implications for school-based prevention, assessment, and intervention.

Chapter 2 provides an introduction to school-based suicide prevention, including a review of the effectiveness of these programs, what we know works well and what does not, the recommended components of effective and comprehensive school-based programs, the reasons schools should be involved in youth suicide prevention, liability and ethical issues in school-based suicide prevention, and the roles and responsibilities of school personnel—particularly school-based mental health professionals—in suicide prevention efforts. Chapter 3 reviews the many advantages of taking a public health approach to youth suicide prevention. This chapter also reviews the effectiveness of various community-based suicide prevention programs, such as means-restriction methods, telephone hotlines, and public education. Information is also provided here about how a public health approach to suicide prevention can be used effectively in schools.

Chapter 4 provides information on how to develop school-based universal prevention programs designed for all students in a particular school or district. Chapter 5 discusses issues and procedures for identifying students who may be at risk or at high risk for suicide, and how to effectively link assessment information to the development of appropriate interventions. Chapter 6 describes selected interventions for students who are at risk for suicide, as well as tertiary and crisis interventions for high-risk students and those students experiencing a suicidal crisis in school.

Chapter 7 deals with the issue of postvention—that is, procedures school personnel should implement if and when a student dies by suicide, including how to effectively respond to and meet the needs of students, school staff, and the media. Postvention procedures may also include those situations in which a student returns to school after exhibiting suicidal behavior, such as making a suicide attempt and being subsequently hospitalized. A brief epilogue presents overall conclusions as well as some final thoughts on school-based suicide prevention, assessment, and intervention. Finally, two appendices are included at the end of the book. The first appendix provides interested readers with a summary of student suicide case law in public schools, authored by two national experts on this topic. The second appendix lists recommended resources, including useful websites, books, and training programs for school personnel interested in further enhancing their knowledge and skills in the area of school-based suicide prevention, assessment, and intervention.

WHY SCHOOL PRACTITIONERS SHOULD READ THIS BOOK

Because youth suicide is such an incredibly tragic, sad, and emotionally overwhelming topic, some might wonder why anyone would want to read about it. Isn't it too morbid a subject? I can think of no better response to this question than one supplied by Joiner (2010), who said, "There's nothing morbid about working to prevent an agonizing cause of death and a massive public health problem" (p. 269). A similar notion is expressed in a different way by an inscription above the door of the Anatomical Institute in Vienna, Austria, where autopsies are performed: *Hic locus est ubi mors gaudet succurrere vitae*, or "This is the place where death rejoices in helping the living" (quoted in Shneidman, 2004). I would add that although death is a natural and an inevitable part of life, death by suicide is neither natural nor inevitable. By enhancing their knowledge and understanding of youth suicidal behavior, as well as how to more effectively prevent, assess, and respond to it, school personnel can help decrease its occurrence.

It is my hope that this book, at least in some small way, can shed some light on the dark topic of suicidal behavior in children and adolescents, and consequently reduce some of the misunderstanding regarding it as well as the stigma experienced by suicidal youth and their families. Most important, I hope it can be a useful and practical resource to professionals working in our nation's schools. The ultimate purpose of school-based suicide prevention, assessment, and intervention is to save young lives. The purpose of this book is to provide school-based practitioners with a better understanding of how to more effectively accomplish that goal.

ACKNOWLEDGMENTS

No author writes a book alone, and this book is no exception. I owe debts of gratitude to many people, beginning with Kristin Miller of Siena College. In addition to being an outstanding college instructor, expert consultant, and the single best example I know of a true scientist-practitioner, she is also my spouse, my best friend, and the love of my life. Kris provided unwavering encouragement and support throughout the writing of this book, as well as ideas and resources that were critical in its development and execution; my debt to her is more than I have the ability to express. I would also like to acknowledge Richard Fossey of the University of North Texas and Perry Zirkel of Leigh University, nationally recognized experts on the liability of educational institutions for student suicides, for authoring Appendix A (Student Suicide Case Law in Public Schools). I am especially grateful to Kenneth W. Merrell, Professor of School Psychology at the University of Oregon and Editor of The Guilford Practical Intervention in the Schools Series; Guilford Editor Natalie Graham; and Guilford Senior Editor Craig Thomas for their encouragement, assistance, patience, and support in moving this project forward. To have this book published by Guilford, and to have it included in their Practical Intervention in the Schools Series, is an honor and one of the highlights of my career.

I would be remiss in not acknowledging my mentors at Lehigh University, where I was fortunate enough to be a doctoral student in the school psychology program. In particular, I would like to acknowledge and thank three professors who made me a better writer as well as a better school psychologist: Christine Cole, Edward Shapiro, and especially George DuPaul, who served as my dissertation chair and coauthored my first professional publication—a literature review of school-based suicide prevention programs that began as a class assignment in one of his courses. The examples of dedication and professionalism provided by these three noteworthy scholars, as well as the clear enthusiasm they had (and continue to have) for their work, inspired me to pursue an academic career in school psychology—a decision I have never regretted. Special thanks are also due to my friend and colleague Tanya Eckert of Syracuse University, with whom I have collaborated on many projects related to school-based suicide prevention—a process that began when we were both graduate students at Lehigh. I would also like to thank another former Lehigh classmate, school psychologist Kevin Kelly of the Quakertown (Pennsylvania) Community School District, for his ongoing friendship and support.

I first became interested in school-based suicide prevention while a doctoral student at Lehigh, and I would like to acknowledge some of the many people who have taught me so much since that time about suicidal behavior and its prevention, particularly among children and adolescents. In particular I would especially like to thank Alan (Lanny) Berman, Executive Director of the American Association of Suicidology and one of the leading suicidologists in the world, for generously contributing the foreword to this book. I would also like to thank Jim Mazza of the University of Washington for reading over the manuscript and providing many helpful suggestions. Other individuals I both respect and admire and whose research and/or writings on this topic have genuinely influenced and greatly inspired me include David Brent, Steve Brock, David Goldston, Madelyn Gould, Pete Gutierrez, Keith Hawton, Kay Redfield Jamison, David Jobes, Thomas Joiner, Cheryl King, Phil Lazarus, Rich Lieberman, Cynthia Pfeffer, Scott Poland, William Reynolds, M. David Rudd, Jonathan Sandoval, David Shaffer, Morton Silverman, Anthony Spirito, Barry Wagner, and Frank Zenere, as well as the late John Kalafat and the late Edwin S. Shneidman. Without the outstanding work done by these and other professionals dedicated to the study and practice of suicide prevention, this book would not have been possible.

I would also like to thank those (now retired) faculty members from the Counseling and Psychological Services Department at SUNY Oswego who first introduced me to the field of school psychology when I was a graduate student there many years ago, including Tom Cushman, Bruce Lester, Andy Steinbrecher, and particularly Gene Perticone, who continues to challenge me to be better. In addition, I would like to thank the members of the Binghamton (New York) City School District Special Services Department for their friendship, support, and collegiality during the period from 1989 to 1991 when I was employed there as a school psychologist, particularly Judy Bode, Carol Fish, Barbara Gilbert, Marena Gonz, Lisa Redecko, Beverly Rosen, and Pat Urban. I have many fond memories of those days at the beginning of my career, working with many talented and dedicated school practitioners in my hometown.

Thomas Power, Professor of School Psychology in Pediatrics at the Children's Hospital of Philadelphia and former editor of *School Psychology Review*, deserves special thanks for his support of school-based suicide prevention and his willingness to publish a special issue of *SPR* on that topic. I would also like to thank Brad Arndt, my brother-in-law, for leading me to some useful information on firearms and their relationship to violent crime that appears in this book. John Draper, Project Director of the National Suicide Prevention Lifeline, has my thanks for answering questions I had about suicidal youth calling 911 for assistance. Several graduate students in the University at Albany, SUNY school psychology program provided valuable assistance in completing this project and deserve to be acknowledged for their hard work, particularly Jeannette Ellis and Jaime Savoie.

Also deserving acknowledgment are the students, faculty, and staff at Centennial School of Lehigh University, an exemplary alternative day school for students with severe emotional and behavioral disorders, where among other things I gained valuable experience conducting suicide risk assessments and engaging in suicide prevention efforts. I would particularly like to thank the Director of Centennial School, Michael George. I have never encountered anyone who knows more about organizational leadership or possesses greater knowledge and skill working with students with emotional and behavioral disorders than Michael, who also happens to be the best boss I ever had. I have been extremely fortunate in having many important mentors in my career; Michael is among these and second to none.

Finally, I would like to acknowledge and thank my parents: my late mother, Mary J. (Wilcox) Miller, and my father, Donald A. Miller, to whom this book is dedicated. My parents lived in the same town in upstate New York where they grew up, and were married for 58 years until my mother's death in 2005. A natural teacher although never trained as one, my mother exhibited compassion for others and instilled in me both a sense of confidence and a love of learning that were instrumental in my development; my life has become immeasurably better because of her presence in it. My father, who nearly single-handedly took care of my mother for 12 years after she had a debilitating stroke, is an inspiration to me and the greatest man I have ever known.

Contents

CHAPTER 1

Suicidal Behavior
in Children and Adolescents

An Introduction and Overview

Each way to suicide is its own: intensely private, unknowable, and terrible . . . and any attempt by the living to chart this final terrain of a life can be only a sketch, maddeningly incomplete.

—KAY REDFIELD JAMISON

To understand suicide we must understand suffering and psychological pain and various thresholds for enduring it; to treat suicidal people (and prevent suicide) we must address and then soften and reduce the psychache that drives it.

—EDWIN S. SHNEIDMAN

To say that people who die by suicide are lonely at the time of their deaths is to begin to approximate the truth, rather like saying the ocean is wet. Loneliness combined with alienation combined with isolation combined with rejection and ostracism – this is better still, but it does not capture it fully. In fact, I believe that it is impossible to capture the phenomenon fully in words, because it is so beyond ordinary experience, much as it is difficult to conceive of what might be beyond the edge of the universe.

—THOMAS JOINER

Suicide is an enormous public health problem of global dimensions. The World Health Organization (WHO) estimates that approximately *one million people* die by suicide every year, a number that is equivalent to approximately 3,000 deaths per day or 1 death every 40 seconds. The annual number of worldwide fatalities that result from suicide is truly staggering, and is much higher than the annual number of deaths caused by homicide or wars. Moreover, according to the WHO, suicide has increased over 60% worldwide during the last half-century and is the second leading cause of death among young people ages 10–24 in the world.

> **Approximately one million people die by suicide every year, a number that is equivalent to approximately 3,000 deaths per day or 1 death every 40 seconds**

1

Suicide has increased over 60% worldwide during the last half-century and is the second leading cause of death among young people ages 10 to 24 in the world.

In the United States, approximately 32,000 people die as a result of suicide each year, the equivalent of about 80 people per day. Information regarding other suicidal behaviors among Americans was revealed in a recent landmark study conducted by the Substance Abuse and Mental Health Services Administration (SAMHSA; 2009). Involving over 46,000 adults 18 years of age and older who completed the National Survey on Drug Use and Health (NSDUH) in 2008, the study found that an estimated 8.3 million adults (3.7% of the U.S. adult population) had serious thoughts of suicide during the past year, 2.3 million (1.0%) had made a suicide plan, and 1.1 million (0.5%) had attempted suicide, with over 60% of this last group requiring some form of medical treatment and 46% requiring hospitalization. In addition, young adults from the ages of 18–25 were found to be more likely than older adults to have had serious thoughts of suicide, to have made suicide plans, and to have attempted suicide during the year.

As alarming as these figures are, perhaps even more disturbing is the finding that many school-age children and adolescents also engage in suicidal behavior to a significant degree. Although death rates of children and adolescents have decreased steadily and substantially during the last several decades due to continuing medical advances, the youth suicide rate in the United States has remained persistently high (King & Apter, 2003). In fact, despite some encouraging declines in recent years, the rate of youth suicide has increased significantly since the 1950s (Berman, Jobes, & Silverman, 2006), and many contend it is likely to further increase in the future (e.g., Gutierrez & Osman, 2008). On average, approximately five children and adolescents between the ages of 10 and 19 currently die by suicide every day in the United States (Wagner, 2009). If this same daily number of deaths had been the result of school shootings rather than suicide, it is likely it would be treated as a national crisis requiring immediate attention.

Although death rates of children and adolescents have decreased steadily and substantially during the last several decades due to continuing medical advances, the youth suicide rate in the United States has remained persistently high.

Unfortunately, youth suicides are only part of the problem. For every youth who dies by suicide, it is estimated that at least 100 to 200 young people make suicide attempts, and thousands more engage in serious thoughts about killing themselves (Miller & Eckert, 2009). In fact, nonfatal but still serious forms of suicidal behavior (e.g., suicidal ideation; suicide attempts) negatively affect an enormous amount of children, adolescents, and families each year. For example, youth who attempt suicide but do not die from it may still have serious injuries as a result, including possible brain damage, broken bones, or organ failure. In addition, youth who seriously contemplate or attempt suicide often experience depression and other mental health issues, and family and friends of suicidal youth are also at risk for developing these problems. Consequently, the psychological, emotional, behavioral, social, medical, and financial cost of youth suicidal behavior, not only

On average, approximately five children and adolescents between the ages of 10 and 19 die by suicide every day in the United States. If this same daily number of deaths had been the result of school shootings rather than suicide, it is likely it would be treated as a national crisis requiring immediate attention.

> **For every youth who dies by suicide, it is estimated that at least 100 to 200 young people make suicide attempts, and thousands more engage in serious thoughts about killing themselves.**

for individuals but also for families and entire communities, is frequently devastating (Miller, Eckert, & Mazza, 2009). Clearly, youth suicidal behavior is a vast public health problem deserving much greater attention than it currently receives (Satcher, 1998).

Because school personnel have daily contact with children and adolescents, they are uniquely and ideally positioned to prevent youth suicide. Although there are many significant challenges confronting our nation's schools, few if any are more important than youth suicidal behavior, and certainly none are more urgent. Many schools have experienced a significant increase in the amount of referrals for students who are seriously depressed, self-injurious, and/or suicidal, and this appears likely to continue (Lieberman, Poland, & Cassel, 2008). Unfortunately, few school personnel appear adequately trained to provide needed services for these children and adolescents. Even school-based mental health professionals frequently report being ill-prepared to effectively prevent or respond to youth suicidal behavior (Darius-Anderson & Miller, 2010; Debski, Spadafore, Jacob, Poole, & Hixson, 2007; Miller & Jome, 2008, in press).

For example, a recent survey found that 86% of a national sample of school psychologists reported they had counseled a student who had threatened or attempted suicide, 35% reported that a student in their school had died by suicide, and 62% reported that they knew a student at their school who made a nonfatal suicide attempt. However, only 22% of the school psychologists in this sample believed their graduate training had sufficiently prepared them to adequately intervene with suicidal youth, or to effectively contribute to postvention procedures following the suicide of a student (Berman, 2009). If school-based mental health professionals are indicating *they* are inadequately trained to address youth suicidal behavior, one can only imagine the lack of preparation teachers, administrators, and other school personnel must be experiencing regarding this topic. Clearly, school-based practitioners have a need for much more information on youth suicidal behavior, particularly information that can serve as a practical guide to effective prevention, assessment, and intervention strategies.

If school personnel are to respond proactively and effectively to youth suicidal behavior, they will need to become knowledgeable and skilled in a number of different areas. These areas include implementing and sustaining school-based suicide prevention programs, conducting suicide risk assessments, intervening with suicidal youth, and responding proactively and effectively if and when a suicide occurs. These issues are critical because the manner in which school practitioners respond to suicidal youth can literally mean the difference between life and death (Miller & Eckert, 2009).

SUICIDAL BEHAVIOR

The first step in the process of effectively preventing and responding to youth suicidal behavior involves adequately understanding what is meant by that term, one used throughout this book. For our purposes, *suicidal behavior* will refer to four separate but frequently overlapping conditions that exist on a con-

> **Suicidal behavior refers to four separate but frequently overlapping conditions that exist on a continuum: suicidal ideation, suicide-related communications, suicide attempts, and suicide.**

tinuum: suicidal ideation, suicide-related communications, suicide attempts, and suicide. The behaviors along this continuum vary and are not mutually exclusive, nor do all suicidal youth advance sequentially through them (Mazza, 2006; Silverman, Berman, Sanddal, O'Carroll, & Joiner, 2007a, 2007b). Moreover, although the frequency of each behavior *decreases* as individuals move along this continuum, the level of lethality and probability of death *increases* (Mazza & Reynolds, 2008). Consequently, suicidal behavior includes and incorporates a much larger set of behaviors than suicide alone. Each of these four types of suicidal behavior is now described in greater detail.

Suicidal Ideation

Suicidal ideation occurs at the beginning of the suicidal behavior continuum and refers to cognitions or thoughts about suicide. These cognitions may range from more general thoughts such as wishes about never being born or about being dead, to more specific thoughts such as developing detailed plans regarding when, where, and how suicide might occur (Mazza, 2006). Depending on the degree and type of suicidal ideation, it may be a precursor to more serious forms of suicidal behavior. For example, an adolescent who thinks infrequently about suicide and quickly rejects this idea when it occurs would generally not be considered at high risk for suicide, particularly if he did not have a history of previous suicide attempts or mental health problems. In contrast, an adolescent who engages in frequent suicidal ideation characterized by a detailed and specific plan to die by suicide should be considered at high risk for it.

Transient thoughts about suicide appear to be quite common and even somewhat normative during adolescence (Rueter, Holm, McGeorge, & Conger, 2008). For example, one study indicated that up to 63% of a sample of high school students reported some level of suicidal ideation (Smith & Crawford, 1986). However, when cross-sectional assessment measures are used, studies generally find that about 20% of adolescents report having serious thoughts about suicide at some time (Bridge, Goldstein, & Brent, 2005). Research indicates that the prevalence of suicidal ideation increases as children grow older, peaking at about age 14–16 and declining thereafter (Rueter & Kwon, 2005). Although a serious form of suicidal behavior, youth who engage in some form of suicidal ideation do not always or even typically move on to more serious suicidal behaviors, such as planning or attempting suicide (Lewinsohn, Rohde, Seeley, & Baldwin, 2001).

It is critical that school personnel understand the conditions under which suicidal ideation is likely to lead to more serious forms of suicidal behavior. Steinhausen, Bösiger, and Metzke (2006) assessed suicidal risk among a group of adolescents at age 13 and then again at age 20, identifying four different subgroups of youth in terms of their level of suicidal ideation. Rueter and colleagues (2008) studied 552 adolescents and young adults over a 13-year period, beginning when they were at a mean age of 14 until they were a mean age of 27. They identified three subgroups: nonideators (i.e., youth who did not exhibit suicidal ideation at age 14 or age 27); decreasers (i.e., youth who decreased in their level of suicidal ideation over time), and increasers (i.e., youth who increased in their level of suicidal ideation over time). The probability of making plans to die by suicide in these groups was found to be greatest among those with increasing suicidal ideation over time. The probability of attempting suicide was found to be highest among males with decreasing suicidal ideation and females with increasing suicidal ideation (Rueter et al., 2008). These results suggest that following the trajectory of suicidal ideation over time may be useful for identifying youth who are at highly at risk for more serious forms of suicidal behavior.

Suicidal ideation becomes clinically significant when "it is more than transient, possibly a preoccupation, and when it is accompanied by the possibility of being translated into behavioral actions" (Berman et al., 2006, p. 99). Many youth who die by suicide had previously thought about, planned, and attempted it (Rueter et al., 2008). For example, Greening and colleagues (2007) conducted a path analysis of suicidal behavior and found a significant direct effect for suicidal ideation on suicide attempts. Moreover, when there is a history of a previous suicide attempt, current suicidal ideation is significantly related to the probability of future suicide attempts.

Suicide-Related Communications

Suicide-related communications refer to "any interpersonal act of imparting, conveying, or transmitting thoughts, wishes, desires, or interest [about suicide] for which there is evidence (either explicit or implicit) that the act of communication is not itself a self-inflicted behavior or self-injurious" (Silverman et al., 2007b, p. 268). This category includes both verbal and nonverbal communications that may have suicidal intent but result in no injurious outcomes for the individual. Within this category are two subsets: suicide threat and suicide plan.

A *suicide threat* refers to "any interpersonal action, verbal or nonverbal, without a direct self-injurious component, that a reasonable person would interpret as communicating or suggesting that [more extreme forms of] suicidal behavior might occur in the near future" (Silverman et al., 2007b, p. 268). This communication may be either direct (e.g., a student telling one of his peers that he wants to kill himself) or indirect (e.g., a student engaging in highly dangerous, risky, and self-destructive behavior), and varies in regards to level of planning, communication, and concealment from others (Kingsbury, 1993). A *suicide plan* refers to "a proposed method of carrying out a design that will lead to a potentially self-injurious outcome; a systematic formulation of a program of action that has the potential for resulting in self-injury" (Silverman et al., 2007b, p. 268). Youth who make either suicide threats or suicide plans are communicating to others an intent to die.

Silverman and his colleagues (2007b) suggest that suicide-related communications be viewed as a halfway point between suicidal ideation and more extreme forms of suicidal behavior, such as suicide attempts. This category of suicidal behavior is interpersonally motivated and frequently involves somehow communicating to others how an individual might advance from suicidal ideation to pre-action (suicide threat), or from suicidal ideation to action (suicide plan).

It is important to realize that not all suicidal youth make suicidal threats, nor are all youth who make suicidal threats actively suicidal (Mazza, 2006). For example, a significant majority of the adolescents who attempt or die by suicide, perhaps as much as 80%, are preceded by threats or warnings. Conversely, the large majority of suicide threats are not followed by suicidal actions, are often not intended to be followed, or are deferred from being acted on because of the presence of contingent reinforcers, such as desired attention from others (Berman et al., 2006). However, understanding that not all youth who threaten suicide follow through with genuine suicide attempts should not be viewed as a rationale or justification for minimizing or ignoring such behavior. As noted by Berman and his colleagues (2006): "All threats and communications about suicide should be taken seriously, responded to, and evaluated as indicators of potential clinical significance and potential risk. To not do so and to be proved wrong by eventual [suicide] is a cost we believe to be most preventable and unacceptable" (p. 99).

Suicide Attempts

A suicide attempt is the third form of suicidal behavior on this continuum and may be defined as "a self-inflicted, potentially injurious behavior with a nonfatal outcome for which there is evidence (either explicit or implicit) of intent to die" (Silverman et al., 2007b, p. 273). There are different types of suicide attempts, with some being considered *high-intent attempts* and others considered *low-intent attempts*. What distinguishes these two types is generally the level of lethality of the method used in making the attempt (Berman et al., 2006). For example, high-intent suicide attempts are associated with higher levels of lethality (e.g., the use of guns). Most suicide attempts made by children and adolescents are of low lethality, allowing for a higher probability of rescue. For example, a gun is a much more lethal method of attempting suicide than taking an overdose of pills, and a student is much more likely to die from a suicide attempt if a more lethal method is used. Fortunately, the typically low level of lethality in the methods chosen by youth attempting suicide suggests that the vast majority are ambivalent about taking their own lives (Mazza, 2006). In fact, the great majority of youth suicide attempts (approximately seven out of every eight) are of such low lethality as to not require medical or other forms of attention and are never even reported (Berman et al., 2006).

Some youth who attempt suicide engage in what Berman and his colleagues (2006) refer to as *low-lethality self-destructive behavior.* The intent of most youth who engage in this behavior generally appears to be to mobilize or cause changes in other people's behavior. For example, an adolescent who cuts himself in front of others in an area that is not likely to result in extensive blood loss (e.g., elbow) may be engaging in low-lethality self-destructive behavior. These low-lethality behaviors are sometimes viewed as a *cry for help* or as a *suicidal gesture.* Both terms are unfortunate because each in its own way minimizes the significance of the behavior through the implication that the youth is not "serious" about suicide, and/or that the individual is "only looking for attention." Although youth who engage in low-lethality attempts may well be seeking attention and/or attempting to change the behavior of others, in such situations it is worth reflecting on *why* these youth would be compelled to engage in such behavior. It may be that other methods for accomplishing these same goals were repeatedly attempted but proved unsuccessful. Regardless, as was noted in the previous section on suicide-related communications, *all* communications regarding suicidal behavior made by youth should be responded to immediately and in a serious and thoughtful manner by caring adults.

Repeated suicide attempters are those youth who engage in "chronic, habitual self-destructive behavior" (Berman et al., 2006, p. 98). These individuals often appear to have more chronic symptoms associated with suicide, as well as poorer coping strategies and histories, and to be members of families that evidence more chaotic and chronic dysfunctional behavior patterns (including suicidal behavior and substance abuse) than individuals who make less frequent suicide attempts. Although the initial suicide attempts of these individuals are usually less lethal than their later attempts, it is not uncommon for the level of lethality of their suicide attempts to increase along with their occurrence. Consequently, repeated suicide attempters are at high risk for eventually dying by suicide because a history of multiple suicide attempts is one of the most pernicious risk factors for suicide. Not surprisingly, repeated suicide attempters are frequently hospitalized and often make significant demands on hospitals and other treatment systems (Berman et al., 2006).

Although most youth suicide attempts result in nonlethal outcomes, this does not mean these behaviors should not be treated seriously by adults. Along with the presence of mental health problems and psychiatric disorders, prior suicide attempts are one of the most important risk factors for individuals who later die by suicide. Although most youth who attempt suicide will do so only once and not die as a result, a substantial number of individuals who attempt suicide later die by it (Berman et al., 2006). Youth who attempt suicide have a greatly increased risk for repeated suicide attempts and an increased risk for later death (Groholt & Ekeberg, 2009). In addition to an increased probability of additional suicidal behavior, engaging in a suicide attempt places youth at risk for a host of other mental health problems. For example, one study followed a group of adolescents 8 to 10 years after they made a suicide attempt. Of the 71 individuals in the sample, 79% had at least one psychiatric disorder at follow-up, the most common of which was depression. In addition, one-third of the sample had received some form of inpatient treatment, 78% received some form of psychiatric treatment, and 44% made additional suicide attempts (Groholt & Ekeberg, 2009).

Suicide

Suicide is the last and obviously the most lethal behavior on the suicidal behavior continuum (Mazza & Reynolds, 2008). Suicide may be defined as a fatal, self-inflected act with the explicit or inferred intent to die (Mazza, 2006). For suicide to occur, an individual must have exhibited suicidal ideation, developed the intent to die by suicide, and used a sufficiently lethal method to carry out this intention. The determination of intentionality is often difficult and rests on evidence that the decedent (i.e., individual who died) understood that the self-inflicted act would produce death. For cause of death to be considered suicide, it must be certified as such by a coroner or medical examiner (Brock, 2002).

A key difference between youth who attempt suicide and those who die by it is the presence of psychopathology, particularly mood disorders, substance abuse disorders, and disruptive behavior disorders, respectively (Fleischmann, Bertolote, Belfer, & Beautrais, 2005). In fact, research suggests that 90% or more of youth who die by suicide have at least one diagnosable mental disorder at the time of their deaths (Berman et al., 2006). The issue of child psychopathology and its relationship to youth suicide is a critical one and will be addressed more extensively in Chapter 4.

Summary

Accurately defining different forms of suicidal behavior is sometimes a complex process and has led different researchers and theorists to define suicidal behavior in different ways (Silverman et al., 2007a, 2007b). For the purposes of this book, suicidal behavior has been broadly defined to include not only suicide but other serious and closely related behaviors as well, including suicidal ideation, suicide-related communications, and suicide attempts.

The profiles of individuals who engage in different forms of suicidal behavior vary significantly. For example, the typical youth who *attempts suicide* is an adolescent female who ingests drugs at home in front of others (e.g., parents), whereas the typical youth who *dies by suicide* is an adolescent male using a firearm (Berman et al., 2006). Children and adolescents who attempt suicide should therefore not be seen as synonymous with youth who die by it. There are often important differences between them, just as there are important differences between youth who "only" engage in suicidal ideation and youth who make suicide attempts. A com-

> **Approximately 1 out of 7 high school students engage in serious suicidal ideation, 1 in 10 make a suicide plan, and 1 in 14 make a suicide attempt, some to a degree that will require medical treatment or hospitalization.**

mon element shared by young people who engage in *any* form of suicidal behavior, however, is that these children and adolescents are exhibiting serious and significant problems to a degree that will require urgent attention and active intervention on the part of caring adults.

YOUTH SUICIDAL BEHAVIOR: THE SCOPE OF THE PROBLEM

The scope of the problem of youth suicidal behavior becomes apparent when considering the prevalence of suicidal ideation, suicide-related communications (i.e., suicide threats and plans), and suicide attempts in addition to suicide. The Youth Risk Behavior Surveillance System (YRBSS) conducted a National Youth Risk Behavior Survey in 2007, resulting in over 14,000 completed questionnaires from students in grades 9 through 12 in 39 states across the United States. This survey, the most comprehensive of its kind at the time of this writing, found that approximately 14.5% of U.S. students seriously considered attempting suicide, including 18.7% of females and 10.3% of males. During this same one-year period, 11.3% of students made a plan about how they would attempt suicide (13.4% of females and 9.2% of males), 6.9% reported making at least one suicide attempt (9.3% of females and 4.6% of males), and 2% reported making at least one attempt that resulted in an injury, poisoning, or overdose that had to be treated by a doctor or nurse (Centers for Disease Control and Prevention [CDC], 2008). Collectively, these data suggest that each year approximately 1 out of 7 high school students engage in serious suicidal ideation, 1 in 10 make a suicide plan, and 1 in 14 make a suicide attempt, some to a degree that will require medical treatment or hospitalization.

Information on the suicidal behavior of students in alternative high schools, including students with emotional and behavioral disorders, or students at risk for failing or dropping out of school, is cause for even greater concern (Berman et al., 2006). When compared to students in "regular" high schools, students placed in alternative high schools were found to be 1.5 times more likely to report having seriously considered suicide or to have made a specific suicide plan. These students were also twice as likely to report having made a suicide attempt and three times as likely to report having made a suicide attempt serious enough to require medical treatment (Berman et al., 2006).

Across all age groups, adolescents have been found to have the highest ratio of nonfatal suicide attempts to actual suicides (King, 1997). Based on the data reported in the YRBSS, as well as data from other sources (Berman et al., 2006), it appears that for every occurrence of youth suicide there are perhaps hundreds of students making suicide attempts. Once a suicide attempt is made at *any* level of lethality, the risk for more serious suicide attempts, as well as actually dying by suicide, increases significantly (Berman et al., 2006).

YOUTH SUICIDE IN PERSPECTIVE

It is important to provide a context for youth suicidal behavior so it can be viewed in appropriate perspective. For example, although suicide is the 11th leading cause of death among Americans overall, it is the third-leading cause of death among adolescents ages 15 to 19 in the United States, and the fourth-leading cause of death among children and early adolescents ages 10 to 14 (CDC, 2006). Among youth between 15 and 19 years

> **More teenagers and young adults die from suicide than die from cancer, heart disease, HIV-AIDS, birth defects, stroke, pneumonia and influenza, and chronic lung disease *combined*.**

of age, only unintentional injury (i.e., accidents) and homicide annually result in greater loss of life than suicide. More teenagers and young adults die from suicide than die from cancer, heart disease, HIV/AIDS, birth defects, stroke, pneumonia and influenza, and chronic lung disease *combined*. For youth ages 10–14, suicide follows unintentional injury, malignant neoplasms (i.e., cancer), and homicide, respectively, as a leading cause of death. Moreover, although overall suicide rates among youth ages 10–19 declined from 1990 to 2004, from 2003 to 2004 suicide rates for females ages 10–19 and males ages 15–19 increased significantly (CDC, 2007).

Despite fluctuating rates of youth suicide over the last several decades, including notable decreases during the 1990s and early 21st century, the overall suicide rate for children and adolescents has increased over 300% in the last 50 years (Berman et al., 2006). Adding to this sobering statistic is the possibility that the number of reported youth suicides may be an underestimate of their actual occurrence (Lieberman, Poland, & Cassel, 2008). For example, some deaths that occur as the result of suicide may not be classified as such if the cause of death is somewhat ambiguous, if another cause of death cannot be conclusively ruled out, or if medical examiners certifying the death are reluctant to identify its cause as suicide to avoid "stigmatizing" the victim's parents/guardians. Although research indicates that if underreporting does take place it is likely to be fairly minimal (Kleck, 1988), the stigma that surrounds it suggests that some degree of youth suicide underreporting may well occur.

Precisely why the rate of youth suicide has risen so dramatically in the last half-century or so is unclear, although a number of possibilities have been suggested, including diminished cohesion in families and an increase in youth depression, drug and alcohol use, and the availability of firearms (Hendin et al., 2005). Reasons for the more recent decline in overall youth suicide rates is even less clear, although it has been suggested that this has occurred as a result of positive economic influences, safer firearm practices, and the increased use of antidepressant medication with children and adolescents (Wagner, 2009).

Because the topic of youth suicide is a tragic and highly painful one, it understandably results in highly emotional reactions among many people. This emotionality is sometimes reflected in exaggerated and hyperbolic statements about youth suicide that may, despite good intentions, sometimes result in misperceptions and distortions about its pervasiveness (Berman et al, 2006). Clearly, youth suicide is a widespread public health problem of major proportions and is a "crisis in need of attention" (Mazza, 2006, p. 156). This is especially true when taking into account the entire spectrum of youth suicidal behavior, including suicidal ideation, suicide-related communications, and suicide attempts in addition to suicide. However, using words such as "epidemic" (e.g., Woods, 2006) or other inaccurate terms to describe youth suicide communicates an unnecessarily alarmist message about a very real and significant problem.

DEMOGRAPHICS OF YOUTH SUICIDE

Ethnicity

Various ethnic groups differ in their rates of youth suicide, the context in which suicide occurs, and in their patterns of help seeking (Goldston et al., 2008). Among the larger ethnic groups in the United States, European Americans have the highest youth suicide rate, followed by African Americans and Latinos (Berman et al., 2006). Although historically African American youth have consistently had a lower suicide rate than European American youth, the suicide rate of African American males has risen substantially in recent decades. For example, between 1960 and 2000 the suicide rate among African American males ages 15 to 19 more than tripled, increasing over 200% during that time (Berman et al., 2006).

The highest rates of youth suicide *proportionally* are among Native Americans, with the lowest rates tending to be among Asian/Pacific Islanders (Mazza, 2006). Several hypotheses regarding the high suicide rate among Native American youth have been proposed, including a proportionally higher use of both alcohol and firearms as well as a frequent lack of social integration in this group (Middlebrock, LeMaster, Beals, Novins, & Manson, 2001). However, there are wide variations in rates of suicide among Native American youth, and suicide rates in this group are affected by a number of different variables, including geography (Berman et al., 2006). Native American youth also tend to have the highest rates of suicidal ideation and nonfatal suicidal behavior of all ethnic groups, followed by Latina/o, African American, and European American youth (Joe, Canetto, & Romer, 2008).

Disparities based on race and ethnicity have frequently been reported in regards to receiving mental health services related to suicide. For example, Freedenthal (2007) conducted a study involving over 2,000 African American, Hispanic, and European American youth ages 12 to 17, each of whom had reported suicidal ideation or made a suicide attempt during the previous year. The results of the study indicated that African American and Hispanic youth were significantly less likely than European American youth to have received professional help for mental health problems during that period.

Gender

Gender appears to have a stronger influence on youth suicidal behavior than ethnicity. Research has consistently found a strong but paradoxical relationship between gender and suicidal behavior (Canetto & Sakinofsky, 1998). Specifically, although adolescent females report much higher rates of suicidal ideation than adolescent males and attempt suicide at rates *two to three times* the rate of males, males commit suicide at a rate *five times* more often than females (Berman et al., 2006). This gender paradox appears across different ethnicities as well (Joe et al., 2008). Plausible reasons for the much higher suicide rate among young males in comparison to females include the higher rates of significant suicide risk factors among males (e.g., access to firearms, alcohol abuse) as well as their being less likely than females to engage in a number of protective behaviors, such as seeking help, being

> **Although adolescent females report more suicidal ideation than adolescent males and attempt suicide at rates *two to three times* the rate of males, males commit suicide at a rate five times more often than females.**

adequately aware of warning signs, having flexible coping skills, and developing effective social support systems (Maris, Berman, & Silverman, 2000).

Age

The probability of suicide increases in both males and females as children grow older. For example, adolescents who are 15 years of age and older are at much higher risk for suicide than youth ages 10 to 14, who are at higher risk for suicide than younger children under the age of 10 (Berman et al., 2006). To put this into perspective, for the year 2006 the CDC reported that young people between the ages of 15 and 19 died by suicide at a rate approximately seven times that of youth between the ages of 10 and 14. More specifically, in that year 1,565 adolescents between the ages of 15 and 19 died by suicide in the United States, whereas the total number of deaths by suicide for children between the ages of 10 and 14 was 216. A declining trend in suicide among youth ages 10–14 has recently been observed, although the rate of suicide in this age group is (like others) substantially higher than it was in previous decades. Between 1981 and 2004, for example, suicide rates increased 51% among children between the ages of 10 and 14 (American Association of Suicidology, 2006).

Youth are at increased risk for suicide as they grow older, with adolescents at higher risk for suicide than younger children.

Suicide *does occur* in children under the age of 10, and there have even been some documented cases of suicidal behavior in preschool children. For example, Rosenthal and Rosenthal (1984) identified 16 preschoolers, ages 2 to 5, who engaged in nonlethal suicide attempts. In the past, mental health professionals widely believed that young children should not be considered suicidal because they could not possibly understand and conceptualize the finality of death (Pfeffer, 2003). However, direct observations of children's behavior has indicated that self-destructive behavior may occur in young children, that children as young as 3 years of age can have concepts of death, and that intent to carry out suicidal behavior does not necessarily require that a child have a mature concept of death (Pfeffer, 1986). In general, however, suicide among children below the age of 10 is extremely rare, with typically only a few reported cases each year. When suicide at this age level does occur, it is typically associated with severe dysfunction and psychopathology in the child's family system.

In sum, suicide can and does occur in children, but is more likely to occur among adolescents, particularly those between the ages of 15 and 19. This finding should not be interpreted, however, as minimizing or discounting the need for school-based suicide prevention efforts designed for elementary and middle school students. First, as will be seen later in this book, many risk factors for youth suicide develop during childhood, and effectively addressing these risk factors while students are in elementary or middle school may decrease the risk for suicide as children grow older. Second, as previously described, suicidal behavior is a broader concept than suicide alone, and includes suicidal ideation, suicide-related communications, and suicide attempts. Each of these behaviors does occur in elementary and middle school students, placing them at increased risk for suicide during adolescence and adulthood. Consequently, it is critical that *all school personnel at all levels*—elementary, middle, and high school—be cognizant of youth suicidal behavior and how to effectively prevent, assess, and respond to it.

Sexual Orientation

It has frequently been suggested that gay and lesbian youth may be at higher risk for suicidal behavior than heterosexual youth. Earlier research supporting this contention has been criticized on methodological grounds, including possible inaccuracies in the reporting of sexual orientation and/or behavior (Hendin et al., 2005) and a lack of accurate youth suicide rates specific to the lesbian and gay population (Berman et al., 2006; Lieberman et al., 2008). There is emerging evidence, however, suggesting that lesbian, gay, and bisexual (LGB) youth may be at elevated risk for suicidal behavior in comparison to their heterosexual peers (Jacob, 2009).

> **There is emerging evidence suggesting that gay, lesbian, and bisexual (GLB) youth may be at elevated risk for suicidal behavior in comparison to their heterosexual peers.**

For example, based on data from the National Longitudinal Study of Adolescent Health, a recent study found that GLB youth were much more likely to report suicidal ideation (17.2% vs. 6.3%) and attempt suicide (4.9% vs. 1.6%) than non-LGB youth (Silenzio, Pena, Duberstein, Cerel, & Knox, 2007). However, data specifically linking suicide deaths to a homosexual orientation currently is lacking (Berman et al., 2006).

The term *transgender* is a general term used to describe individuals whose self-identification or expression "transgresses established gender categories or boundaries" (Grossman & D'Augelli, 2007, p. 528). Very little information is currently available regarding the suicidal behavior of transgender individuals. In the first published study examining the suicidal behavior of young people in this group, a sample of 55 transgender adolescents (ages 15–21) were asked to report on their life-threatening behaviors. The results of the study indicated that nearly half the sample reported having suicidal ideation to a serious degree, and one quarter reported making suicide attempts (Grossman & D'Augelli, 2007). In general, having a sexual minority status, including individuals who are gay, lesbian, bisexual, or transgender, may put an individual at increased risk for suicidal behavior, particularly suicidal ideation or suicide attempts.

Geography

> **Youth suicide rates are highest in the Western states and Alaska and lowest in the Northeastern states.**

As with adults, youth suicide rates are highest in the Western states and Alaska and lowest in the Northeastern states (Berman et al., 2006; Gould & Kramer, 2001). For example, in 2006 Wyoming had the proportionally highest suicide rate of any state in the United States across all age groups. For adolescents and young adults ages 15 to 24, the suicide rates were proportionally highest in Alaska, North Dakota, South Dakota, New Mexico, Montana, Nevada, Arizona, Colorado, Wyoming, Nebraska, Oregon, and Idaho, respectively. All of these states are located west of the Mississippi River, and most of them are in the far Western portion of the United States. The five states with the lowest proportion of suicides in this age group during this same period were Vermont, Massachusetts, New York, New Jersey, and Rhode Island—all located in the Northeast.

It has been suggested that the proportionally larger suicide rate in Western states may at least partly be due to the greater population density in other areas of the country (e.g., the Northeast) compared to many Western states (Berman et al., 2006). The sparser population, greater physical isolation, fewer mental health facilities, and limited opportunities for social interaction that characterize many states in the Western portion of the United States may lead to greater social disconnection, a variable highly associated with suicide (Joiner, 2005). Consistent with this hypothesis is the finding that suicide rates are typically higher in rural areas than in urban areas (Berman et al., 2006). Joiner (2005) also hypothesizes that individuals (particularly males) in many Western states and rural areas live by a "culture of honor" (p. 99) ethos characterized by the use of violence to protect one's perceived reputation, which may lead to increased suicidal behavior. Because of a cultural emphasis on hunting in many Western states and rural sections of the country, gun ownership is highly prevalent among individuals living in these areas, which may also be a factor in the higher suicide rates in these geographical locations.

Socioeconomic Status

Research regarding the influence of socioeconomic status (SES) and suicidal behavior has been described as "mixed and contradictory" (Berman et al., 2006, p. 31). Although suicide occurs across all socioeconomic levels, research generally suggests that there is an inverse relationship between SES and suicide rates in both the United States and other countries (Stack, 2000; Ying & Chang, 2009). That is, the degree to which individuals are struggling economically is associated with an increased risk for suicidal behavior. Research on SES and youth suicide is lacking, although one study examining the socioeconomic differences among more than 20,000 Danish youth who died by suicide found that individuals in the lowest socioeconomic quartile had more than five times the risk of suicide compared to their more affluent peers (Qin, Agerbo, & Mortenson, 2003).

COMMON MYTHS ABOUT YOUTH SUICIDE

There are a number of myths about suicide in general (for more information on this topic, the reader is referred to Joiner, 2010) and youth suicide in particular. Perhaps the most significant and dangerous myth about youth suicide is that asking questions or talking about suicide with children and adolescents will increase the probability that suicide will occur (Kalafat, 2003). Despite fears to the contrary, there is no evidence for this belief (Gould et al., 2005). In

> Perhaps the most significant and dangerous myth about youth suicide is that asking questions or talking about suicide with children and adolescents will increase the probability that suicide will occur. Despite fears to the contrary, there is no evidence for this belief.

fact, research suggests that youth who are able to openly and candidly discuss the topic of suicide with trusted adults typically have more beneficial outcomes, as do their peers who may be at risk (Mazza, 2006). Moreover, the direct questioning of youth suspected of possibly engaging in suicidal behavior is an essential component of effective suicide risk assessment (Miller & McConaughy, 2005), a subject that will be explored in greater detail in Chapter 5.

A second myth is that parents/caregivers are cognizant of their child's suicidal behavior (Mazza, 2006). One study found that 86% of parents were unaware of the suicidal behavior of their children, including their suicide attempts (Kashani, Goddard, & Reid, 1989). This myth underscores the notion that youth typically do not communicate their suicidal thoughts or actions to their parents/caregivers, and reinforces the need for school personnel to directly ask youth about their suicidal behavior rather than relying on parents or other adults for this information (Miller & McConaughy, 2005).

A third myth is that youth who attempt suicide usually receive medical attention or some other form of treatment for it (Mazza, 2006). Unfortunately, research suggests this typically does not occur. For example, Smith and Crawford (1986) found that only 12% of a sample of 313 adolescent suicide attempters received medical treatment, leaving 88% untreated. Given that many school-age youth are not old enough to drive, transportation for medical or other forms of treatment would require informing a parent/caregiver or older sibling about their suicidal behavior, an approach most of these youth do not appear to be taking (Mazza, 2006).

A fourth myth is that most young people who die by suicide leave suicide notes (Martin & Dixon, 1986). Garfinkel, Friese, and Hood (1982), however, found that only 5% of children and adolescents wrote a suicide note prior to their suicide attempts, a finding consistent with other research indicating that the majority of people who die by suicide (including children, adolescents, and adults) do not leave suicide notes (Jamison, 1999). Like the treatment myth mentioned earlier, it has been suggested that one of the primary reasons why youth typically do not write suicide notes is that they do not want to reveal what they are thinking or feeling to their parents. They may believe that their parents are overly involved in their lives and that writing a suicide note only increases the probability of parental interference (Mazza, 2006). In addition, in most cases suicide notes are not particularly revealing, and among individuals who die by suicide there are frequently no significant differences between those who leave suicide notes and those who do not (Callahan & Davis, 2009).

A fifth myth is that individuals who are suicidal are impulsive, often dying by suicide "on a whim" (Joiner, 2010). This myth seems to be commonly believed because individuals often appear to make suicide attempts or to die by suicide suddenly, without much forethought or planning. Actually, the opposite is true. In most cases, individuals who attempt or die by suicide have given suicide a great deal of thought, and made careful and specific plans regarding it. As noted by Joiner (2010), "people who die by suicide have thought of the possible methods and locations and so forth well in advance, often years in advance" (p. 75). Although a particular suicide may appear to others to be a sudden or an impulsive act, this is generally not the case.

Other common myths about youth suicide include the belief that it is caused primarily by family and social stress rather than mental health problems or disorders (Moskos, Achilles, & Gray, 2004), that individuals who talk about suicide are only doing so to get attention and are not "seriously" considering it (Martin & Dixon, 1986), that people who are suicidal are "crazy" or "out of their mind," that suicides are primarily a way to show anger or gain revenge, that suicides follow a lunar cycle and peak during a full moon, and that once an individual decides to commit suicide little or nothing can be done to prevent it (Joiner, 2010). This last myth has particular implications for suicide prevention because underlying it is the mistaken notion that preventing an individual from suicide is ultimately pointless because the individual will simply attempt or die by suicide at another time. Research suggests, however, that this is regularly not the case, as will be seen in the next chapter.

YOUTH SUICIDE: WHEN, WHERE, AND HOW

When Is Youth Suicide Most Likely to Occur?

Several studies have examined temporal variations in suicide (e.g., Blachly & Fairly, 1989; Lester, 1979), although none to date has been specific to youth suicide. Research indicates that suicides in general occur with relatively similar frequency across the different months of the year, with spring being the peak season. A common myth is that suicide rates increase in December, particularly around the many holidays (i.e., Christmas, Hanukkah, Kwanzaa) celebrated during that month (Joiner, 2010). However, there are actually *fewer* suicides in December than in any other month, a finding consistent with research indicating that suicide rates tend to decrease somewhat before and during major holidays (Berman et al., 2006; Bradvik & Berglund, 2003; Phillips & Feldman, 1973). The reason for the decreased suicide rate at such times is likely due to the increased social interaction and support available to people as a result of holiday gatherings (Joiner, 2010).

Researchers have also examined the most likely days of the week and time of day that suicides occur. In general, suicides appear to occur most often on Mondays and least often on weekends (Bradvik & Berglund, 2003). The reason for this finding is not entirely clear, although one possibility is that during weekends people are more likely to engage in social and enjoyable activities, which often end abruptly on Mondays with the start of a new week of work or school. An alternative hypothesis has been provided by Joiner (2010), who suggested that because suicide "is an activity that requires reflection, planning, and a kind of determined resolve . . . those who die on Monday may have spent their weekend building up their will to do a very daunting and difficult thing" (p. 266). Regarding time of day, the majority of youth suicides occur in the afternoon or evening rather than in the morning. (Hoberman & Garfinkel, 1988; Shafii & Shafii, 1982). Temporal trends in youth suicide should be interpreted with caution, however, both because of the limited data currently available and because death certificates may not accurately reflect when a suicide actually occurred (Berman et al., 2006).

Where Is Youth Suicide Most Likely to Occur?

Research on this topic is limited, but it appears that most youth suicides occur in the residences where students live, where the primary means for suicide (e.g., firearms) are typically available (Berman et al., 2006; Hoberman & Garfinkel, 1988). The majority of nonfatal youth suicide attempts involve ingesting drugs, also typically kept in the youth's home (Berman et al., 2006). A much smaller percentage of youth suicides and suicide attempts occur in schools or in areas other than the child's or adolescent's place of residence.

How Is Youth Suicide Most Likely to Occur?

The risk of suicidal behavior often is a function of intention, and intention is closely linked to the method an individual uses to attempt suicide (Miller & Eckert, 2009). Although there are exceptions (e.g., an individual may have a strong intention to die but use a low lethality method), in general the stronger the intention to die by suicide, the greater the potential lethality of the method selected to carry out that intention (Berman et al., 2006). For example, firearms and hanging typically are more lethal methods than wrist cutting, carbon monoxide poisoning, or drug ingestion overdose. Choice of suicide method is strongly influenced by a number of factors, including (1) accessibility and readiness for use; (2) knowledge, experience, and familiarity; (3) meaning and cultural significance; and (4) state of mind of the person at risk (Berman et al., 2006; Berman, Litman, & Diller, 1989)

The suicide attempts of most children and adolescents tend to be of low lethality and allow for a high likelihood of being rescued (Garfinkel et al., 1982). For example, research conducted with 469 adolescent suicide attempters found that the two most common methods were drug ingestion overdose (i.e., taking pills) and wrist cutting, respectively (Reynolds & Mazza, 1993). These same results have been found in other studies as well, suggesting the ambivalence many youth appear to experience in regards to taking their own lives (Mazza, 2006).

The use of firearms is the most frequently used method among males ages 10–19 who die by suicide. Historically, firearms were the most frequently used suicide method among females in this age group as well. Beginning in 2001, however, and continuing through 2004, young females were more likely to use hanging/suffocation rather than firearms to commit suicide (CDC, 2007).

THE BIG QUESTION: WHY DO YOUNG PEOPLE DIE BY SUICIDE?

One of the most difficult, elusive, and complex questions to answer is what makes some children and adolescents engage in suicidal behavior? Why do people die by suicide, and in particular why do young people die by suicide? Unfortunately, there is not now and likely never will be simple answers to these questions. Variables that may help to explain or predict youth suicidal behavior include risk factors and warning signs (to be discussed extensively in Chapter 4), but they cannot fully account for why individuals engage in suicidal behavior. In fact, no single factor can provide a complete explanation of why suicide, including youth suicide, occurs. A comprehensive understanding of the causes of youth suicidal behavior requires sensitivity to a broad and complex range of interrelated variables, including genetic, neurobiological, social, cultural, and psychological influences (Berman et al., 2006; Goldston et al., 2008). Although a detailed discussion of these causal variables is outside the scope of this book, interested readers are encouraged to review the seminal work by Berman and his colleagues (2006) for more information on this topic.

In addition to understanding that suicidal behavior is the result of a variety of interconnected variables, school personnel should also be cognizant of some of the more prominent theories regarding suicidal behavior, including earlier theories as well as more contemporary ones. The primary function of a theory is to generate new ideas and discoveries that can then be subjected to rigorous evaluation (Higgins, 2004). A brief overview of these theories is provided in the next section (for more compre-

> No single factor can provide a complete explanation of why suicide, including youth suicide, occurs. A comprehensive understanding of the causes of youth suicidal behavior requires sensitivity to a broad and complex range of interrelated variables, including genetic, neurobiological, social, cultural, and psychological influences.

hensive overviews, see Berman et al., 2006; Joiner, 2005). Because of its comprehensiveness, its growing empirical support, and the clear implications it has for school-based suicide prevention and intervention, particular attention is given to Joiner's (2005, 2009) interpersonal-psychological theory of suicidal behavior.

Early Theories of Suicidal Behavior

One of the earliest theories of suicide that is still influential today was proposed over 100 years ago by the French sociologist Emile Durkheim (1897), who emphasized the impact of social factors on suicidal behavior. Durkheim suggested that collective social forces were much more central to suicidal behavior than individual factors, and his theory focused on the importance of social integration and moral regulation (Joiner, 2005). Durkheim's theory is overly dismissive of individual variables (e.g., genetics; psychiatric disorders) that clearly play a prominent role in suicidal behavior, but it remains influential because there has been empirical support for some aspects of it and because it was the first comprehensive and testable theory of suicide (Joiner, 2005).

Although Durkheim's work is often considered the classic sociological statement on the topic of suicide, other sociological models of suicide have also been proposed, as well as approaches that attempt to synthesize both social and psychological variables that may lead to suicidal behavior. For example, Hendin's (1987) theory of youth suicidal behavior attempts to explain suicide from both epidemiological and psychodynamic perspectives, whereas Lester (1988) has proposed a social-psychological perspective that attempts to explain youth suicidal behavior as a function of quality of life.

More psychologically oriented theories of suicide began to appear in the 20th century, dominated initially by psychoanalytic models. One of the most influential psychoanalytically oriented theorists of suicide was Karl Menninger (1933), who in works such as *Man against Himself* (1938) elaborated on and extended some of Freud's theoretical formulations of suicide while adding some of his own (Berman et al., 2006). Psychodynamic theories of suicide, including the well-known hypothesis that suicide results largely from hate or anger turned inward, have been rejected by many theorists and researchers due to their lack of empirical evidence (Joiner, 2005).

There does appear to be some disagreement, however, about the value of this theoretical perspective among contemporary suicidologists. For example, Berman et al (2006) state that "the psychoanalytic tradition, both past and present, has greatly contributed to suicide theory building and our understanding of the phenomenon" (pp. 54–55). In contrast, Joiner (2005) states that "it is difficult to think of a lasting contribution to the understanding of suicide from this (i.e., psychoanalytic) perspective" (p. 35). Although some theorists continue to promote a psychodynamic approach to understanding suicide (e.g., Hendin, 1991), in general the influence of this theoretical framework has significantly declined in recent decades.

In my view, although understanding suicidal behavior clearly requires a holistic approach involving the consideration of a number of variables, a *cognitive-behavioral perspective* provides a valuable and practical theoretical model for conceptualizing suicidal behavior in general and youth suicidal behavior in particular. For example, Rudd, Joiner, and Rajab (2001) provide a comprehensive, cognitive-behavioral approach to the treatment of suicidal behavior, and argue convincingly that any viable approach to intervention must be based on a theoretically based conceptual model. Their model is an integrated one in which the interactions of different systems of personality (i.e., cognitive, affective, behavioral, and motivational schemas) are emphasized, and provides an excellent example of linking theory with practice.

The relationship between theory and practice is important, especially for those mental health professionals in schools who may be working most often and most closely with suicidal youth. For these professionals, one's theoretical orientation in regards to suicidal behavior (or any other psychological or mental health problem, for that matter) is by no means merely an abstract, impractical, "academic" exercise. On the contrary, an individual's theoretical orientation provides a "lens" for how to perceive and conceptualize a problem, and therefore how to approach its resolution. In the words of the prominent psychologist Kurt Lewin, "There is nothing so practical as a good theory" (1951, p. 169).

Contemporary Theories of Suicidal Behavior

A useful theory is one that is coherent, economical, testable, generalizable, and can explain previously known findings (Higgins, 2004). More recent theories of suicidal behavior have received greater empirical support than earlier ones, and usually provide a more useful and practical framework for generating coherent predictions and testable hypotheses (Van Orden, Witte, Selby, Bender, & Joiner, 2008). Although developmental (e.g., Emery, 1983), family systems (Richman, 1986), and neurobiological and genetic (Mann, 1998) models of suicide have been proposed, many contemporary theories of suicide conceptualize it from a cognitive-behavioral perspective, focusing in particular on thinking patterns and cognitions that may contribute to the development and maintenance of suicidal behavior (for more information on the current status and empirical support of these theories, the reader is referred to Berman et al., 2006; Joiner et al., 2009; Van Orden et al., 2008).

For example, Aaron Beck and his colleagues (1975, 1989) proposed a cognitive theory of suicide that emphasized the role of *hopelessness*, which they viewed as more highly characteristic of suicide than depression, a contention that has received some research support. Beck and his colleagues (Beck, 1996; Beck, Rush, Shaw, & Emery, 1979) have for many years emphasized the important role that *cognitive errors* and *distorted thinking* play in suicidal behavior. In particular, Beck's concept of the *cognitive triad* (i.e., negative thoughts about oneself, others, and the future) is a central component of his cognitive theory of depression, with distinct and important implications for understanding suicide and intervening with suicidal individuals (Berman et al., 2006).

The British psychologist Mark Williams also views suicidal behavior from a cognitive perspective. In discussing suicidal ideation and suicide attempts, Williams (2001) contends that although suicide is commonly viewed by many people as a "cry for help," it is more accurate to view it as a "cry of pain." As Williams notes:

> The cry for help, which many have misinterpreted as a lack of genuineness, is better seen as a cry of pain. Suicidal behavior can have a communication outcome without communication being the main motive. The behavior is elicited by a situation in which the person feels trapped. . . . Suicidal behavior may be overtly communicative in a minority of cases, but mainly it is "elicited" by the pain of a situation with which the person cannot cope—it is a cry of pain first, and only after that a cry for help. (p. 148)

The experience of pain also plays a central role in suicide, according to Edwin S. Shneidman, an influential theorist and founder of the American Association of Suicidology (AAS). Shneidman (1985, 1996) posited that individuals engage in suicidal behavior because of severe, intolerable *psychological pain*—a condition he described as *psychache*—that results from unmet psychological needs. Shneidman suggested that all people who die by suicide experience psychache prior to their deaths, although only a small percentage of people who experience psychache die by suicide. This indicates his belief that psychache is a necessary but not sufficient condition for suicide to occur. According to Shneidman, the additional factor of *lethality* is also necessary for suicide to take place. "Suicide happens," said Shneidman (1996), "when the psychache is deemed unbearable and death is actively sought to stop the unceasing flow of painful consciousness" (p. 13).

Like Shneidman, Roy Baumeister's (1990) *escape theory of suicidal behavior* also posits that mental or psychological pain is a key factor in suicidal behavior, although Baumeister places a greater emphasis on the role of *aversive self-awareness* in his conceptualization of suicidal behavior. According to Baumeister, for suicidal behavior to emerge, several sequential steps must take place. First, an individual must experience a severe discrepancy between one's expectations and actual events. Once this occurs, a high level of aversive self-awareness develops, leading to highly negative emotional experiences. To escape from these negative emotions and aversive experiences of self-awareness, the individual retreats into a state referred to as "cognitive deconstruction." In this state, the individual becomes essentially "numb" in regards to his or her emotions and self-awareness, developing reduced inhibitions and impulse control, and subsequently a heightened risk for suicide.

The desire to escape negative, aversive emotions that is such an important component of Baumeister's theory is similar to the primary risk factor in Marsha Linehan's (1993) *emotional dysregulation theory of suicidal behavior*. Linehan's theory posits that suicide results from emotional dysregulation, a condition that develops from the joint influences of biological predispositions and invalidating environments (e.g., child abuse). Linehan initially developed her theory in the context of treating individuals with borderline personality disorder and self-injury. For Linehan, self-injury is a primary example of a maladaptive attempt to regulate emotions when an individual's usual emotion regulation mechanisms have broken down or have not adequately developed. Dialectical behavior therapy, the cognitive-behavioral treatment derived from her theory, has been applied to the treatment of suicidal adolescents (Miller, Rathus, & Linehan, 2007) and will be discussed in greater detail in Chapter 6.

Joiner's Interpersonal–Psychological Theory of Suicidal Behavior

Thomas Joiner's interpersonal–psychological theory of suicidal behavior (Joiner, 2005, 2009; Joiner et al., 2009) has received significant attention in recent years due to its comprehensiveness and its growing empirical support. More importantly for the purposes of this book, it also has useful and practical implications for preventing youth suicidal behavior, conducting suicide risk assessments, and intervening with suicidal youth. Consequently, this theory will be reviewed in some detail here, and the implications of it will be discussed in subsequent chapters in this book.

Joiner's theory of suicidal behavior was not designed to replace the theories of individuals such as Beck and Shneidman, but rather to build on them, to incorporate their strengths, and to be both broader and more conceptually precise than these earlier theories (Joiner, 2005). For example, even if one accepts Beck's theory that hopelessness is a key variable in causing suicide, "what in particular are suicidal people hopeless about? If hopelessness is key, why then do relatively few hopeless people die by suicide?" (Joiner, 2005, p. 39). Shneidman's (1985, 1996) psychache theory of suicidal behavior has similar problems, given that he does not indicate precisely what a suicidal person is experiencing psychache about, or what leads to its development. Neither Beck nor Shneidman adequately articulated why some individuals who exhibit hopelessness or psychological pain die by suicide but many others do not.

According to Joiner (2009), people (including children and adolescents) die by suicide essentially "because they can, and because they want to" (p. 244). In other words, individuals are at increased risk for suicide if they have both the *capability* to die by suicide and the *desire* to do so. How does an individual become capable of suicide, given that evolutionary forces operate to promote self-preservation and avoid self-destruction? Joiner and his colleagues (2009) suggest that an answer to this question can be found by considering what "is obvious after a moment's reflection and yet has been very neglected in past work, namely, that lethal self-injury is associated with so much fear and/or pain that few people are capable of it . . . a fact that applies even to most of those who have ideas about and the desire for suicide" (p. 4).

> Young people die by suicide essentially because they can and because they want to. In other words, individuals are at increased risk for suicide if they have both the *capability* to die by suicide as well as the *desire* to do so.

Consequently, according to Joiner's theory, the only individuals who are capable of suicide are those who have been through enough past experiences involving pain and provocation (especially involving intentional self-injury) to have *habituated* to the fear and pain associated with death, so that the self-preservation instinct is altered. Although the self-preservation instinct cannot be eliminated entirely, it can be substantially reduced, particularly through the frequent exposure and eventual habituation to pain and fear. Furthermore, although previous self-injury (especially with the intent to die) is the most powerful habituation experience for decreasing fear and pain about future episodes of self-injury, it is not the only kind of experience that can serve this function.

To varying degrees, *any* fear- and/or pain-inducing experience—such as injuries, accidents, violence (either as victim, perpetrator, or witness), and/or "daredevil" behaviors—may effectively function to habituate an individual from a fear of death. Much like a skydiver who overcomes his fear after repeatedly jumping from airplanes, Joiner's theory suggests that individuals overcome their fear of death by suicide through frequent encounters with painful and/or provocative experiences that lead to eventual habituation. This theory may help at least partially explain why adults in such varying occupations as medical doctors, police officers, and soldiers have elevated suicide rates compared to individuals in many other lines of work; the common denominator in each of these professions is the frequent exposure to, and presumably eventual habituation to, physically painful or provocative experiences (Joiner, 2005).

Joiner and colleagues (2009) add that the capability to die by suicide requires both time and practice, and is in fact very hard to do. Indeed, there is ample evidence that killing others or oneself is often a highly difficult task. Grossman (1995) points out how within-species fights are often nonlethal, including fights involving humans. For example, soldiers in battle frequently miss each other when using firearms at rates that far exceed chance. Grossman quoted an eyewitness of the Civil War during the battle of Vicksburg in 1863, who said that "it seems strange that a company of men can fire volley after volley at a like number of men and not over a distance of fifteen steps and not cause a single casualty. Yet such was the facts in this case" (p. 11). The instinctive prohibition against killing one's own kind appears to also extend to killing oneself. Although highly lethal means aimed at highly vulnerable areas (e.g., pulling the trigger on a gun aimed at one's head) will likely lead to a quick death, many suicidal individuals have learned about how difficult it is, both physically and psychologically, to engage in self-destructive behavior.

The *physical* difficulty of suicide is illustrated by Runyon (2004), who at age 14 doused himself with gasoline and set himself on fire in an attempt to kill himself. Prior to that suicide attempt, he had made several other attempts, as he describes in the following passage:

> I wonder why all the ways I've tried to kill myself haven't worked. I mean, I've tried hanging. I used to have a noose tied to my closet pole. I'd go in there and slip the thing over my head and let my weight go. But every time I started to lose consciousness, I'd just stand up. I tried to take pills. One afternoon, I took twenty Advil, but that just made me sleepy. And all the times I tried to cut my wrists, I could never cut deep enough. That's the thing—your body tries to keep you alive no matter what you do. (p. 13)

The *psychological* difficulty of suicide is illustrated by this quote by Knipfel (2000), speculating on why his multiple suicide attempts did not result in death:

> It was clear that it was cowardice that had kept me from going all the way before. I had never succeeded because I didn't have the nerve. . . . No matter how hard I tried, nothing worked. I threw myself down a flight of stairs, drank bleach, cut my wrists, stepped in front of buses, all to no avail. (pp. 13, 33)

The notion that suicide is a cowardly act is a common one. Writer Tom Hunt, author of *Cliffs of Despair* (2006), interviewed a man who for many years had served on a team that recovered the bodies of people who had jumped to their deaths from the seaside cliffs of Beachy Head in the United Kingdom. When the man was asked if he thought it took courage to jump off Beachy Head, he responded that it was "the coward's way out." He then added that "it would take far more courage to actually face up to life, to face up to the problems, depression or whatever it is, that's bringing them to that point than to actually take, in a way, the easy option" (p. 115). Although this view appears to be one that is widely held, the fact remains that dying by suicide is not a cowardly act but rather one that requires a great deal of resolve as well as personal courage, in the sense that to die by suicide typically requires great effort as well as successfully defeating the life preservation instinct (Joiner, 2005).

The capacity or capability to die by suicide, however, does not necessarily entail a *desire* for suicide. For example, individuals trained in the martial arts have the capacity to inflict physical harm upon others, but except in self-defense situations they do not have the desire to do so and therefore do not typically behave aggressively (Joiner, 2009). Similarly, according to Joiner's theory, the capability to engage in suicidal behavior is a necessary but not sufficient condition for suicide to occur. Along with capability, the desire for suicide is also required.

As to what constitutes suicidal desire, Joiner postulates that for suicide to take place an individual must experience two co-occurring, interpersonally relevant states of mind: perceived burdensomeness and failed belongingness. *Perceived burdensomeness* refers to the belief that an individual's existence is somehow burdensome to others, such as family, friends, or society as a whole (Joiner et al., 2009). When applied to children and adolescents, the notion of perceived burdensomeness may also incorporate perceptions of *expendability* and *ineffectiveness* (Joiner, 2005). That is, children and adolescents who perceive themselves as being expendable and/or ineffective often view themselves as being a burden to their family or to others in their environment. In essence, these youth view their death as being worth more than their life.

Understanding the concept of perceived burdensomeness is a useful antidote to the common myth that suicide is a "selfish" act (Jamison, 1999; Joiner, 2010), in the sense that by killing themselves individuals are selfishly disregarding family and friends who will be emotionally devastated as a result of their suicide. From the perspective of suicidal individuals, however, their suicide is not viewed as a selfish act but rather as a beneficial one, because it would result in fewer burdens for their families and friends, who would be better off without them anyway. It is important to recognize that this viewpoint, common among many suicidal people, represents a significant and potentially life-threatening *misperception*—one that can result in fatal consequences (Joiner, 2009).

Kay Redfield Jamison, a recognized authority on both bipolar disorder and suicide, possesses firsthand knowledge of this phenomenon, as described in her book *Night Falls Fast: Understanding Suicide* (1999):

> I had tried years earlier to kill myself, and nearly died in the attempt, but did not consider it either a selfish or non-selfish thing to have done. It was simply the end of what I could bear, the last afternoon of having to imagine waking up the next morning only to start all over again with a thick mind and black imaginings. It was the final outcome of a bad disease, a disease it seemed to me I would never get the better of. No amount of love from or for other people— and there was a lot—could help. No advantage of a caring family and fabulous job was enough to overcome the pain and hopelessness I felt; no passionate or romantic love, however strong, could make a difference. . . . I knew my life to be a shambles, and I believed—incontestably— that my family, friends, and patients would be better off without me. There wasn't much of me left anymore, anyway, and I thought my death would free up the wasted energies and well-meant efforts that were being wasted on my behalf. (p. 291)

Similarly, Jamison (1999) quotes a young chemist who stated the following, presumably in a suicide note, shortly before his death by suicide:

> The question of suicide and selfishness to close friends and relatives is one that I can't answer or even give an opinion on. It is obvious, however, that I have pondered it and decided I would hurt them less dead than alive. (p. 292)

Consistent with Joiner's theory, and like other individuals with a history of suicidal behavior, neither Jamison nor the chemist considered their desire to die as reflecting a selfish impulse. Instead, both appeared to view suicide as a reasonable response to the emotional suffering they were experiencing, and as a way to decrease the burden they perceived themselves as having on others.

Although Joiner proposes that perceived burdensomeness is a necessary condition for the desire for suicide to develop, he does not see this condition as being sufficient. In addition to perceived burdensomeness, failed belongingness is also required. *Failed belongingness* refers to "the experience that one is alienated from others and not an integral part of a family, circle of friends, or other valued groups" (Joiner, 2009, p. 245). It is roughly, though not perfectly, synonymous with loneliness and social alienation (Joiner et al., 2009). Like perceived burdensomeness, failed belongingness is a *perceptual state*. For example, a suicidal youth could have many friends, but if the youth *perceives* that this is not the case, and perceives himself as someone who is socially isolated and does not belong, the risk for suicide increases. When individuals simultaneously experience significant degrees of perceived burdensomeness *and* failed belongingness, Joiner (2009) asserts that "the desire for death develops because of the perception that there is nothing left to live for" (p. 245).

To briefly summarize Joiner's theory, why do people, including children and adolescents, die by suicide? Because they have both the capability and the desire to do so. Who has the capability to die by suicide? Those individuals who, through habituation, have acquired the ability to enact lethal self-injury. Who has the desire to die by suicide? Those individuals who perceive themselves as being a burden on others (e.g., family members, friends) and as not sufficiently belonging to a valued group or relationship (Joiner, 2009).

Like the other theories presented here, a comprehensive discussion of Joiner's theory of suicidal behavior is outside the scope of this book. Readers interested in a more extensive review of the interpersonal–psychological theory of suicidal behavior, as well as the empirical and anecdotal evidence that supports it, are encouraged to review works by Joiner and his colleagues (Joiner, 2005, 2009; Joiner et al., 2009).

THE IMPORTANCE OF
REDUCING SUFFERING IN SUICIDAL YOUTH

A common theme in each of the contemporary theories described in this chapter is their emphasis on psychological pain and suffering as a primary causal variable in the development of suicidal behavior. However, although the words "pain" and "suffering" are often used and interpreted synonymously by many theorists, they are not identical and there are actually important distinctions between them. For example, Kabat-Zinn (1990) distinguishes between pain and suffering as follows:

> Pain is a natural part of the experience of life. Suffering is one of many possible responses to pain. Suffering can come out of either physical or emotional pain. It involves our thoughts and emotions and how they frame the meaning of our experiences. Suffering, too, is perfectly natural. In fact the human condition is often spoken of as inevitable suffering. But it is important to remember that suffering is only *one* response to the experience of pain . . . it is not always the pain per se but the way we see it and react to it that determines the degree of suffering we will experience. And it is the suffering that we fear the most, not the pain. (pp. 285–286)

Similarly, it is important to recognize that emotional suffering is often the result of cognitive variables, as noted by DeMello (1998):

> What causes suffering? Mental activity, constructing our thoughts. Sometimes the mind is in repose, and all is well. But sometimes it begins to act, elaborating what Buddha calls the con-

struction of thoughts. It begins to make judgments, evaluations, different and varied thoughts. The mind moves along in a way that means evaluating things and judging persons and events. Suffering is the result of evaluation, judgments, and mental constructs. (p. 94)

School personnel, particularly school-based mental health professionals, should recognize the importance of reducing psychological and emotional suffering in their attempts to prevent suicidal behavior and intervene with suicidal youth. Indeed, a critical point to understand is that individuals contemplating or attempting suicide often do not want to die as much as they want their suffering to end (Shneidman, 1996). In other words, suicidal people, including suicidal youth, are often not motivated by a wish to die as much as they are motivated by a desire to *escape* from what they perceive to be an otherwise unbearable situation (Williams, 2001). For many suicidal children and adolescents, their multiple and varied attempts to decrease or end their suffering has not been successful, and as a result they may view death as the only viable option for accomplishing this goal. Consequently, individuals exhibiting suicidal behavior are often seeking relief from a kind of suffering that is "prolonged, intense, and unpalliated" (Jamison, 1999, p. 24). For suicidal youth, this suffering is experienced to such a degree that it is eventually perceived as being unendurable.

> **Individuals contemplating or attempting suicide often do not want to die as much as they want their suffering to end.**

Although psychological pain and the suffering that so often accompanies it is not sufficient to cause suicidal behavior, when experienced in conjunction with the desire for death and the acquired ability to engage in potentially lethal self-harm, the risk for suicide may increase significantly (Joiner, 2005). Although school personnel may not play the primary role in providing treatment for suicidal youth, they clearly can and should be an important part of this process. Specific practices school personnel can engage in to prevent youth suicidal behavior and respond effectively when it does occur will be discussed in subsequent chapters in this book.

CONCLUDING COMMENTS

Youth suicidal behavior is a significant public health problem in the United States and throughout the world. Despite fluctuating rates over time, the number of child and adolescent suicides has increased significantly in recent decades, a trend that is likely to continue. The purpose of this chapter was to provide a definition of suicidal behavior, as well as some basic demographic information about suicidal youth to put this national and international problem into an appropriate context. Information was also presented regarding when, where, and how youth suicide most often occurs, as well as a brief overview of some prominent theories as to why people in general—and children and adolescents in particular—die by suicide. Joiner's interpersonal-psychological theory of suicidal behavior was given particular emphasis because of its clear and practical implications for suicide prevention, assessment, and intervention—topics that will be discussed more extensively in later chapters. First, however, it is important to better understand the role of schools and school personnel in preventing youth suicide, including liability issues and ethical responsibilities. These important topics are addressed in Chapter 2.

CHAPTER 2

Youth Suicidal Behavior and the Schools

Because the school is the community institution that has the primary responsibility for the education and socialization of youth, the school context has the potential to moderate the occurrence of risk behaviors and to identify and secure help for at-risk individuals.

—John Kalafat

A very real and practical question that school personnel need to ask concerns the responsibility and liability of the school system with regard to suicide.

—Scott Poland

The noblest goal of an organization or individual is to save lives.

—Gene Cash

Because the problem of youth suicidal behavior is so serious and pervasive and because children and adolescents spend much of their time in school, it has frequently been suggested that schools take on a more prominent role in youth suicide prevention efforts. For example, in their excellent text *Adolescent Suicide: Assessment and Intervention* (2006), Alan L. Berman, David A. Jobes, and Morton M. Silverman ask the reader to do the following:

> Imagine yourself sitting at a symposium on adolescent suicide called in response to media reports of an alarming increase in the incidence of youth suicide. An interdisciplinary panel of distinguished speakers has gathered to present views and explanations for the problem and suggestions for its resolution. The panel focuses on the schools and the intensely competitive pressures of the times as sources of stress. Youth suicide is noted by some panelists to be an international problem. Others question the validity and adequacy of official statistics; still others comment on the problem of journalistic sensationalism. Concerns are raised about suicide clusters, the role of suggestibility and imitation, as well as the availability of guns. Various preventive and intervention strategies are proposed, and the educational system is singled out as uniquely positioned to play a key role in prevention. (p. 21)

Any contemporary school-based mental health professional, including school psychologists, school counselors, or school social workers, could imagine attending such a symposium at any number of conferences. What is perhaps most interesting about this example, however, is that the symposium it describes occurred in 1910. The chair of the symposium was Sigmund Freud, and it was one of the last meetings of the Vienna Psychoanalytic Society (whose members included Carl Jung and Alfred Adler), which was presided over by Freud and held on Wednesday nights in his living room (Berman et al., 2006). The fact that issues similar to those confronting us today were being discussed over a century ago is a useful reminder that the problem of youth suicide is not new, and that this topic has been a vexing and perplexing one for a very long time (Berman, 2009).

SUICIDE PREVENTION IN THE SCHOOLS

The ominous and troubling increases in youth suicide that occurred during the second half of the 20th century in the United States and other countries spawned the development and growth of suicide prevention programs in schools. The first U.S. studies and subsequent literature reviews that attempted to examine and evaluate these programs began appearing in the 1980s (e.g., Ashworth, Spirito, Colella, & Benedict-Drew, 1986; Nelson, 1987; Overholser, Hemstreet, Spirito, & Vyse, 1989; Ross, 1980; Spirito, Overholser, Ashworth, Morgan, & Benedict-Drew, 1988) and grew more prevalent during the 1990s (e.g., Ciffone, 1993; Eggert, Thompson, Herring, & Nicholas, 1995; Garland & Zigler, 1993; Kalafat & Elias, 1994; Klingman & Hochdorf, 1993; LaFromboise & Howard-Pitney, 1995; Mazza, 1997; Miller & DuPaul, 1996; Orbach & Bar-Joseph, 1993; Reynolds & Mazza, 1994; Shaffer, Garland, Vieland, Underwood, & Busner, 1991; Shaffer et al., 1990; Zenere & Lazarus, 1997) and the first decade of the 21st century (e.g., Aseltine & DeMartino, 2004; Ciffone, 2007; Kalafat, 2003; Mazza, 2006; Mazza & Reynolds, 2008; Miller, Eckert, & Mazza, 2009; Randall, Eggert, & Pike, 2001; Zenere & Lazarus, 2009).

Developed initially in the 1970s, school-based suicide prevention programs grew rapidly during the 1980s. For example, Garland, Shaffer, and Whittle (1989) conducted a national survey of these programs and reported that the number of schools using them increased from 789 in 1984 to 1,709 in 1986. After a period of declining interest in these programs occurred during the 1990s, a renewed interest in them was generated by federal government actions, such as the Surgeon General's *Call to Action to Prevent Suicide* (U.S. Department of Health and Human Services, 1999).

Earlier, so-called first-generation school-based suicide prevention programs (i.e., many of the programs that were the subject of studies published in the 1980s) were criticized for their lack of focus regarding their target audience and their objectives (Kalafat, 2003). An additional criticism of these programs, and one that may have actually undermined their effectiveness, was the finding that a large majority of student informational programs appeared to subscribe to a so-called stress model of suicidal behavior (Garland et al., 1989). Although well-intended, this model presents a distorted and inaccurate view of suicidal behavior in youth. Specifically, it represents suicide as "a response to a significant or extreme amount of stress, ignoring the substantial amount of research that has shown that adolescent suicide and suicidal behavior is strongly associated with mental illness or psychopathology" (Mazza, 1997, p. 390).

The "stress model" of suicide has also been criticized because it essentially "normalizes" suicide and suicidal behavior by suggesting that given enough stress anyone would be vulnerable to suicide (Mazza, 1997; Miller & DuPaul, 1996). Program directors who used a stress model in their suicide prevention programs indicated that they avoided using a mental illness model because they feared that linking suicide to mental health problems would discourage youth from disclosing their own suicidal behavior or that of their peers (Garland et al., 1989). However, Shaffer, Garland, Gould, Fisher, and Trautman (1988) took the opposite position. They argued that by "normalizing" suicide, a stress model would make it a more acceptable behavior among students. They also argued that emphasizing the relationship between suicide and mental illness would make suicide a less appealing method for dealing with problems among potentially suicidal youth. Finally, their review of the literature suggested that informational programs appeared to be least beneficial to those students most likely to be suicidal. The recommendations made by Shaffer and his colleagues at this time, which included essentially putting a "moratorium" on certain prevention programs, aroused significant controversy and discussion about the possible unintended side effects of such programs.

> **More recent school-based suicide prevention programs provide students with the accurate information that suicide is not the result of stress but rather a possible by-product of serious mental health problems, most typically depression.**

More recent "second-generation" school-based suicide prevention programs generally provided students with the more accurate information that suicide is not the result of stress but rather a possible by-product of serious mental health problems, most typically depression. These programs were also focused to a greater extent on preparing students to respond effectively to their at-risk peers and to get help from adults, and demonstrated positive effects on student knowledge and intentions to seek help on behalf of their troubled peers. However, these programs, like most other programs evaluated both before and since, often did not specifically examine the effects of prevention programming on the *behavior* of students considered at risk or high risk for suicide. These programs have also been criticized for assuming that changes in knowledge and attitudes will lead to behavioral change, which is not necessarily the case (Berman et al., 2006; Miller & DuPaul, 1996).

The typical school-based suicide prevention program appears to be a curriculum-based, classroom-centered, lecture-discussion program, usually provided at the high school level during three to six classes (Goldsmith, Pellmar, Kleinman, & Bunney, 2002). The goals of these programs have typically included increasing awareness about youth suicide, discussing and dispelling various myths and misinformation about suicide,

> **The typical school-based suicide prevention program appears to be a curriculum-based, classroom-centered, lecture-discussion program, usually provided at the high school level during three to six classes.**

increasing student recognition of risk factors and possible warning signs, changing attitudes about accessing help, and providing information about resources in the school and community. Many programs also provide similar information and gatekeeper education sessions for school staff members. Some programs also use additional components in their program, such as teaching students problem-solving and crisis management skills (Berman et al., 2006).

The increased proliferation of suicide prevention programs in the schools during the last few decades does not necessarily imply that all school personnel approve of or support this development. In fact, school personnel may have several reasonable and legitimate questions in regard to this issue. For example, how effective are school-based prevention programs? Why should schools be involved in youth suicide prevention? Is this really the responsibility of the schools?

HOW EFFECTIVE ARE SCHOOL-BASED SUICIDE PREVENTION PROGRAMS?

As noted earlier in this chapter, the evaluation of school-based suicide prevention programs is a relatively recent development. Leenars and his colleagues (2001), in reviewing the international status of school-based suicide prevention programs, indicated that the United States and Canada were "in the forefront" (p. 381) of these efforts. An increasing number of countries are adopting some form of suicide prevention programming in their schools (e.g., Ireland; Lithuania), including Japan, where suicide has been a taboo subject for centuries. Nevertheless, many undeveloped countries have no school-based suicide prevention programs to speak of (or, for that matter, suicide prevention programs of any kind). Even among developed countries (e.g., Japan, Australia), school-based suicide prevention efforts are "only beginning . . . lagging some 20 years behind" the United States and Canada (Leenars et al., 2001, p. 381).

Given the recent development of these programs, it is not surprising that much more research is needed to evaluate their effectiveness. An increasing number of studies examining the effectiveness of school-based suicide prevention programs are available, but they remain relatively few in number. Furthermore, among those studies that have been published, most exhibit serious methodological problems that make at least some of their conclusions questionable (Miller, Eckert, & Mazza, 2009). This kind of research is also inherently challenging to conduct for a variety of reasons, including the relatively low base rate of suicide in the general student population (which is fortunate, of course, but makes studying this topic more difficult).

Much remains to be learned about school-based suicide prevention and what components of it are most effective for identifying suicidal youth, responding effectively to students when they are identified, and ultimately reducing youth suicidal behavior. The most recent literature review examining the effectiveness of these programs at the time of this writing was conducted by me and my colleagues (Miller, Eckert, & Mazza, 2009). We evaluated the effectiveness of 13 studies involving school-based suicide prevention programs that were published between 1987 and 2007. All studies were analyzed according to eight methodological indicators based on the Task Force on Evidence-Based Interventions in School Psychology Procedural and Coding Manual (Kratochwill & Stoiber, 2002). Each study was coded on a 4-point rating of evidence (i.e., 0 = no evidence; 1 = marginal or weak evidence; 2 = promising evidence; 3 = strong evidence). Our review found that most of the published studies exhibited significant methodological problems. For example, very few studies demonstrated promising evidence of educational/clinical significance, identifiable components linked to statistically significant primary outcomes, and program implementation integrity (Miller, Eckert, & Mazza, 2009).

What *do* we know about school-based suicide prevention programs? We actually know a great deal, and our knowledge regarding what works in suicide prevention—and what does not—continues to accumulate. For example, we know that presenting information to students and school personnel can increase the knowledge those groups have about youth suicidal behavior and can lead to an increased number of referrals to school mental health professionals (Mazza, 1997; Miller & DuPaul, 1996). We know, too, that presenting information to students about youth suicide can help change their attitudes about it (Kalafat, 2003), and that discussing possible warning signs of suicide does not result in negative and unintended side effects, such as increasing negative mood or having the counterintentional effect of increasing suicidal behavior (Rudd et al., 2006; Van Orden et al., 2006).

We know that providing information to students regarding suicide awareness and intervention, teaching them problem-solving and coping skills, and reinforcing protective factors while addressing risk factors may lead to improvements in students' problem-solving skills as well as reductions in self-reported suicide vulnerability (Miller, Eckert, & Mazza, 2009). We know that there are reliable and valid screening and assessment measures and methods available (Goldston, 2003; Gutierrez & Osman, 2009; Reynolds, 1991), that these can be used at schoolwide, classwide, and/or individual levels (Gutierrez & Osman, 2008), that they can effectively identify students who are at risk or at high risk for suicide (Gutierrez & Osman, 2008, 2009), and that the use of these screening devices does not lead to an increased level of self-reported distress or suicidal behavior among students (Gould et al., 2005), as some had feared.

We also know some approaches to school-based suicide prevention that will likely *not* be effective. For example, one-time-only programs, such as assembly presentations, do not provide sufficient time and resources to be effective, nor do they allow the opportunity to monitor all students' reactions to the material presented. Prevention programs should not include media depictions of suicidal behavior, or presentations by youth who have made previous suicide attempts, because research suggests these may be counterproductive for vulnerable youth (the topics of dealing with the media and possible contagion effects related to suicide will be discussed extensively in Chapter 7). Outsourcing prevention programs rather than developing local expertise among existing school personnel fails to enhance available local resources and is therefore not recommended either. Poorly implemented programs (i.e., those that lack treatment integrity), regardless of their quality or the frequency of their use, will likely not have positive effects on student behavior. Finally, solitary prevention programs should be avoided because their use oversimplifies the complexity of youth suicidal behavior, and as a result they will likely be ineffective in preventing it (Kalafat, 2003)

Unfortunately, there is still much we do not know about the effects of school-based suicide prevention programs. Perhaps the most glaring problem is the need for research to conclusively demonstrate that suicide prevention programs in schools can reduce suicidal behavior, particularly its most extreme forms (e.g., suicide attempts and suicide). That is not to say, however, that we have *no* evidence in this area. In fact, data collected over an 18-year period in the Miami–Dade Public School District provides some compelling evidence that school-based suicide prevention can indeed reduce the incidence of youth suicide.

The suicide prevention programs implemented in Miami–Dade public schools is particularly interesting because it provides one of the few examples in the professional literature of a school-based suicide prevention program demonstrating long-term reductions in actual suicidal behavior, rather than simply changes in students' knowledge and attitudes about suicide. In addition, the programs implemented at Miami–Dade are noteworthy in their universal, districtwide focus.

Suicide Prevention in the Miami–Dade County Public School District

Located in Miami, Florida, the Miami–Dade County Public School District is the nation's fourth largest, serving over 350,000 students in 392 school sites. The district is urban and highly diverse, with over 60% of the student body being Hispanic, over a quarter of the students African American, and less than 10% of the students of European American descent. In 1988, 18 Miami–Dade students died by suicide. The level of alarm and concern generated by these suicides provided the impetus for developing a districtwide suicide prevention program, which formally began the following year. The prevention program included a number of components at multiple levels, which have been modified as needed in the intervening years since the program began. Zenere and Lazarus (1997) examined the effects of this comprehensive program on various aspects of suicidal behavior, including suicidal ideation, suicide attempts, and suicide, over a 5-year period. Although no significant reductions were observed in suicidal ideation during this time, both the number of student suicide attempts and the number of student suicides decreased substantially after program implementation.

Despite its methodological limitations, this case study provided initial evidence that school-based suicide prevention programs can potentially reduce youth suicidal behavior, including its most serious forms (i.e., suicide attempts and suicide). It is also the only study found in a recent literature review to demonstrate promising evidence for educational/clinical (as opposed to merely statistical) significance (Miller, Eckert, & Mazza, 2009). A follow-up longitudinal study over an 18-year period (1988–2006) indicated that the reduction in the number of both student suicide attempts and student suicides was sustained over time (Zenere & Lazarus, 2009).

Although Miami–Dade is the only school district of which I am aware that has collected and published data on the effects of its suicide prevention programs on various forms of youth suicidal behavior over an extensive period, it is not the only major metropolitan school district implementing suicide prevention programs on a massive, districtwide level. The Los Angeles Unified School District, which includes over 1,200 schools, serves approximately 850,000 students, and is second in size only to the New York City Public Schools, began implementing a youth suicide prevention program in the 1980s. The program is coordinated by a school psychologist who provides a variety of services, including training school personnel about the risk factors and warning signs of suicide, providing consultative support services, training crisis teams, and providing postvention support in the aftermath of a student, staff, or parent death by suicide (Lieberman et al., 2008).

COMPONENTS OF COMPREHENSIVE SCHOOL-BASED SUICIDE PREVENTION PROGRAMS

Berman and colleagues (2006) identified seven components of comprehensive school-based suicide prevention programs: (1) early detection and referral-making skills; (2) resource identification; (3) help-seeking behavior; (4) professional education; (5) parent education; (6) primary prevention; and (7) postvention.

Early detection and referral-making skills refers to the need to teach students and staff the risk factors and (especially) possible warning signs of suicide, as well as what they should do and what procedures they should follow in making a referral if they suspect a student might be suicidal. *Resource identification* is necessary because an effective referral requires having competent professionals in the school to conduct suicide risk assessments and competent professionals in the community to whom referrals can be made if necessary. Community resources, mental health agencies, psychiatric hospitals, and private practitioners can be evaluated to ensure the competencies of those professionals to whom at-risk or high-risk students may be sent. Resources in the school designed to help students should also be clearly communicated to them (Berman et al., 2006).

One of the collateral benefits of resource identification for students is that it makes the idea of *help-seeking behavior* more normative. When schools and communities demonstrate concern for the services to suicidal youth and the quality of these services, awareness increases, as does the potential for greater destigmatization of suicidal people. As a result, a greater acceptance of resource utilization may be created; it is even possible that student compliance with referred treatments might increase. Also related to resource identification is *professional education*, in the sense that an improvement in school personnel's education regarding youth suicide increases the schools' identified resources (Berman et al., 2006).

> **When schools and communities demonstrate concern for the services to suicidal youth and the quality of these services, awareness increases as does the potential for greater destigmatization of suicidal people.**

If the broad view of the school's role includes educating all segments of the community, then *parent education* regarding youth suicide is an important component of school-based suicide prevention efforts as well. Parents/caregivers should be provided with information regarding risk factors and warning signs for suicide in much the same way that this information is provided to students and

> **Parents/caregivers should be provided with information regarding risk factors and warning signs for suicide in much the same way that this information is provided to students and school personnel.**

school personnel. In addition, given that most youth suicides occur by use of a handgun and take place in the home, outreach programs on gun management and safety can be provided to parents (Simon, 2007), particularly those with sons or daughters considered at risk or at high risk for suicidal behavior (Berman et al., 2006).

Primary prevention strategies (what are described as "universal" strategies in this book) are likely "the most effective and probably the most cost-effective" (Berman et al., 2006, p. 320) procedures available for school personnel in suicide prevention efforts. Berman and his colleagues recommend that these programs teach health-enhancing behaviors through teaching behavioral skills. They recommend that these programs begin in elementary school, that they be reinforced through follow-up training, and that they focus on building students' adaptive skills and competencies. Finally, these authors suggest that comprehensive, school-based suicide prevention programs should contain *postvention* procedures. As defined by Berman and colleagues (2006), these include procedures that should be followed not only if or when a student dies by suicide, but also in those situations in which a serious but nonfatal suicide attempt occurs. For example, postvention procedures would be used in situations in which a student made a damaging suicide attempt, was then hospitalized for several days as a result, and is now returning to school.

In addition to its comprehensive approach to school-based suicide prevention, one of the clear advantages of the components described earlier is the relative ease with which they can be implemented. Unlike other schoolwide initiatives, such as schoolwide positive behavior support, implementing the recommendations listed above is not particularly costly either financially or in terms of time and effort of school staff. Consequently, a comprehensive suicide prevention program would likely be implemented much more easily, and therefore much more quickly, than other schoolwide initiatives. Just because it may not be overly difficult (at least logistically) to implement such programs, however, should not be viewed as a sufficient reason for doing so. There are many more important reasons why schools should be involved in suicide prevention, as described below.

WHY SHOULD SCHOOLS BE INVOLVED IN SUICIDE PREVENTION?

> **Given the substantial amount of time children and adolescents spend in school, educational facilities provide an ideal place for focused, suicide prevention efforts.**

In addition to some emerging evidence that school-based suicide prevention programs can be effective (e.g., Kalafat, 2003; Miller, Eckert, & Mazza, 2009; Zenere & Lazarus, 1997, 2009), schools should be involved in youth suicide prevention efforts for many other reasons. First, as was mentioned previously, given the substantial amount of time children and adolescents spend in school, educational facilities provide an ideal place for focused, suicide prevention efforts. Schools are places where "student attention is held relatively captive, where teaching and learning are normative tasks, and where peer interactions can be mobilized around a common theme" (Berman et al., 2006, p. 313). Second, as is discussed in greater detail later, school personnel have an ethical responsibility to make reasonable and appropriate efforts to prevent youth suicide whenever possible, including creating clear policies and procedures on this topic (Jacob, 2009).

> **School personnel have an ethical responsibility to make reasonable and appropriate efforts to prevent youth suicide whenever possible, including creating clear school policies and procedures on this topic.**

Third, as will be discussed in Chapter 4, a strong relationship exists between youth suicide and mental health problems (Mazza, 2006), and school personnel are being increasingly asked to take on a greater role in addressing these issues, particularly in the area of prevention and mental health promotion (Miller, Gilman, & Martens, 2008; Power, DuPaul, Shapiro, & Kazak, 2003). Although some school personnel may question the appropriateness of this responsibility, they ultimately have little choice in the matter, given that no institution other than the school system oversees the mental health needs of children and adolescents (Mazza &

> **A strong relationship exists between youth suicide and mental health problems, and school personnel are being increasingly asked to take on a greater role in addressing these issues, particularly in the area of prevention and mental health promotion.**

Reynolds, 2008). As we shall see, the presence of mental health problems is a primary risk factor for the development of suicidal behavior, and both preventing and providing treatment for mental health problems is a major characteristic of effective suicide prevention programs.

A fourth reason schools should be involved in suicide prevention is the lack of personnel adequately trained to respond to youth suicidal behavior. Given that recent national surveys indicate that even school-based mental health professionals (e.g., school psychologists) perceive themselves as requiring additional training in suicide risk assessment (Miller & Jome, 2008), prevention, and intervention (Darius-Anderson & Miller, 2010; Debski et al., 2007; Miller & Jome, in press), a variety of school practitioners would clearly benefit from additional information on this topic. Moreover, in those tragic cases in which a student does die by suicide, schools can play an important role in developing postvention procedures (discussed in Chapter 7) designed to prevent additional suicidal behavior, including possible contagion effects (Brock, 2002).

Another important reason for school personnel to be more actively involved in suicide prevention is its relationship to the school's primary function—education. For example, one recent study found that adolescents with poor reading ability were more likely to experience suicidal ideation or attempts and to drop out of school than youth with typical reading ability, even when controlling for psychiatric and demographic variables (Daniel et al., 2006). Similarly, there may also be a relationship between *perceived* academic performance and youth suicidal behavior. For example, a study found that perceptions of failing academic performance were associated with an increased probability of a suicide attempt among a group of adolescents, even when controlling for self-esteem, locus of control, and depressive symptoms (Richardson, Bergen, Martin, Roeger, & Allison, 2005). A longitudinal follow-up study found that perceived academic performance, along with self-esteem and locus of control, were significantly associated with suicidal behavior, with perceived academic performance found to be a particularly good long-term predictor of suicidal behavior (Martin, Richardson, Bergen, Roeger, & Allison, 2005). Additional research in this area is needed, especially given the hypothesized relationship discussed in the previous chapter between perceived ineffectiveness and suicide (Joiner, 2005).

To avoid any possible confusion, I should add that these findings should not be interpreted as suggesting that child or adolescent problems in reading, or even perceived problems in reading, will generally or inevitably result in increased student suicidality. Based on what we know about the causal factors associated with suicide, these academic problems would not, by themselves and in isolation, lead to the development of suicidal behavior. Nevertheless, these and other studies illustrate the significant relationship often found between mental health problems and academic difficulties.

These studies also provide the useful reminder that improvement in one of these areas can and often does have positive effects on the other (Miller, George, & Fogt, 2005). Indeed, research clearly indicates that improving students' academic success often has the collateral effect of enhancing students' behavior and mental health (Berninger, 2006). For example, when mental health interventions were compared to a typical school treatment (i.e., regular academic program), the mental health interventions were found to be no more effective than the regular academic program in promoting mental health (Weiss, Catron, Harris, & Phung, 1999). These and other studies strongly support the notion that effective mental health interventions and effective academic interventions should be viewed as complementary and integrally related.

LIABILITY ISSUES,
ETHICAL RESPONSIBILITIES, AND BEST PRACTICES

If these reasons are not persuasive enough, there are also legal and ethical reasons school personnel should adopt school-based suicide prevention programs. Liability issues involving schools and youth suicide, the ethical responsibilities school personnel have in preventing youth suicide and responding to youth suicidal behavior, and the importance of using best practices when implementing school-based prevention programs are discussed in the following section.

Liability Issues

Many people have pointed out that school districts, as well as school employees, can and have been sued by parents/caregivers under conditions in which a student dies by suicide (e.g., Berman, 2009; Poland, 1989). This is certainly true, and all school personnel should be aware of it. In particular, some school personnel may fear being held liable for a student's suicide if they fail to adequately warn others about a student's potentially suicidal behavior. This concern is likely the result of the well-known case of *Tarasoff v. Regents of the University of California* (1976), which established that a psychotherapist has a duty-to-warn if the therapist's client poses a serious threat to others. What does *not* appear to be widely known, however, is that the *Tarasoff* decision has not been universally adopted by other courts, and even California's highest court refused to extend the *Tarasoff* duty-to-warn requirement to cases involving suicide.

> **A review of published court decisions in which families have sought to hold school officials liable for students' suicides reveals that the vast majority of these decisions were found in favor of school officials.**

A review of published court decisions in which families have sought to hold school officials liable for students' suicides reveals that the vast majority of these decisions were found in favor of school officials (Fossey & Zirkel, 2004; Zirkel & Fossey, 2005). In addition, none of these decisions resulted in a school-based mental health professional or other school employee being held liable for a damages award. Although this is of course subject to change in future judiciary decisions, at the time of this writing courts have clearly been reluctant to hold school personnel liable for youth suicides under a variety of circumstances (for a detailed discussion of relevant court cases and their rulings through 2009, the reader is referred to Appendix A: Student Suicide Case Law in Public Schools).

School personnel should understand that liability issues involving schools and suicide typically involve issues of *negligence* and *foreseeability*. For example, if a student dies by suicide and the student's parents/caregivers believe that school personnel were negligent in not preventing their

> **School personnel should understand that liability issues involving schools and suicide typically involve issues of *negligence* and *foreseeability*.**

child's death when they could have reasonably done so (e.g., school personnel failed to monitor a student in school when it was known the student was imminently suicidal), school personnel may be held liable by the courts. Similarly, school personnel put themselves at risk for potential lawsuits if they do not act appropriately to prevent a *foreseeable* suicide.

According to Jacob (2009), all school personnel have a duty to protect students "from reasonably foreseeable risk of harm" (p. 243). It should be clearly understood, however, that "foreseeability is not synonymous with predictability" (Berman, 2009, p. 234). That is, school personnel have *not* been held liable by the courts for failing to accurately predict and/or identify which students may become suicidal. Rather, foreseeability refers to a "reasonable assessment of a student's risk for potential harm" (Berman, 2009, p. 234). Of course, what is considered "reasonable" is open to interpretation, but in general the courts have given schools wide latitude in this regard.

School personnel can and have been sued for actions such as failing to notify parents regarding their child's suicidal communications, failing to intervene in situations in which a student communicated a suicide plan, and failing to follow established school policies and procedures related to youth suicidal behavior (Berman, 2009). Although schools and school employees who have been sued under these conditions have typically not been found liable by the courts, any school administrator, school board member, or school staff member

> **School personnel can and have been sued for actions such as failing to notify parents regarding their child's suicidal communications, failing to intervene in situations in which a student communicated a suicide plan, and failing to follow established school policies and procedures related to youth suicidal behavior.**

will attest that lawsuits directed against one's own school district—or to a specific school district employee—is something to be avoided whenever possible. The cost of such lawsuits, not only in monetary terms but also in time, labor, and the bad publicity such lawsuits generate, is extensive regardless of the outcome.

What should school personnel do to decrease the probability of becoming targets of a lawsuit related to youth suicidal behavior? First, they should be aware that lawsuits have seldom, if ever, occurred except under the condition that a student dies by suicide and the parents/caregivers of the deceased youth believed school personnel could have prevented it but failed to do so. Many school administrators and other school practitioners, dealing with the numerous challenges confronting our nation's schools, may understandably react to this last statement with a sigh of relief. For example, some school personnel may have experienced a student's suicide rarely if at all, depending on their years of experience and other variables.

Although even one case of a child or an adolescent suicide is one too many, the relative infrequency of youth suicide (though *not* suicidal behavior, as we saw in Chapter 1), at least compared to other problems faced by schools, may give school personnel a false sense of security. Youth suicide does occur, frequently when it is least expected, and school personnel are often left confused, scared, and floundering about what to do when it does, let alone how to better prevent it from occurring in the first place. This lack of planning and foresight also creates the heightened probability that mistakes will be made in response to youth suicidal behavior, resulting in the increased possibility of (successful) litigation.

To begin to address this issue, all school districts and schools should have clear policies and procedures regarding youth suicidal behavior and how to respond to it. The desire to avoid possible litigation is one reason for this recommendation, but it is not the only one, and not even the most important one. For example, Jacob and Hartshorne (2007) indicated that results of court cases such as *Eisel v. Board of Education of Montgomery County* (1991) have been interpreted to suggest that schools should develop clear suicide prevention policies and procedures, including notifying parents/guardians of any suspected or possible suicidal behavior exhibited by their child, and ensuring that school personnel be adequately oriented to the school's policies and procedures regarding youth suicidal behavior. As of this writing, however, most states do not legally require specific policies and procedures in schools regarding youth suicidal behavior.

Of course, just because there is no legal mandate requiring that all schools have suicide prevention policies and procedures in place does not mean they *cannot* or *should not*, or that the absence of clearly outlined policies and procedures is a wise decision. In a nutshell, developing school-based policies and procedures related to youth suicidal behavior is recommended not because it is legally required, but rather because it is a prime example of both *professional ethical behavior* and *best practice*.

Ethical Responsibilities

In contrast to laws, which are "a body of rules of conduct prescribed by the state that has binding legal force," *professional ethics* refers to "a combination of broad ethical principles and rules that guide the conduct of a practitioner in his or her professional interactions with others" (Jacob & Hartshorne, 2007, p. 21). Individuals working in schools are professionals, regardless of their role and function, and therefore they have ethical responsibilities to the children and adolescents they serve. Engaging in a professionally ethical manner involves the application of ethical principles and specific rules to the problems that inevitably arise in professional practice (Jacob & Hartshorne, 2007).

Many professionals working in the schools, including school-based mental health professionals, are considered responsible for exhibiting professional behavior typically outlined in so-called codes of conduct. These professional codes of conduct often require that school personnel behave in ways that are "more stringent" (Ballantine, 1979, p. 636) than required by law, and frequently require that professionals alter their behavior accordingly to meet these higher ethical standards.

> **Professional codes of conduct often require that school personnel behave in ways that are more stringent than required by law, and frequently require that professionals alter their behavior accordingly to meet these higher ethical standards.**

To illustrate what is meant by this, consider this situation: imagine you are relaxing by a lake, reading a favorite book on a warm summer's day. The sun has recently set, and the lifeguard who was on duty has left for the day. Suddenly, you hear someone screaming for help. You look up and see an adolescent boy flailing in the water, his arms waving wildly, a look of panic on his face, and clearly giving the appearance of not being able to swim. You quickly perceive that unless someone helps this adolescent immediately, he may drown. You also realize that the lifeguard previously on duty has left, that no one else is around, and that you are the only one in earshot of the boy able to hear his increasingly urgent pleas for help. What would you do? There is clearly no legal obligation requiring you to jump into the water and attempt to rescue the person in distress, and your failure to do so would have no legal ramifications. Would you therefore ignore his plea for help? Of course not. Why? Because although attempting to help the person in this situation is not a legal mandate, most would agree it is the ethically appropriate and responsible thing to do. Or, said another way, it is the morally "right" thing to do, given widely accepted cultural and societal values.

What is the relationship between professional ethical responsibilities and school-based suicide prevention and intervention? First, school personnel are ethically required to act within their level of competence and not exceed their training and knowledge (Davis & Sandoval, 1991). This suggests that school-based mental health professionals, who most likely possess knowledge, skill, and competence in the area of suicide and other mental health problems experienced by youth, should take the lead in developing school-based suicide prevention programs. By virtue of their training and experience, school-based mental health professionals would be considered more appropriate for this task than other school employees (e.g., teachers, administrators), who likely lack the necessary knowledge and skills for this role.

Second, as stated in ethical codes such as the National Association of School Psychologists (NASP) Principles for Professional Ethics, professionals are expected to "act as advocates for their students/clients" and assure a "high quality of professional service." In the context of suicide prevention, this suggests that school psychologists (and, by extension, other school-based mental health professionals) should strive to advocate for suicidal youth, who may frequently be stigmatized and perhaps marginalized by other students, even by school personnel, for their behavior. Mental health professionals in the schools are also the most appropriate members of the school community to advocate for prevention and other programs designed to address and hopefully reduce suicidal behavior, as well as provide high-quality services for children and adolescents in need of mental health services.

Although "high quality" is not defined in the NASP Principles for Professional Ethics, use of this term clearly implies that the services provided demonstrate utility for their designated purposes. Providing high-quality services in schools for the purpose of enhancing and promoting students' academic, behavioral, social, and emotional development is considered best practice (Power et al., 2003) and is a goal to which all school personnel should aspire.

Best Practices

Best practice refers to methods, strategies, or techniques that have been demonstrated to lead to more beneficial outcomes for students. Best practice is *informed* by legal requirements and ethical responsibilities, but need not be *limited* by them. That is, although school personnel should behave in ways congruent with legal mandates and their

> **Best practice is *informed* by legal requirements and ethical responsibilities, but need not be *limited* by them.**

particular code of professional ethics, meeting both of these requirements should simply be viewed as the minimum standard expected and does not necessarily reflect or limit what professionals *could or should do.*

For example, providing evidence-based prevention and intervention strategies in schools, whether these are the suicide prevention programs described in this book or other types of prevention and/or intervention programs with emerging empirical support for their effectiveness (e.g., substance abuse, bullying), is neither legally nor ethically required. However, the use of such programs is not only justified but also strongly recommended because they serve the broader and best interests of children and adolescents. In other words, such programs exemplify best practices.

Based on liability issues and professional and ethical codes of conduct, what should schools and school personnel *minimally* do in regards to youth suicide prevention? Neither court cases nor ethical principles provide specific guidance in this area. Poland (1989) recommends that all schools (1) detect potentially suicidal students; (2) assess the severity level of potentially suicidal students; (3) notify the parents/caregivers of a suicidal student; (4) work with parents/caregivers to secure the needed supervision and services for the student; and (5) monitor the student and provide ongoing assistance. Handout 2.1 (at the end of the chapter) provides a slightly more extensive list of several recommended practices that, in my view, schools should minimally do to address this issue. School personnel who adopt these practices will better protect themselves from possible litigation and, more importantly, will be engaging in ethically and professionally responsible behavior.

ROLES AND RESPONSIBILITIES OF SCHOOL-BASED MENTAL HEALTH PROFESSIONALS

Although all students and all school personnel have a role to play in effective school-based suicide prevention efforts, school-based mental health professionals (e.g., school psychologists, school counselors, and school social workers) are particularly important in this process. It is these professionals who ultimately can and should take leadership roles and responsibilities in school-based suicide prevention programs, and they should be integrally involved in implementing, sustaining, and evaluating them.

Berman (2009) indicates that school psychologists (and, by implication, other school-based mental health professionals) can "play a vital role in lowering the incidence of suicidal behavior among students and in responding to suicidal events and their effects" (p. 237). To accomplish this, he suggests that all school-based mental health professionals will require the following:

- To be knowledgeable about risk factors and warning signs of suicidal behavior.
- To understand legal issues and best practices regarding suicide prevention in the schools.
- To understand evidence-based practices in regards to suicide prevention.
- To know how to formulate and conduct a suicide risk assessment.
- To be able to differentiate between suicidal behavior and nonsuicidal self-injury.
- To understand the differences between and advantages of safety plans versus no-harm contracts.
- To be knowledgeable and skilled in the areas of crisis assessment and intervention.
- To know how to involve parents of potentially suicidal youth in the intervention process.
- To know how best to reintegrate a student back into the classroom following a student suicide attempt.
- To know about issues related to suicide contagion and clusters.
- To know how to effectively implement effective suicide postvention procedures.

Readers of this book will gain knowledge in each of these areas. Additional resources on youth suicide and its prevention are provided in Appendix B. Moreover, the AAS offers an online school suicide prevention accreditation program that provides school personnel with training in these domains (see www.suicidology.org). As noted by Berman (2009), school psychologists and other school-based mental health professionals should avail themselves of various training opportunities "to be better prepared to meet the challenges of preventing the next, if not the first, suicide in their schools" (p. 237).

CONCLUDING COMMENTS

Robert Horner, Professor of Special Education at the University of Oregon, once gave a guest lecture at Lehigh University to a crowded group of graduate students training to work in schools. "The job of school personnel," he said at one point, "is broader than education alone. It is to alter the trajectory of our students' lives." This memorable statement is a useful reminder of the powerful influence school practitioners have in modifying students' behaviors, improving their outcomes, and even changing their lives. Effective school-based suicide prevention programs can potentially do all these things. Indeed, not only can they change lives, they can save them.

> **School-based suicide prevention programs attempt to accomplish one of the most significant and meaningful goals imaginable—to save young lives from an unnecessary and premature death.**

The primary justification for school-based suicide prevention programs is not because their use may better avoid legal entanglements or potential lawsuits, although this is certainly a possible and advantageous outcome. Rather, the primary justification for implementing them is that it is the ethically and morally responsible thing to do. It is ethically and morally responsible because these programs attempt to accomplish one of the most significant and meaningful goals imaginable—to save young lives from an unnecessary and premature death. What could be more important than that?

Responding to Youth Suicidal Behavior: Minimal Recommendations for Schools

- Each school should have a written policy and procedure regarding youth suicidal behavior, including prevention, risk assessment, intervention, and postvention strategies.

- All policies and procedures should be presented and taught to school personnel on an annual basis. It is not merely expected that school personnel will be *exposed* to these policies and procedures; they should demonstrate that they have *learned* them.

- All school personnel should receive inservice training on the topic of youth suicide, including training on its demographic variables, common myths and misunderstandings about suicidal behavior, risk factors and possible warning signs of suicide, and what to do and who to contact if any school employee even *suspects* that a student may be suicidal.

- Mental health (e.g., school psychologists; school counselor; school social workers) and other appropriate professionals (e.g., school nurse) should be identified in each school to provide inservice training, conduct suicide risk assessments as needed, and serve on crisis intervention teams within each school. These duties should be included in their job descriptions.

- These professionals should be responsible for keeping abreast of any federal or state requirements in regards to youth mental health issues in general and suicide prevention in particular, including keeping up to date on court decisions involving schools and suicide.

- These professionals should be familiar with the ethical codes of their professions regarding suicide and should be required to continually improve their skills through a programmatic approach to professional development. This commitment to professional development should be fully supported by school district administration, including providing funding for professional development activities (e.g., attending conferences).

- School and community resources to assist potentially suicidal youth should be identified and shared with students and school personnel. Health and mental health professionals should be cognizant of these resources and know how to access them quickly.

- When any member of the school even suspects that a student might be suicidal, this suspicion should be immediately reported to the school principal as well as to the designated mental health professional in the school who has training in conducting suicide risk assessments and in suicide prevention.

- Any youth suspected of possibly being suicidal should be supervised at all times and should never be left alone under any circumstances. Any device that is a weapon (e.g., gun) or that could be used as a weapon (e.g., sharp object) should be confiscated from the student.

(cont.)

- Each time a student is identified as potentially suicidal, the procedures that were followed should be recorded, in detail, on the day the incident occurred. Use of a standardized incident report is recommended. All recorded incidents should be filed and stored in a secure location.

- If a student is suspected of engaging in possible suicidal behavior and a suicide risk assessment is conducted, parents/caregivers of the student should be immediately contacted and apprised of the results.

- In situations in which it is determined that a student is at moderate to high risk for suicide, the student should not be allowed to leave the school by bus or to walk home unless accompanied by a parent or other responsible adult. Parents/caregivers in such situations should be asked to come to the school to receive their child. Depending on the severity of the situation, the student should be taken by appropriate school personnel, the police, or an ambulance to a hospital or psychiatric facility for a more extensive assessment.

- If a student is hospitalized or is out of school for any time as a result of suicidal behavior, when the student returns to school a designated professional (e.g., school-based mental health professional) should be available to greet, meet with, and monitor the student on an as-needed basis.

- Non-mental health professionals employed by the school (e.g., teachers) who work directly with a potentially suicidal student should be informed of their status on a need-to-know basis, and should be given clear instructions regarding what to do if they observe any form of suicidal behavior.

CHAPTER 3

A Public Health Approach to Youth Suicide Prevention

A large number of people at small risk may give rise to more cases of disease than a small number who are at high risk.
— GEOFFREY ROSE (Rose's Theorem)

By directing professional practice toward populations and institutions rather than individual clients, and by focusing our energies on the creation of environments that prevent the emergence of problems and facilitate the promotion of competence, public health methodologies offer a unique platform on which to build a powerful future.
— TERRY B. GUTKIN

School suicide prevention programs attempt, in general, to reach the greatest number of adolescents, hoping to detect the smaller number most at risk and then to identify and refer them for intervention (assessment and possible treatment) before they become acutely suicidal.
— ALAN L. BERMAN

Writing in 1998, former U.S. Surgeon General David Satcher noted that "the public health problems of suicide and injuries from suicidal behavior have not been adequately addressed in this nation" (1998, p. 325). Since that time, there have been increased attempts at the federal level to address the problem of suicide, particularly among young people. Many of these initiatives were instigated by Satcher during his tenure as Surgeon General. For example, his *Call to Action to Prevent Suicide* (U.S. Department of Health and Human Services [USDHHS], 1999), the first report on suicide to appear from the Surgeon General's Office in its 200 years of existence (Jamison, 1999), emphasized that suicide is a national public health problem. The report called for greater public awareness about suicide and its risk factors, an improvement in population-based and clinical services, and an increased investment in the science of suicide prevention (Jamison, 1999).

That same year, Satcher produced the document *Mental Health: A Report of the Surgeon General* (USDHHS, 1999), which provided an overview of the significant role of mental health and substance abuse services in suicide prevention. In late 2000, he convened a conference called Children's Mental Health: Developing a National Action Agenda, in which he emphasized the need to improve early identification of mental disorders in children and adolescents within all systems that serve them, and to remove barriers and increase access to services.

These and other efforts led to the landmark publication of the *National Strategy for Suicide Prevention: Goals and Objectives for Action* (U.S. Public Health Service, 2001). Described by Satcher as "a strategy for the American people for improving their health and well-being through the prevention of suicide" (p. 1), the *National Strategy for Suicide Prevention* uses a public health approach to suicide prevention. The purpose of this document is to "promote and provide direction to efforts to modify the social infrastructure in ways that will affect the most basic attitudes about suicide and its prevention and that will also change judicial, educational, and health care systems" (Berman et al., 2006, p. 304). The *National Strategy for Suicide Prevention* represented the United States' first attempt to prevent suicide using a coordinated approach involving both public and private sectors. Two years after its development, the President's New Freedom Commission on Mental Health (2003) called for its advancement and implementation. A list of the goals and objectives of the *National Strategy for Suicide Prevention* is provided in Handout 3.1 (at the end of the chapter).

These reports signaled an important shift in federal health priorities. Specifically, they "were thematically linked around the premises that (a) mental health was an integral, core, and significant component of the public health system; (b) reducing stigma and increasing early identification of mental health problems was essential to a sound public health system; and (c) strengthening the link between research and practice will achieve the greatest yield for the public" (Hoagwood & Johnson, 2003, p. 3).

These initiatives were further strengthened when the nation's first youth suicide prevention bill, the Garrett Lee Smith Memorial Act, was signed into law in 2004. The purpose of this legislation was "to support the planning, implementation, and evaluation of organized activities involving statewide youth suicide early intervention and prevention strategies, to provide funds for campus mental and behavioral health service centers, and for other purposes" (p. 1). The Garrett Lee Smith Memorial Act was named in honor of the late son of Senator Gordon Smith of Oregon, one of the sponsors of the bill; Garrett Lee Smith died by suicide at the age of 21. In passing this landmark piece of legislation, the U.S. Congress noted that "youth suicide is a public health tragedy linked to underlying mental health problems and that youth suicide early intervention and prevention activities are national priorities" (p. 1).

> **In passing the Garret Lee Smith Memorial Act, the U.S. Congress noted that "youth suicide is a public health tragedy linked to underlying mental health problems and that youth suicide early intervention and prevention activities are national priorities."**

Collectively, these actions led to the increasing realization that suicide is a significant public health problem, particularly among young people. Understanding and conceptualizing suicide as a public health problem led many individuals and groups to conclude that a public health model would also be a useful approach for preventing it. The remainder

> **Understanding and conceptualizing suicide as a public health problem led many individuals and groups to conclude that a public health model would also be a useful approach for preventing it.**

of this chapter discusses various public health approaches that have been successful in reducing suicide and introduces the concept of applying a public health approach to youth suicide prevention in the schools. Subsequent chapters in the book will then describe in more specific detail how this approach could be implemented at various levels. Before beginning that process, however, it is first necessary to briefly discuss public health in general.

PUBLIC HEALTH: A BRIEF OVERVIEW

There are many definitions of public health, but one of the most concise and useful was provided by the Institute of Public Health (1988). Specifically, "public health is what we, as a society, do collectively to assure the conditions in which people can be healthy" (p. 1). The issue of public health first gained notoriety in the 19th century, when physicians and government officials began considering various societal and environmental variables as potentially causing, contributing to, or exacerbating existing health problems (Doll & Cummings, 2008b). The first public health programs began as simple policies to clean up communities, with later efforts focusing on medical intervention as we know them today in the form of vaccines and environmental improvements (Strein, Hoagwood, & Cohn, 2003; Woodside & McClam, 1998).

Beginning in the 1970s, the health status of U.S. populations, rather than simply individuals, has been a national priority and has led to significant changes in local and federal policies (Strein et al., 2003). Many public health initiatives have been implemented since that time, including those designed to accomplish such varied goals as decreasing smoking and alcohol consumption, increasing physical exercise, decreasing the number of highway fatalities, and increasing "safe" sexual behavior to prevent pregnancy and sexually transmitted diseases.

There have also recently been public health initiatives designed to reduce suicide. A summary of what we currently know about community-based public health approaches to suicide prevention is provided in the following section. Although these approaches are not specifically focused on schools, school personnel will greatly benefit from an understanding of which community-based public health approaches have been most effective in preventing suicidal behavior, as this information has important implications for school-based suicide prevention efforts.

COMMUNITY-BASED PUBLIC HEALTH APPROACHES TO SUICIDE PREVENTION

A literature review published in 2002 found that 68% of people who died by suicide were not seen in a mental health setting for a 12-month period prior to their deaths (Luoma, Martin, & Pearson, 2002). To put this in perspective, given that approximately 32,000 people die by suicide in the United States each year, it would mean that nearly 22,000 of them would not be reached by traditional psychotherapeutic approaches (Joiner et al., 2009). It also means that if we want to most effectively and efficiently prevent suicide from occurring, traditional treatment approaches are not the solution. This does *not* mean that direct individual

> **Suicide prevention is best accomplished when more traditional, individual approaches are combined with public health approaches that attempt to prevent suicide on a more universal level.**

or group treatment of suicidal individuals is not worthwhile or that these approaches are ineffective. There is a significant need for mental health practitioners who are skilled at providing effective interventions for those who are imminently suicidal or at high risk for suicide. However, suicide prevention is best accomplished when more traditional, individual approaches are combined with public health approaches that attempt to prevent suicide on a more universal level (Joiner et al., 2009).

Several community-based approaches informed by a public health model have been proposed. Four approaches—restricting access to lethal means, the use of telephone crisis hotlines, the Internet, and public education campaigns aimed at providing information about suicide—are discussed next. Information is also provided on a program developed by the U.S. Air Force, which has demonstrated notable success in its public health approach to suicide prevention.

Restricting Access to Lethal Means

Restricting access to lethal means refers to limiting the availability of potentially life-threatening objects, such as guns or certain medications, and/or limiting access to tall buildings and bridges. The logic behind means restriction is that it would theoretically allow the impulse to attempt suicide to wane, or at least force the suicidal individual to consider and locate an alternative means (one that would most likely be less immediately lethal) and therefore allow greater time and opportunity for intervention (Berman et al., 2006). A long-standing counterargument to this position, however, is that limiting access to a lethal means of suicide would only prevent suicides temporarily because an individual thwarted from attempting suicide through one method will simply adopt another one (Stengel, 1967). According to this position, commonly referred to as *method substitution*, restricting access to lethal means in one area (e.g., restricting access to guns) would simply result in an increase in another, nonrestricted suicide method (e.g., carbon monoxide poisoning), and the overall suicide rate would remain unchanged.

Despite its intuitive appeal, method substitution does not inevitably occur, suggesting that means restriction should be considered a viable form of suicide prevention. For example, concerned about the large number of suicides resulting from carbon monoxide poisoning in Great Britain, the British government modified the source of its domestic heating gas in 1970 to one containing one-sixth the amount of carbon monoxide content of earlier supplies. Prior to this modification, 40% of all British suicides occurred as the result of asphyxiation due to carbon monoxide poisoning. After this modification, carbon monoxide poisoning accounted for fewer than 10% of all suicides. Perhaps most interesting, the overall suicide rate in Britain also declined, with no appreciable increase in the use of alternative suicide methods (Shaffer et al., 1988). Moreover, this overall reduction in the suicide rate occurred despite increasing unemployment, a variable associated with increased suicide (Joiner et al., 2009; Kreitman & Platt, 1984).

Another example involves the site of more annual suicides than any other single place in the world: the Golden Gate Bridge in San Francisco (Blaustein & Fleming, 2009). More than 1,200 people have died by suicide at the bridge since its completion in 1937 (the exact number is unknown), and the number grows by approximately 20 additional suicides per year (Joiner et al., 2009). Despite the number of suicides that have occurred at this site, and even though the idea of constructing suicide prevention barriers was first proposed in the 1950s, it was not until September 2006 that an agreement was made to create a suicide deterrent system for the bridge in the form of a horizontal net or some other type of physical barrier. At the time of this writing, the Golden Gate Bridge Physical Suicide Deterrent System Project is underway but has not yet been completed.

Over the past several decades, many people have objected to enacting a barrier on the Golden Gate Bridge, typically citing costs, aesthetics, and the common belief that a bridge barrier would not ultimately prevent suicides (Colt, 2006; Friend, 2003). With regard to this belief, a study published in 2006 asked a national sample of 2,770 respondents a hypothetical question about what effect a suicide barrier might have had on the fate of the more than 1,000 people who had already died by suicide at the Golden Gate Bridge. Thirty-four percent of the respondents indicated their belief that every single person would have found another way to commit suicide if a suicide prevention barrier was present at the bridge. An additional 40% believed that most would have done so (Miller, Axrael, & Hemenway, 2006).

Neither these respondents nor the many opponents of constructing a barrier on the Golden Gate Bridge are likely aware of a now classic study conducted over 30 years ago. Richard Seiden (1978) examined the records of 515 individuals who were restrained from attempting suicide at the Golden Gate Bridge from 1937 through 1971. The method substitution theory would predict that most of these individuals, possibly the large majority, would have died by suicide at a later date after they were prevented from jumping off the bridge. What Seiden found, however, was that *94% of these individuals did not later die by suicide.* Many subsequent studies examining the effects of bridge barriers on suicidal behavior have found similar results (e.g., Beautrais, 2007; Bennewith, Nowers, & Gunnell, 2007; O'Carroll & Silverman, 1994; Reisch & Michel, 2005), indicating that putting physical barriers on bridges to prevent suicides can save lives. Many sites that are also notorious for their attraction to potentially suicidal individuals (e.g., the Empire State Building in New York, the Sydney Harbor Bridge in Australia, Mount Mihara in Japan) have constructed barriers, and at each of these sites suicide has been reduced to near zero levels (Friend, 2003).

These findings should not be interpreted, however, as meaning that method substitution does not occur. Some individuals will use a different suicide method if a certain method is unavailable, or if they are prevented from using it (Caron, Julien, & Huang, 2008; Reisch, Schuster, & Michel, 2007). For example, De Leo, Dwyer, Firman, and Nellinger (2003) demonstrated a correlation between a decrease of suicide by firearms and an increase of suicide by hanging. Similarly, another study found that the number of suicides by hanging increased as suicides by firearms decreased following the passage of gun control legislation (Rich, Young, Fowler, Wagner, & Black, 1990).

Given that most youth (as well as adults) who die by suicide use guns as their suicide method, the issue of means restriction has particular relevance when considering firearms. In a nutshell, there is clear and compelling evidence that the presence of guns in a young person's home, particularly unlocked, loaded handguns, are associated with a significantly increased risk for suicide (Simon, 2007). Moreover, the risk conferred by guns is proportional to their accessibility and number available, and if a gun is used to attempt

> There is clear and compelling evidence that the presence of guns in a young person's home, particularly unlocked, loaded handguns, are associated with a significantly increased risk for suicide.

suicide a fatal outcome will occur 78–90% of the time (Berman et al., 2006). Public policy initiatives that have restricted the access to guns (especially handguns) are associated with a reduction of suicide by firearms and also suicide overall, especially in young people. Consequently, one of the potentially most powerful youth suicide prevention strategies is removing guns from the home environment (Berman et al., 2006).

> **The risk conferred by guns is proportional to their accessibility and number available, and if a gun is used to attempt suicide a fatal outcome will occur 78–90% of the time.**

> **Public policy initiatives that have restricted the access to guns (especially handguns) are associated with a reduction of suicide by firearms and also suicide overall, especially in young people. Consequently, one of the potentially most powerful youth suicide prevention strategies is removing guns from the home environment.**

However, gun control is an emotionally charged issue, and the passage of more restrictive gun laws is not likely given the current political climate. Moreover, although reducing the easy availability of guns may reduce suicides, opponents of gun control have argued that there is some evidence indicating that gun ownership is associated with an increased likelihood of deterring violent crime, and that in the vast majority of cases no actual shots are fired in accomplishing this outcome (e.g., Kleck & Delone, 1993; Tark & Kleck, 2004). Furthermore, the issue of gun control and gun rights represents not only a political divide but a cultural one as well. For many Americans living in rural areas or small towns, particularly in Western states, hunting is a popular and long-standing cultural tradition, and guns are often passed down from one generation to the next as family heirlooms (Bageant, 2007). Historically, legal attempts to place restrictions on gun ownership in such areas have not been well received, and that is unlikely to change in the immediate or near future.

Nevertheless, restricting access to guns has much to recommend it. A Consensus Statement on Youth Suicide by Firearms (1998) emphasized the importance of gun safety, training, and education regarding the relationship between guns and suicide, and making guns inoperable by and inaccessible to youth. Garland and Zigler (1993) provided additional recommendations in regards to firearms, including providing youth and adults with gun safety training and requiring mandatory background checks and waiting periods prior to making gun purchases. Attempts at passing legislation in these areas, however, have largely been defeated at both state and federal levels.

Finally, because drug ingestion and overdose is the most widely used method of suicide attempts among adolescent females, it has been suggested that restricting access to drugs and medications might be a useful suicide prevention procedure. For example, restrictions in Denmark on the availability of barbiturates and on household gas with carbon monoxide content was associated with a decline both in the number of overall suicides (55%) and the number of suicides by self-poisoning (Nordentoft, Qin, Helweg-Larsen, & Juel, 2007). Berman and colleagues (2006) suggest that limiting prescription doses of potentially lethal medications to a restricted time frame might be beneficial. Hawton (2002) reported a national legislative mandate to decrease the number of analgesics that could be purchased at any one time, and found a reduction in suicides using analgesics and in drug overdoses after the new law took place.

Crisis Hotlines

Because of their easy accessibility, crisis hotlines are in a unique position to intervene with individuals at various points during a suicidal crisis, including those moments, minutes, or hours prior to a possible suicide attempt (Joiner et al., 2007). Telephone crisis hotlines offer callers immediate help, with 24-hour, 7-days-per-week availability to resolve crises of a suicidal or potentially suicidal nature through active intervention (Berman et al., 2006). For children and adolescents, "the anonymity and comfort and familiarity of the telephone and the typically non-professional staffing of these services theoretically make this form of entry to the help-giving system more acceptable than direct, face-to-face contact with an office-based professional" (Berman et al., 2006, p. 310).

Crisis hotlines have many other advantages for youth: They offer some level of service at times when other suicide prevention or intervention services may be unavailable; they can be useful for providing information about other possible treatment resources; they provide a safe and nonjudgmental environment in which youth can articulate complex feelings; and they allow the caller to freely initiate and terminate contact (Gould, Greenberg, Munfahk, & Kleinman, & Lubell, 2006). Suicidal crises may be resolved after calls to hotlines are made, and if they are not referrals for more intensive intervention can be provided. Furthermore, given the ubiquitous presence of portable cell phones among children and adolescents, access to crisis hotlines has never been easier.

How effective are crisis hotlines? The evidence indicates that hotlines can be beneficial to people who are suicidal (Gould, Kalafat, Munfakh, & Kleinman, 2007) and nonsuicidal (Kalafat, Gould, Munfakh, & Kleinman, 2007), and that youth who use hotlines are often helped by them. Telephone crisis counseling has resulted in significant decreases in suicidal behavior and significant improvements in the mental state of youth during the course of the call (King, Nurcombe, Bickman, Hides, & Reid, 2003). Unfortunately, despite a high level of awareness about hotlines among youth as well as high satisfaction among those who use them, few adolescents appear to use hotlines (Gould et al., 2006). Adolescents also access crisis hotlines less often and perceive them more negatively than other sources of help (Vieland, Whittle, Garland, Hicks, & Shaffer, 1991).

> The evidence indicates that hotlines can be beneficial to people who are suicidal and nonsuicidal, and that youth who use hotlines are often helped by them.

Gould and colleagues (2006) conducted a study of 519 high school students and found that only a few of the students (2.1%) reported using crisis hotlines. The most common reasons for hotline nonuse related to feelings of self-reliance and shame, respectively. For example, the 10 most frequently endorsed reasons for the nonuse of hotlines among this sample was (1) I thought the problem was not serious enough (35.3%); (2) I wanted to solve the problem by myself (33.1%); (3) I thought a family member or friend would help me (24.6%); (4) I thought it probably would not have done any good (24.0%); (5) I thought the problem would get better by itself (22.8%); (6) the problem was too personal to tell anyone (15.1%); (7) I did not know where to call (13.1%); (8) I was concerned what my family might think or say (10.9%); (9) I would not have trusted the advice or help they would give me (9.7%); and (10) I was ashamed to call (7.1%).

Perhaps most disconcerting is that objections to using hotlines was strongest among those students most in need of them. First, and consistent with previous research (Mishara & Daigle,

2001), female adolescents were more likely to access hotlines than male adolescents. As noted in Chapter 1, although adolescent females are more likely to attempt suicide than adolescent males, males have a much higher rate of suicide. This finding may reflect the widespread reluctance among males to ask for assistance for their problems by engaging in help-seeking behavior (Gould et al., 2006).

Second, students who reported impaired functioning or feelings of hopelessness objected to hotlines more than students who did not exhibit these conditions. For example, youth who reported impaired functioning were more likely than unimpaired youth to endorse items related to self-reliance as their rationale for their nonuse of hotline services. This finding is consistent with previous research which found that depressed youth and youth exhibiting suicidal behaviors are more likely than their mentally healthier counterparts to believe that people should be able to handle their own problems without outside help (Gould et al., 2004). Students with functional impairment also reported being more ashamed to use hotlines. Adolescents who reported feelings of hopelessness indicated that their nonuse of hotlines was more related to issues such as never having heard of crisis hotlines, not knowing where to call, and having problems accessing a private telephone. These perceptions may also reflect the negative cognitions and loss of motivation that often accompany hopelessness (Gould et al., 2006).

Objections to using hotlines were also found to be consistently stronger among those adolescents who had seen a mental health professional, even when controlling for the presence of functional impairment and hopelessness. Of the few adolescents in this study who reported using hotlines, the vast majority used other services as well. Gould and colleagues (2006) suggested that these findings may indicate that adolescents' needs are already being addressed through this system of care, and that once they enter the mental health system these youth may perceive using hotlines as unwanted or unnecessary.

The low rate of hotline use by adolescents, particularly by students who may be most at risk for suicidal behavior, is a serious problem. It is also not clear how crisis hotlines should best be used or marketed to youth. As noted by Gould and colleagues (2006), "The question remains of whether hotline use should be promoted as an independent source of short-term relief, an entry to accessing other more long-term resources of help, and/or as an adjunct to other service use" (p. 611). There have also been some concerns about the quality of suicide risk assessments that are conducted using hotlines, and there have been recent attempts to establish standards for the assessment of suicide risk among callers to hotlines such as the National Suicide Prevention Lifeline (Joiner et al., 2007).

Berman and colleagues (2006) also suggest the need for increased contact between suicidal youth and those who can provide needed services through hotlines. Because the large majority of youth suicides are males, targeting this group for greater utilization of crisis hotlines would appear to be essential (Shaffer et al., 1988). If hotlines are to be more readily accessed by youth, particularly those highest at risk for suicidal behavior, they "must work to promote a specific function that can be provided to [youth] in a manner that fits with the [youth's] sense of his or her needs and is compatible with a [youth's] lifestyle" (Gould et al., 2006, p. 611).

One final note about crisis hotlines is worth mentioning. Specifically, a student who is experiencing a suicidal crisis and wants to call a hotline might not have quick and easy access to a crisis hotline phone number. In many cases, these students may simply call 911, given that this number is highly recognizable to most people. Are responders to 911 calls skilled at dealing with suicidal crises? The answer to this is unclear. According to John Draper, Project Director of the National Suicide Prevention Lifeline, there are several 911 call officer training organizations in the United States, and all have training modules for officers (operators) responding to suicidal callers. The level of skills these officers possess appears to vary considerably, based on their amount and quality of training. Attempts are being made to increase the collaboration between 911 call centers, local crisis centers, and national organizations devoted to suicide prevention (e.g., National Suicide Prevention Lifeline; SAHMSA). This enhanced level of collaboration will hopefully result in 911 operators who are able to respond more effectively to suicidal callers.

The Internet and Other Electronic Communication Devices

One possible avenue for increasing access to crisis services by youth is the Internet. Like cell phones and other electronic communication devices (e.g., Twitter, YouTube, MySpace), the Internet is widely used by youth of all ages. Adolescents have been found to be as likely to access the Internet for help as they are to see a school counselor or other mental health professional (Gould, Munfakh, Lubell, Kleinman, & Parker, 2002). Despite its great potential as a community-based approach to suicide prevention, however, the Internet also presents significant problems. Because it is not regulated for content, much information on the Internet regarding suicide is incorrect and even harmful (e.g., "pro-suicide" websites). For example, Mandrusiak and colleagues (2006) found that although many websites present lists of possible warning signs for suicide, there is relatively poor agreement among them. However, because of the popularity of the Internet with youth, particularly in comparison to crisis hotlines, ways to use it to support youth suicide prevention efforts is warranted and should be given greater attention.

Public Education about Suicide

Thousands of people who die by suicide in the United States each year are never seen in a mental health setting prior to their deaths. However, most of these suicide victims came into contact with other people before and right up to their deaths. The people with whom they came into contact could have potentially been important "gatekeepers" in preventing a suicide from occurring, had these individuals been cognizant of some basic facts about suicide, including its warning signs, and how to assist the person in getting needed help (Joiner et al., 2009). For this help to be accomplished, however, it is necessary to widely disseminate accurate and helpful information to people about suicide, and what they can do about it. The Internet is ideally suited to this purpose, but as already noted the many websites that provide this information are of varying quality and are not regulated for quality assurance.

Public education about suicide and campaigns aimed at the general population are relatively recent developments, and only limited data is currently available evaluating its effectiveness (Mann et al., 2005). Some studies have begun to examine this issue and have demonstrated some positive results. For example, the suicide rate in rural areas in Japan was reduced by 50% after a community-based intervention emphasizing public awareness of the problem of suicide, health promotion initiatives, programs designed to promote a sense of purpose among senior citizens (middle-aged and senior citizens were the primary focus of intervention efforts), and creation of a community network (Motohashi, Kaneko, Sasaki, & Yamaji, 2007) was implemented.

Another study examined the effects of improving its citizens' *mental health literacy* (Goldney & Fisher, 2008). This term refers to the knowledge and beliefs individuals have about mental disorders that aid in their recognition, management, and prevention. Because it is also a determinant in help-seeking behavior, it is presumed to be an important component of community-based suicide prevention programs (Joiner et al., 2009). The researchers examined the effects of providing information on the mental health literacy of three groups: individuals who were diagnosed with major depression and who exhibited suicidal ideation; individuals who were diagnosed with major depression but did not exhibit suicidal ideation; and individuals who were neither depressed nor exhibited suicidal ideation. The results indicated that the intervention produced a significant improvement in the mental health literacy of all three groups, although there was less change among those who most needed it (i.e., individuals with both major depression and suicidal ideation). There were also fewer changes in appropriate treatment seeking in this group (Goldney & Fisher, 2008).

The findings in this study are consistent with previous research demonstrating that individuals who are suicidal often lack effective problem-solving and decision-making skills, indicating that there are clear limits to widespread, community-based education programs designed to reduce suicide. Similar results have been found when examining the effects of school-based curriculum programs providing information to students, as was discussed in the previous chapter. This is not surprising given what we know about suicide and what we know about public health models. That is, we know that universal interventions (e.g., providing information to individuals about the warning signs of suicide) can be helpful, but that by themselves they are not sufficient to meet the needs of individuals who are at risk for suicidal behavior (who may require selected-level interventions) or individuals who are at high risk for suicidal behavior (who may require tertiary-level and/or crisis intervention services).

The U.S. Air Force Model of Suicide Prevention

In response to an alarming increase in suicide rates among members of the U.S. Air Force in the mid-1990s, Air Force leaders made proactive efforts to conceptualize suicide prevention as a communitywide responsibility rather than as an individual medical problem, as it had been viewed previously. Key components of the suicide prevention program included (1) ongoing commitment from Air Force leaders; (2) consistent and frequent communication around the topic of suicide prevention with Air Force personnel; (3) destigmatization of seeking help for mental health problems; (4) improved collaboration among prevention agencies within the Air Force community; and (5) identification and training of "everyday" gatekeepers. A significant and sustained drop in suicide rates among Air Force personnel was observed following the communitywide dissemination of this suicide prevention program (Knox, Conwell, & Caine, 2004).

Knox and colleagues (2004) noted that "the Air Force prevention program potentially serves as the first demonstration of the relevance of Rose's Theorem for preventing suicide: improving overall community mental health can reduce the events of suicide more effectively than extensive efforts to identify the imminently suicidal individual" (p. 42). The Air Force suicide prevention program, as well as the other community-based suicide prevention programs described in this chapter, also illustrates how a public health approach can be applied to suicide prevention.

MENTAL HEALTH AS PUBLIC HEALTH

In the last two decades, there have been many national initiatives (such as the ones mentioned at the beginning of this chapter) to expand the public health model to focus not only on prevention but also on health promotion, especially mental health promotion, particularly among children and adolescents (Miller, Gilman, & Martens, 2008; Power, 2003). Mental health is increasingly being viewed as an important aspect of public health. For example, in contrast to past dichotomies of mental health and illness, current thinking conceptualizes mental health, mental health problems, and mental illness or disorders as points along a continuum (Nastasi, Bernstein Moore, & Varjas, 2004). Handout 3.2 (at the end of the chapter) provides the U.S. Surgeon General's definitions of these terms, and it is important and useful for school personnel to adequately understand the differences between them.

In contrast to the traditional "medical model," which is largely focused on disorders presumed to reside within an individual and is concerned primarily with issues related to diagnosis and treatment, the contemporary public health model of the USDHHS is focused more broadly on "surveillance of mental health within the population at large, mental health promotion and illness prevention, person–environment links, access to services, and evaluation of services" (Nastasi et al., 2004, pp. 4–5). Consequently, a public health perspective as applied to mental health issues implies (1) a comprehensive provision of services, characterized by a continuum of services from prevention to treatment; (2) an ecological model that considers cultural, social, and physical environmental factors; (3) service provision that is easily accessed by the general population, such as through schools; (4) a science-based approach to practice that includes data collection and ongoing evaluation; and (5) methods for surveillance of mental health needs (Nastasi et al., 2004).

APPLYING THE PUBLIC HEALTH APPROACH TO SCHOOLS

> **A public health approach to prevention and intervention in schools is being increasingly viewed as an important and recommended educational practice.**

A public health approach to prevention and intervention in schools is being increasingly viewed as an important and recommended educational practice (Doll & Cummings, 2008a, 2008b; Merrell et al., 2006; Power, 2003; Strein et al., 2003). The impact of the federal initiatives launched to address suicide as well as mental health issues generally has perhaps been strongest in the schools, given repeated findings that mental health is critical to academic success (Hoagwood & Johnson, 2003) and that the two are reciprocally and integrally related (Adelman & Taylor, 2006; Doll & Cummings, 2008b). Handout 3.3 (at the end of the chapter) provides a comparative listing of essential public health services along with their equivalent mental health services in schools.

> **Mental health is critical to academic success, and the two are reciprocally and integrally related.**

Specific aspects of the public health approach that have particular relevance for schools include (1) applying scientifically derived, research-based evidence to the delivery of educational and psychological services; (2) increasing and strengthening positive behavior in addition to focusing on reducing problem behaviors; (3) emphasizing school–community collaborative efforts and better linking services in these systems; and (4) using appropriate research strategies to improve the knowledge base and more effectively evaluate services in the schools (Strein et al., 2003). Public health models may also be useful for enhancing *systems capacity* in schools through the identification, selection, and implementation of appropriate prevention programs and intervention strategies to address students' diverse needs (Merrell & Buchanan, 2006). Capacity building refers to the creation of effective "host environments" that support the use of preferred and effective practices (Nelson, Sprague, Jolivette, Smith, & Tobin, 2009).

A public health model has three central, interdependent, and integrally related characteristics. First, it focuses primarily on populations and secondarily on individuals, and it considers the full spectrum of interventions needed to address all levels of risk in a given population. Second, it focuses primarily on preventing problems rather than treating them, although both are important. Third, in addition to a focus on reducing problems, it places an equal emphasis on promoting competencies, health (both mental and physical), and wellness (Doll & Cummings, 2008a; Domitrovich et al., 2010). An additional characteristic of most public health approaches is that the prevention programs and interventions employed should be evidence-based, in the sense that the interventions have been subject to rigorous evaluation through scientific research to determine their effectiveness. Each of these three characteristic of a public health approach in schools is now briefly described.

Population-Based Mental Health Approaches

A hallmark of the public health approach is its emphasis on population-based services. Doll and Cummings (2008a) provide the following description of population-based mental heath services in schools:

> Population-based mental health services refer to services that have been carefully designed to meet the mental health needs of all students enrolled in a school. Their premise is that psychological wellness is a precondition for students success in school and that, as teachers are responsible for teaching all children to read, school mental health providers are responsible for insuring that all students have the psychological competence needed for learning. (p. 3)

Ideally, population-based mental health services have at least four goals: (1) to promote the psychological well-being and developmental competence of all students; (2) to promote supportive environments that can promote and nurture students, allowing them to overcome minor challenges and risk factors; (3) to provide protective supports to students who are at higher risk for problems; and (4) to remediate emotional, behavioral, and social problems so that students can develop competence (Doll & Cummings, 2008a).

Prevention

From a public health perspective, preventing problems before they begin is a more effective and efficient method than attempting to treat them once they have already begun. Satcher (1998) provided an example of a public health approach to prevention in describing a major cholera outbreak that occurred in England in 1854. Many people were dying from the epidemic, and doctors and other medical professionals throughout England were overwhelmed with the number of patients needing to be seen and treated in hospitals and clinics. One doctor, after talking to hundreds of patients about what they had eaten during the last several days and the source of the water they had been drinking, discovered that all of the patients had one thing in common: they were all getting their water from the same pump. Leaving the hospital to go in search of the pump (angering many of the hospital staff in the process), he found that a sewage line was contaminating the water. He promptly removed the handle on the water pump, thereby effectively preventing anyone else from drinking from it. Soon afterward, the cholera epidemic ended.

A wide variety of prevention programs are becoming increasingly popular in schools. Many of these programs have demonstrated to be effective in reducing or preventing a number of academic, social, emotional, and behavioral problems (Durlak, 2009). The most effective prevention programs address both risk factors and protective factors in children and adolescents. They attempt to compensate for factors that place youth at risk for developing problems, but they also seek to promote students' individual strengths and competencies by building on their protective factors (Doll & Cummings, 2008b; Durlak, 2009). Some common principles guiding effective prevention and competency promotion programs appear in Handout 3.4 (at the end of the chapter).

Factors that place youth at risk for a host of mental health problems include early behavior problems, early academic failure, peer rejection, association with deviant peers, neighborhood disorganization, and economic deprivation. Protective factors include personal and social competencies (e.g., self-control; conflict resolution skills; drug refusal skills; problem-solving skills) as well as bonding to school (Durlak, 2009). Schools can also promote students' protective factors. In particular, schools that are characterized by a safe and orderly campus, caring and supportive school staff, high academic expectations, a challenging curriculum, parental involvement in their child's school life, and strong school-family partnerships contribute to the positive development of children and adolescents (Durlak, 2009).

Health Promotion

Health promotion is characterized by a focus on wellness rather than the prevention of disorder or illness. It is distinguished from prevention by its emphasis on the facilitation of healthy outcomes, such as competence or happiness (Stormont, Reinke, & Herman, 2010). Health promotion may include physical health (e.g., nutrition, diet and exercise), mental health (e.g., developing higher levels of hope and optimism), or a combination of the two (Miller, Gilman, & Martens, 2008). Research increasingly suggests that focusing exclusively or even primarily on preventing and treating disorders or problems may not be as effective as building and developing students' strengths and competencies (Doll & Cummings, 2008a).

An important aspect of health promotion in schools is the emerging development of positive psychology, the scientific study of human strengths and virtues (Snyder & Lopez, 2007). Positive psychology emphasizes that wellness is more than simply the treatment and removal of disease or disorder, and advocates a change from a preoccupation with addressing deficits to promoting mental health and well-being (Miller, Nickerson, & Jimerson, 2009).

Evidence-Based Practices

There has recently been a strong emphasis on the importance of evidence-based practices in schools (Stoiber & DeSmet, 2010), which essentially refers to intervention and prevention programs that have demonstrated some recognized scientific research support for their effectiveness. Unfortunately, schools have historically been and largely continue to be institutions in which highly touted interventions and prevention programs are frequently adopted despite little or no evidence of their effectiveness. Short-term fads and unproven trends often develop and flourish, only to be eventually replaced by other well-intentioned but typically fleeting educational initiatives (Miller & Sawka-Miller, in press). Not only are many of these faddish trends and programs implemented with little or no research support, but in many cases they also are ineffectively evaluated or not evaluated at all (Merrell et al., 2006; Rodgers, Sudak, Silverman, & Litts, 2007). Similarly, many individuals in schools are not sufficiently aware of which interventions are effective for resolving particular problems, let alone how to effectively implement them. There is an unfortunate gap between what we know and what we do in schools, particularly in regards to student mental health issues (Jensen, 2002a).

School personnel should be cognizant of the evidence-based practices in their respective fields. For example, school-based mental health professionals such as school psychologists, school counselors, and school social workers should be aware of the prevention programs and interventions that have an evidence base for effectively preventing or treating a variety of psychological and mental health disorders and problems, including suicidal behavior. Possessing the knowledge of what has scientifically demonstrated to be most effective in solving problems, however, is a necessary but not sufficient condition for real change to occur in schools. This knowledge is only a first step and requires that it be linked to actual and effective behavioral change through the implementation of school-based programs. As noted by Witmer (1907/1996), generally considered to be the founder of both school and clinical psychology, "the final test of what is called science is its applicability" (p. 249).

An Example of the Public Health Approach Applied to Schools: The Three-Tiered Model

A public health approach to prevention and intervention can perhaps best be illustrated by a three-tiered model that is being increasingly adopted in schools (Shinn & Walker, 2010; Walker et al., 1996). This public health model has often been visually represented through use of a triangle, with three overlapping tiers that "collectively represent a continuum of interventions that increase in intensity (i.e., effort, individualization, specialization) based on the corresponding responsiveness" of students (Sugai, 2007, p. 114). The first tier, represented as the base of the triangle, is referred to as the *universal* or *primary* level because all students in a given population (e.g., all students in a particular school) receive a universal set of interventions designed to prevent particular emotional, behavioral, and/or academic problems. The second and

> One potentially effective public health model has often been visually represented through use of a triangle, with three overlapping tiers that collectively represent a continuum of interventions that increase in intensity (i.e., effort, individualization, specialization) based on the corresponding responsiveness of students.

middle tier of the triangle, referred to as the *selected* or *secondary* level, is comprised of more intensive interventions for those students who may be at risk for developing particular problems, or for those students who do not adequately respond to universal strategies. The third, final, and top tier of the triangle, referred to as the *indicated* or *tertiary* level, is characterized by highly individualized, specialized interventions for those students who exhibit clear problems and who have not adequately responded to universal and selected levels of prevention and intervention (Sugai, 2007; Walker et al., 1996).

The original prevention logic that led to the "triangle model" of public health described above was developed in the late 1950s as a systematic response to preventing chronic illness. Later, during the 1980s and 1990s, the "triangle model" was refined and applied to other disciplines, including mental health (Sugai, 2007). More recently, in the late 1990s and early 21st century, the prevention logic of a continuum of interventions to meet individual student needs has focused on prevention and intervention of academic and behavior problems in schools, as exemplified in such recent developments as response to intervention (Burns & Gibbons, 2008) and schoolwide positive behavior support (Sugai & Horner, 2009).

For example, schoolwide positive behavior support is a public health approach designed to reduce antisocial behavior and increase prosocial behavior among students in schools. Emerging research evaluating the effectiveness of schoolwide positive behavior support indicates that it can lead to a significant reduction in the number of office discipline referrals as well as other indices associated with antisocial behavior (Sugai & Horner, 2009). It has been used effectively in a wide variety of schools, including urban schools (McCurdy, Mannella, & Eldridge, 2003; Putnam, McCart, Griggs, & Choi, 2009) and alternative schools for students with severe behavior disorders (Miller, George, & Fogt, 2005; Nelson et al., 2009). For this model to be effective, the intensity of the intervention must be commensurate with the intensity of the problem, and the effectiveness of the individualized, tertiary-level interventions is highly dependent on the effectiveness of universal-level strategies (Sugai, 2007).

Advocates of this approach have demonstrated how it can be useful in addressing a variety of problems confronting schools, including prevention and treatment of academic problems (Martinez & Nellis, 2008), child poverty (Miller & Sawka-Miller, 2009), antisocial behavior (Horner, Sugai, Todd, & Lewis-Palmer, 2005), aggression and bullying (Swearer, Espelage, Brey Love, & Kingsbury, 2008), social and emotional problems (Merrell, Gueldner, & Tran, 2008), substance abuse (Burrow-Sanchez & Hawken, 2007), depression (Mazza & Reynolds, 2008), and nonsuicidal self-injury (Miller & Brock, 2010). A public health approach to school-based suicide prevention (Hendin et al., 2005; Kalafat, 2003; Mazza & Reynolds, 2008; Miller, Eckert, & Mazza, 2009) has also recently been the subject of increased interest. This approach to school-based suicide prevention will be emphasized in the remaining chapters in this book.

MENTAL HEALTH, PUBLIC HEALTH, PUBLIC POLICY, AND THE SCHOOLS

Some individuals oppose the use of school resources for the mental health needs of students, contending that these services surpass the expertise available in school settings (Nelson et al., 2009). For example, some have questioned the ability of school personnel to accurately and adequately identify children and adolescents with mental health conditions, whereas others have raised concerns regarding the limited resources available in most schools for addressing these conditions (Nelson et al., 2009). However, failing to identify students who require mental health evaluation and treatment creates a "catch-22" in which the needs of students with mental health issues can be easily underestimated, with potentially significant and negative implications for those students who fail to receive services (Jensen, 2002b).

The failure to understand children's mental health issues and their pervasiveness may lead policymakers to advocate for even fewer mental health services for children and adolescents. For example, in a highly influential document addressing educational reform, Horn and Tynan (2001) recommended that students identified as having emotional or behavioral adjustment problems should be served through the juvenile justice system rather than through the public schools, despite the fact that juvenile justice systems are often punitive and not geared toward providing useful mental health services. As noted by Nelson and colleagues (2009), "The dangers associated with accepting such an ill-conceived policy position are immense, both for the youth and families needing supports and for society as a whole" (p. 477).

Our failure to accept the need for mental health services in schools has implications that extend beyond students themselves (Knitzer, Steinberg, & Fleisch, 1991). For example, the systems created through a coordinated mental health effort should also provide more support for the teachers serving these students (Nelson et al., 2009). There will always be critics who suggest that general and special education services for children and adolescents in schools are distinctly different from mental health services. However, conceptualizing services for students in schools in terms of universal, selected, and indicated prevention and intervention is bringing "research and practice into closer alignment with a comprehensive and potentially more effective public health model" (Nelson et al., 2009, p. 478).

> **Conceptualizing services for students in schools in terms of universal, selected, and indicated prevention and intervention is bringing research and practice into closer alignment with a comprehensive and potentially more effective public health model.**

CONCLUDING COMMENTS

Suicide is now increasingly viewed as a significant public health problem. Initiatives by the federal government in the 1990s led to an increased focus on suicide and its prevention, both in communities and in schools. Several community-based public health approaches to suicide prevention have been suggested, such as means restrictions, crisis hotline services, and public education, all of which have demonstrated promise and some level of success. Public health approaches to problems of children and adolescents in schools have also been a topic of increasing interest, particularly the three-tiered model that includes universal prevention programming for all students, selected interventions for students identified as at risk, and tertiary interventions for students at high risk for problems or who are already experiencing them.

The first three chapters in this book provided a context for the problem of youth suicide, a rationale for why schools should be involved in youth suicide prevention efforts, and why a public health approach to this problem is a reasonable and sensible response to it. The remaining chapters will focus on specific and practical prevention, assessment, and interventions strategies schools can implement to more effectively prevent youth suicidal behavior.

National Strategy for Suicide Prevention:
Goals and Objectives for Action

- **Goal 1:** Promote awareness that suicide is a public health problem that is preventable.

- **Goal 2:** Develop broad-based support for suicide prevention.

- **Goal 3:** Develop and implement strategies to reduce the stigma associated with being a consumer of mental health, substance abuse, and suicide prevention services.

- **Goal 4:** Develop and implement suicide prevention programs.

- **Goal 5:** Promote efforts to reduce access to lethal means and methods of self-harm.

- **Goal 6:** Implement training for recognition of at-risk behavior and delivery of effective treatment.

- **Goal 7:** Develop and promote effective clinical and professional practices.

- **Goal 8:** Improve access to community linkages with mental health and substance abuse services.

- **Goal 9:** Improve reporting and portrayals of suicidal behavior, mental illness, and substance abuse in the entertainment and news media.

- **Goal 10:** Promote and support research on suicide and suicide prevention.

- **Goal 11:** Improve and expand surveillance systems.

U.S. Surgeon General's (USDHHS, 1999) Definitions of Mental Health, Mental Health Problems, and Mental Illness

- **Mental health** is a state of successful performance of mental function, resulting in productive activities, fulfilling relationships with other people, and the ability to adapt to change and to cope with adversity. Mental health is indispensable to personal well-being, family and interpersonal relationships, and contribution to community or society. It is easy to overlook the value of mental health until problems surface. Yet from early childhood until death, mental health is the springboard of thinking and communication skills, learning, emotional growth, resilience and self-esteem. These are the ingredients of each individual's successful contribution to community and society. Americans are inundated with messages about success—in school, in a profession, in parenting, in relationships—without appreciating that successful performance rests on a foundation of mental health. (USDHHS, 1999, p. 4)

- **Mental illness** is the term that refers collectively to all diagnosable mental disorders. Mental disorders are health conditions that are characterized by alterations in thinking, mood, or behavior (or some combination thereof) associated with distress and/or impaired functioning. . . . Alterations in thinking, mood, or behavior contribute to a host of problems—patient distress, impaired functioning, or heightened risk of death, pain, disability, or loss of freedom. (USDHHS, 1999, p. 5)

- **Mental health problems** [is the term used] for signs and symptoms of insufficient intensity or duration to meet the criteria for any mental disorder. Almost everyone has experienced mental health problems in which the distress one feels matches some of the signs and symptoms of mental disorders. Mental health problems may warrant active efforts in health promotion, prevention, and treatment. . . . (In some cases) early intervention is needed to address a mental health problem before it becomes a potentially life-threatening disorder. (USDHHS, 1999, p. 5)

Traditional Public Health Services
and Their School Mental Health Equivalents

Traditional Public Health Services	Equivalent School Mental Health Services
1. Monitor health status to identify community health problems.	1. Monitor students' mental health status including their academic, social–emotional, and relational competence.
2. Assess and investigate health problems and health hazards in the community.	2. Assess and investigate emotional, behavioral, and mental health problems in students.
3. Inform educate, and empower people about health issues.	3. Inform, educate, and empower students and their families about mental health issues.
4. Mobilize community partnerships to identify and solve health problems.	4. Mobilize school–family–community partnerships to identify and address students' emotional, behavioral, and mental health problems.
5. Develop policies and plans that support individual and community health efforts.	5. Develop policies and plans that support student, family, school, and community mental health efforts.
6. Enforce laws and regulations that protect health and ensure safety.	6. Implement policies and practices that protect students' mental health and ensure developmental competence.
7. Link people to needed personal health services and assure the provision of health care when otherwise unavailable.	7. Link students and their families to universal, selected, and tertiary interventions as needed.
8. Assure a competent public health and personal health care workforce.	8. Provide appropriate staff training and monitor throughout intervention.
9. Evaluate effectiveness, accessibility, and quality of personal and population-based health services.	9. Evaluate effectiveness, accessibility, and quality of school mental health services.
10. Research new insights and innovative solutions to health problems.	10. Research new insights and innovative approaches to promoting mental health.

Compiled from Doll and Cummings (2008a) and the Institute of Medicine (1988).

Common Principles of Effective Prevention and Competency Promotion Programs

Effective prevention and competency promotion programs are:

- Theory-driven.

- Evidence-based.

- Emphasize behavior change as well as the promotion of personal and social competencies.

- Use effective strategies to change behavior and competencies.

- Recognize the importance of multiple environmental influences.

- Foster connections to adults and prosocial peers.

- Permit flexible approaches to fit the needs, preferences, and values of the target population and setting.

- Evaluated and modified as needed based on data.

- Implemented properly and effectively.

Compiled from Bond and Carmola Hauf (2004), Durlak (2009), and Nation et al. (2003).

CHAPTER 4

Universal School-Based Suicide Prevention Programs for All Students

No mass disorder affecting mankind is ever brought under control or
eliminated by attempts at treating the individual.

—George W. Albee

Promoting mental health for all Americans will require scientific know-
how but, even more importantly, a societal resolve that we will make the
needed investment. The investment does not call for massive budgets;
rather, it calls for the willingness of each of us to educate ourselves and
others about mental health and mental illness, and thus to confront the
attitudes, fear, and misunderstanding that remain as barriers before us.

—David Satcher

An ounce of prevention is worth a pound of cure.

—Benjamin Franklin

Universal school-based suicide prevention programs are presented to all students in a given
population (e.g., all students in a classroom; all students in a school; all students in a school district), regardless of their level of risk. The key assumption underlying universal programs is that
the conditions that contribute to suicide risk in youth "often go unrecognized, undiagnosed,
and untreated, and that educating students and gatekeepers [e.g., school personnel] about the
appropriate response will result in better identification of at-risk youth, and an increase in help
seeking and referral for treatment" (Hendin et al., 2005). Universal suicide prevention programs
appear to be the most widely used approach in the schools. In our review of school-based suicide prevention programs, of the 13 studies identified for inclusion, 10 of them were classified as
universal programs (Miller, Eckert, & Mazza, 2009).

The primary purpose of universal suicide prevention programs is to provide useful, relevant, and practical information to both students and staff about suicide and how the school is
attempting to respond to this problem. School-based mental health professionals, such as school
psychologists, school counselors, and school social workers, are typically the most appropriate
professionals for leading these informational sessions.

Universal approaches attempt to reach the greatest number of students and staff possible, in an attempt to identify and detect the much smaller number of students who may be at risk for suicide (Berman, 2009). Historically, many universal suicide prevention programs have been of short duration, frequently promoting a "stress" model of suicide prevention (i.e., suggesting to students that suicidal behavior can occur as a result of extreme levels of stress) and failing to assess program effects on more serious forms of suicidal behavior. Research suggests, however, that these programs should be of longer duration, have a comprehensive mental health focus, and assess and evaluate program effectiveness on a broader spectrum of suicidal behaviors (e.g., suicide communications; suicide attempts) rather than simply focusing on knowledge and attitude change (Miller, Eckert, & Mazza, 2009).

> **Universal approaches attempt to reach the greatest number of students and staff possible, in an attempt to identify and detect the much smaller number of students who may be at risk for suicide.**

Universal suicide prevention programs should include providing students and school personnel with information about suicide in general and youth suicide in particular. Because potentially suicidal youth are more likely to confide in a peer rather than an adult about their suicidal thoughts or actions (Kalafat & Lazarus, 2002), it is particularly important that all students be provided with information regarding suicide. In fact, after receiving information about suicide in a universal program, it is much more likely that a student will contact an adult in the school with concerns about a peer's suicidal behavior than a student will contact a school official to make a self-referral.

> **Universal suicide prevention programs should include providing students and school personnel with information about suicide in general and youth suicide in particular.**

Presenting this information to school staff is also useful because they come into frequent contact with students. Although much of the information presented to students and school staff will be identical, there will be some variations. For example, teachers and other school personnel should be instructed to be attentive to permanent products produced by students in school, such as artwork or written assignments. Drawn or painted pictures from students that clearly suggest possible suicidal preoccupations (e.g., a student who draws a picture of a person hanging from a tree, or a picture of a person with a gun pointed to the person's head) should immediately be brought to the attention of a school mental health professional.

> **Because potentially suicidal youth are more likely to confide in a peer rather than an adult about their suicidal thoughts or actions, it is particularly important that all students be provided with information regarding suicide.**

School personnel should be made aware that student writings and artwork may be quite revealing about a student's emotional state, and that it may function as one possible vehicle for increasing connectedness to school staff through candid and revealing self-expression. As such, teachers who require students to complete artwork or written assignments should be required to carefully review them. I know of one parent who was shocked to see that her son wrote in one creative writing assignment that he was thinking about hurting himself. Given that this statement was written in response to an assignment from his teacher, it was a clear attempt by the student to communicate his emotional problems to his teacher. Unfortunately, the only action taken by the teacher in response to this statement was to place a checkmark by it, indicating her acknowledgment that the student had fulfilled the writing requirement. Though perhaps not intentional, in this case the only thing the teacher communicated to the student about his emotional suffering was her indifference to it.

INFORMATION REGARDING YOUTH SUICIDE
FOR ALL STUDENTS AND STAFF

> **Topics that can and should be presented to students and staff include pertinent demographic information about suicide, dispelling common myths and misinformation regarding it, various risk factors that may increase the probability of suicide, possible warning signs of suicidal behavior, and protective factors that may decrease the probability of suicide.**

Topics that can and should be presented to all students and staff include pertinent demographic information about suicide, dispelling common myths and misinformation regarding it, various risk factors that may increase the probability of suicide, possible warning signs of suicidal behavior, and protective factors that may decrease the probability of suicide. Teaching appropriate responses to peers who come into contact with other students who may be depressed or suicidal is also a useful and recommended universal practice, as is providing information to students and staff about school and community resources for getting help (Kalafat, 2003; Mazza & Reynolds, 2008).

The focus at this level should not be to provide an exhaustive presentation of these issues, but rather to highlight information that has particular relevance for youth suicide prevention. For example, it is often recommended that universal suicide prevention programs provide students with information regarding the many myths that surround it. One such myth (discussed in Chapter 1) is that most youth who die by suicide leave suicide notes. Although one could discuss and dispel this myth with students and staff, it is clear that doing so may provide some interesting information but will likely not lead to meaningful outcomes (i.e., a reduction in the number of student suicide attempts). There are other myths, however, that are particularly pernicious because the extent to which they are believed and acted upon will often actively undermine school-based suicide prevention efforts.

Presented in this chapter is information that, in my view, has the most direct relevance for school-based suicide prevention. I would recommend that mental health professionals present this information to all stakeholders in their schools, especially those in middle and high schools. For example, I would recommend having a school-based mental health professional provide this information to all school personnel, including instructional staff (e.g., teachers, teacher aides), administrative staff (e.g., principals, vice-principals); and support staff (e.g., bus drivers, secretaries, cafeteria workers, maintenance personnel), on an annual basis. Similarly, I would recommend that this information also be annually provided to all middle and high school students. School-based mental health professionals should also make it clear that they will be available for any follow-up questions or consultation after this information is presented.

> **I would recommend having a school-based mental health professional provide information regarding youth suicidal behavior to all school personnel, including instructional staff, administrative staff, and support staff on an annual basis.**

Information presented to students can be communicated in various ways. I would not recommend that presentations to students be conducted at a schoolwide level, in which information is presented in a large auditorium to a large group of students or to all students in the school at the same time and place. Instead, I recommend that this information be shared with students in different classrooms, perhaps as part of a unit in a health class. In my view, this arrangement has multiple advantages. First, it allows the mental health professional to meet and greet students in a smaller, more comfortable setting. Making an initial "good impression" on students is important; the mental health professional should appear relaxed, knowledgeable, friendly, and approachable. Making a good first impression on students can help build rapport with them, and can decrease some of the possible confusion and/or anxiety students may have about the role of mental health professionals in the schools generally, and in the context of suicide prevention efforts in particular.

Meeting with students in classrooms also allows them the time to ask questions about the information provided, in an environment more conducive to asking questions than a large assembly hall or auditorium. The topic of youth suicide is one that is potentially disturbing to students, but is also one of high interest to them. Remember, merely talking about suicide will not "put ideas into their head." In addition, carefully and honestly answering any questions students may have about suicide conveys the clear message that school personnel consider this a serious problem, and that they are willing and able to discuss it in an open manner and to be proactive in doing something about it.

DEMOGRAPHIC INFORMATION

Demographic information regarding suicidal behavior in general and youth suicidal behavior in particular was provided in Chapter 1. Although it is useful for school-based mental health professionals to be fully cognizant of this information, not all of it is directly relevant to students and other school personnel. School-based mental health professionals should make use of the demographic information provided in Chapter 1 in developing their informational presentation, and should periodically update this information as new research findings related to demographic variables are discovered and refined. Demographic information that is relevant and useful for students and school personnel and should therefore be presented to these groups includes:

- The scope of the problem of suicide worldwide and in the United States.
- The scope of the problem of youth suicide worldwide and in the United States.
- The notion that suicidal behavior is broader than suicide alone (e.g., suicidal ideation; suicidal communications; suicide attempts) and explaining what these differences entail.
- Effects of age, gender, ethnicity, geography, sexual orientation, and socioeconomic status on suicidal behavior.

MYTHS AND REALITIES

Common myths regarding youth suicide were also discussed in Chapter 1. Handout 4.1 (at the end of the chapter) lists 10 common myths that in my view are particularly important to be shared with students and school personnel. Some of these myths are elaborated on in other chapters in this book, providing school personnel with additional information. However, the information presented in Handout 4.1 is usually sufficient to dispel some of the more prominent myths about youth suicide. School personnel who would like additional information regarding the many myths that surround suicide and that often impede effective prevention and intervention efforts are encouraged to read *Myths about Suicide* by Joiner (2010).

VARIABLES THAT HELP EXPLAIN OR PREDICT YOUTH SUICIDAL BEHAVIOR

Variables that help explain or predict youth suicidal behavior can be placed into two broad categories: risk factors that may predispose an individual to suicidal behavior and warning signs that may indicate the possibility of a suicidal crisis (Van Orden et al., 2008). Although risk factors and warning signs are frequently linked concepts, there are important distinctions between them. Perhaps the most salient distinctions are that risk factors suggest a more distant temporal relationship to suicidal behavior, whereas warning signs suggest a more proximal relationship (Van Orden et al., 2008). In addition, risk factors are typically long-standing, often unchangeable, and have been derived empirically (i.e., identified through research studies). In contrast, warning signs are more dynamic and have generally been derived from clinical practice and experience rather than the research literature (Joiner et al., 2009; Rudd et al., 2006).

> Variables that help explain or predict youth suicidal behavior can be placed into two broad categories: risk factors that may predispose an individual to suicidal behavior, and warning signs that may indicate the possibility of a suicidal crisis.

RISK FACTORS

Although numerous risk factors for suicide have been identified, the two most prominent are (1) the presence of at least one mental health disorder; and (2) a history of previous suicidal behavior, particularly suicide attempts. In presenting information about youth suicide to students and school personnel, it is essential that these two risk factors be clearly identified as the most significant. Both of these prominent risk factors are discussed in greater detail in this section, followed by a brief review of other risk factors for youth suicidal behavior.

> Although numerous risk factors for suicide have been identified, the two most prominent are (1) the presence of at least one mental health disorder; and (2) a history of previous suicidal behavior, particularly suicide attempts.

Presence of Mental Health Disorders

The most reliable and robust risk factor for youth suicide is the presence of one or more mental health disorders. Findings from "psychological autopsies" (i.e., a systematic collection of data via structured interviews of family members and/or friends of the suicide victim) estimate that approximately 90% of youth who die by suicide experienced at least one mental disorder at the time of their deaths (Miller & Eckert, 2009). This is important information for students and school personnel, and it should be made clear to both groups that the converse of this statement is *not* true (i.e., it is not true that 90% of all people who have mental disorders die by suicide).

The most common mental disorders exhibited by youth who die by suicide are, in order, mood disorders (e.g., major depressive disorder; dysthymic disorder; bipolar disorder), substance-related disorders (e.g., alcohol and/or drug abuse), and disruptive behavior disorders (Fleischmann et al., 2005). Although the large majority of clinically depressed youth are not suicidal and not all suicidal youth are clinically depressed (Reynolds & Mazza, 1994), approximately 42–66% of youth who die by suicide appear to have been experiencing some type of depressive disorder at the time of their deaths (Fleischmann et al., 2005; Shaffer et al., 1996). Both unipolar depressive disorders (e.g., major depressive disorder, dysthymic disorder) and bipolar disorder increase the probability of suicidal behavior in youth.

> **The most common mental disorders exhibited by youth who die by suicide are, in order, mood disorders, substance-related disorders, and disruptive behavior disorders.**

Other types of mental disorders that have been linked to youth suicide include anxiety disorders (e.g., panic disorder; posttraumatic stress disorder), schizophrenia, borderline personality disorder, and adjustment disorder (Brent et al., 1993; Mazza, 2000; Mazza & Reynolds, 2001; Moskos, Olson, Halbern, Keller, & Gray, 2005; Shaffer et al., 1996). The eating disorders of anorexia nervosa and bulimia are also known to confer risk for suicide. However, although both anorexia and bulimia increase risk of suicidal ideation and suicide attempts, only anorexia is associated with an increased risk for death by suicide (Joiner et al., 2009).

Although not a diagnosable mental disorder, the presence of *hopelessness* also is highly associated with youth suicide (Thompson, Mazza, Herting, Randell, & Eggert, 2005) and can be either a risk factor or warning sign for it. In discussing some of the prominent theories of suicide in Chapter 1, you will recall Beck's theory regarding the centrality of hopelessness in the development of suicidal behavior. Hopelessness is a key variable in suicide, and it has implications for both assessment and treatment with or without the presence of particular mental disorders. As noted by Joiner and colleagues (2009): "Regardless of clinical diagnosis or life context, suicide is an act characterized by general hopelessness" (p. 192).

Other variables associated with youth suicide include peer victimization (Brunstein Klomek, Marrocco, Kleinman, Schonfield, & Gould, 2008), sexual and/or physical abuse (Joiner et al., 2006) and self-injury (Miller & Brock, 2010). In fact, most youth who die by suicide have *comorbid* psychiatric disorders and/or mental health problems (Miller & Taylor, 2005). That is, they exhibit the simultaneous occurrence of two or more disorders/problems, which often makes assessment and treatment of these individuals quite challenging. The consistent finding of the substantial presence of comorbid forms of psychopathology strongly indicates that suicide does not occur in isolation but rather is the by-product of other mental health problems (Mazza, 2006).

Previous Suicidal Behavior

In addition to psychopathology, the other prominent risk factor for suicide is previous suicidal behavior, especially previous suicide attempts. This relationship has been found in both youth and adult samples (Joiner et al., 2005). For example, the presence of a prior suicide attempt was

> **The single best predictor of a future suicide attempt is a history of one or more previous suicide attempts.**

found to significantly elevate the risk for future suicide attempts in adolescence (Borowski, Ireland, & Resnick, 2001). A general principle that applies to all behavior, including suicidal behavior, is that the best predictor of future behavior is past behavior. Consequently, the single best predictor of a future suicide attempt is a history of one or more previous suicide attempts.

Other Risk Factors

Children and adolescents who exhibit milder forms of suicidal behavior (e.g., suicidal ideation) but who are undertreated or not treated for it (e.g., not receiving antidepressant medication or psychotherapy) are also at increased risk for suicide. Ethnic minority youth in the United States may also be affected by various risk factors that European American youth may not face, such as racial discrimination, acculturative stress, a fatalistic philosophy, and passive coping strategies (Gutierrez & Osman, 2008). As mentioned in Chapter 1, sexual minority (i.e., lesbian, gay, bisexual, transgender) youth appear to be at higher risk for suicidal ideation and suicide attempts than heterosexual youth. Exposure to suicide through death of a peer also may be considered an accelerating risk factor, particularly among those already predisposed to be at risk (Berman et al., 2006). Consequently, conducting a suicide risk assessment of close friends of a suicide victim is strongly recommended. Methods and procedures for conducting suicide risk assessments are discussed extensively in the next chapter.

Some additional risk factors for youth suicide that have been identified (Brock, Sandoval, & Hart, 2006; Joiner, 2005; Lieberman et al., 2008) include the following:

- Biological deficits in serotonin functioning.
- Social isolation.
- Limited access to mental health facilities.
- Poor problem-solving and coping skills.
- Low self-esteem.
- Dysfunctional parenting or family environments.
- Parental psychopathology.
- Cultural or religious beliefs.
- Access to lethal weapons, particularly firearms.
- Repeated engagement in or exposure to violence.

POSSIBLE WARNING SIGNS OF SUICIDAL BEHAVIOR

As opposed to risk factors, warning signs for suicide are more dynamic and proximal factors that suggest the increased probability of a suicidal crisis (Van Orden et al., 2008). A working group convened by the AAS reviewed the research literature and reached consensus on a set of possible warning signs for suicide (Rudd et al., 2006). These warning signs, which should be shared with all students and school personnel, include:

- Hopelessness.
- Rage, anger, seeking revenge.

- Acting recklessly or engaging in risky activities, seemingly without thinking.
- Feeling trapped, as if there is no way out.
- Increasing alcohol or drug use.
- Withdrawing from friends, family, or society.
- Experiencing anxiety and/or agitation.
- Being unable to sleep or sleeping excessively.
- Dramatic mood changes.
- Perceiving no reason for living or no sense of purpose in life (Rudd et al., 2006).

The AAS has also developed a useful mnemonic for remembering the warning signs of suicide—IS PATH WARM?

- *I* is for suicidal ideation.
- *S* is for substance abuse.
- *P* is for purposelessness.
- *A* is for anxiety and agitation (including being unable to sleep).
- *T* is for trapped (as in feeling trapped).
- *H* is for hopeless.
- *W* is for withdrawal.
- *A* is for anger.
- *R* is for recklessness.
- *M* is for mood fluctuations.

A few caveats regarding warning signs are worth mentioning. First, many of the currently known warning signs have not been validated specifically for youth suicide. More research is needed to determine if signs of acute suicide risk differ between children, adolescents, and adults (Van Orden et al., 2008). Second, although the giving away of possessions has frequently been described as a warning sign for suicide, there is no empirical evidence to support this contention, so it is not listed as a warning sign. Third, and perhaps most important, many if not most youth exhibit some or even several of these warning signs and never engage in suicidal behavior, and it is not clear how many of these warning signs, or what combination of them, are the best predictors of suicide. Similarly, not all youth who die by suicide will necessarily exhibit all or even some of these warning signs. As noted by Joiner (2010), "the vast majority of those who have the risk do not display the outcome (suicide), and many of those who have the outcome do not possess the risk factor" (p. 31). Nevertheless, youth who exhibit several warning signs in addition to the risk factors described above should be viewed as being at high risk for suicide and should be individually assessed by a school-based mental health professional.

SITUATIONAL CRISES, STRESSFUL LIFE EVENTS, AND PRECIPITANTS

Risk for suicidal behavior increases when acute situational crises or stressful life events, such as some type of loss of an interpersonal nature, occurs in conjunction with other, more chronic risk factors, such as depression, substance abuse, and/or access to lethal methods (Gould & Kramer, 2001; Lieberman & Poland, 2002). Several different types of stressful events that may precipitate suicidal behavior in youth have been identified. Although these events do not directly cause suicidal behavior, they may have the potential to "trigger" suicidal behavior in potentially vulnerable students. No one particular stressful event is highly predictive of suicidal behavior, although the risk for suicide increases as the number and emotional intensity of stressful events increase in the lives of youth already predisposed to suicidal tendencies (Miller & McConaughy, 2005). Handout 4.2 (at the end of the chapter) lists several possible stressful events that may trigger or precipitate suicidal behavior.

PROTECTIVE FACTORS

Given the finding that many youth who have a number of prominent risk factors for suicide do not engage in suicidal behavior suggests the presence of various protective or resiliency factors (Beautrais, 2007). Protective factors refer to those variables that have been linked empirically (e.g., as mediators or moderators) to decreased risk for suicidal behavior (Gutierrez & Osman, 2008). Although work in this area is increasing, less research has been devoted to examining protective factors in comparison to risk factors in regards to suicide. As a result, relatively little is known about which factors might mitigate risk factors for suicidal behavior (Berman et al., 2006). Some protective factors that have been tentatively identified, however, include (1) social problem solving and coping skills; (2) self-esteem; and (3) social support, from both peers and (particularly) parents. In addition, although not specific to suicide, a number of other protective factors have been identified that, when present, can often offset other risk factors (Doll & Cummings, 2008a). These include:

- Close peer friendships.
- High self-efficacy.
- High levels of engagement in productive activities (e.g., school).
- Warm relationships and guidance from adults.
- Responsive schools.

TEACHING STUDENTS HOW AND WHERE TO GET HELP

Any universal program for suicide prevention should include information presented to all students regarding what they should do if they are suicidal, or if they suspect that someone they know may be suicidal. Students should be given multiple avenues for how this may occur, giving them various options so that they feel most comfortable in sharing their concerns (e.g., telling a trusted and liked teacher). A major barrier to this process is the consistent finding that youth with the highest risk for suicidal behavior are frequently the least likely to seek help from others (Berman et al., 2006). In other words, suicidal thoughts and other suicidal behaviors may act as a barrier to getting help for some children and adolescents, a phenomenon that has been described

> **It is frequently the case that youth with the highest risk for suicidal behavior are the least likely to seek help from others.**

as *help-negation* (Rudd, Joiner, & Rajab, 1995). A growing literature supports the occurrence of help-negation in nonclinical samples of high school and college students. For example, Carlton and Deane (2000) found that the presence of suicidal ideation was negatively associated with help seeking in a sample of New Zealand high school students. This finding was later replicated among Australian (Deane, Wilson, & Ciarrrochi, 2001) and American university students (Fur, Westfield, McConnell, & Jenkins, 2001). In the study involving American students ($n = 1455$), the authors found that only 20% of the participants who had reported experiencing suicidal ideation had sought counseling for it.

Many of these high-risk youth—typically adolescent males—exhibit attitudes characterized by particular core beliefs that support the use of maladaptive coping strategies in response to depression and suicidal behavior (Gould et al., 2004). For example, many of these adolescents have the strong cognitive belief that people should be able to "handle" their own problems without outside assistance. Unfortunately, peers of students in this group are not likely to be particularly helpful in referring them either because they often have their own mental health issues. Gould and colleagues (2004) suggest that cognitive-behavioral approaches can be useful for assessing students' coping strategies, and for assessing how they perceive the idea of getting help for their problems. School personnel can also frequently communicate and reinforce the notion (as the Air Force program described in Chapter 3 has done) that getting help is not a sign of weakness but rather a sign of strength—a willingness to honestly admit that one has problems. In fact, using the successful Air Force program as an example might be particularly beneficial for males, the group most likely to engage in help-negation.

A variety of factors may affect the help-seeking behaviors of children and adolescents in regards to suicide or other problems (Srebnik, Cauce, & Baydar, 1996). For example, Cigularov, Chen, Thurber, and Stallones (2008) examined the barriers to help seeking among 854 high school students in Colorado. These researchers examined both the barriers students identified to getting help themselves as well as the barriers to getting help for others. The most prominent barriers the students self-identified were (1) an inability to discuss problems with adults, (2) the belief that one should handle such problems oneself, (3) a fear of hospitalization, and (4) a lack of closeness to school adults. The most prominent barriers students perceived for helping their friends get help included (1) concerns about making the wrong judgment about their friends, (2) the perceived lack of approachability of school adults, (3) the fear of a friend's hospitalization, and (4) underestimating their friends' problems.

These results, as well as results from other studies indicating the clear reluctance of vulnerable students to seek help for their problems (e.g., Carlton & Deane, 2000; Zwaaswijk, Van der Ende, Verhaak, Bensing, & Vernhulst, 2003), have important implications for universal school-based suicide prevention efforts. In particular, research suggests that school personnel need to form stronger bonds with students generally, so that students are more likely to perceive school personnel as approachable and helpful people for addressing their concerns, whether it is their own suicidal behavior or that of their peers. The need for school personnel to extend themselves to students and to show their support for them is particularly important for males, given that they are at much higher risk for actually dying by suicide than females. Moreover, students should be taught that mental health problems that often underlie suicidal behavior, such as depression, are very common in children and especially in adolescents, and that getting help for them is analogous to getting help for a physical problem. Indeed, highlighting biological vulnerabilities to depression and suicidal behavior may be helpful for some youth, particularly male

> **School personnel need to form stronger bonds with students generally, so that students are more likely to perceive school personnel as approachable and helpful people for addressing their concerns, whether it is their own suicidal behavior or that of their peers.**

students, who may be reluctant to identify themselves as suffering from mental (rather than physical) health issues, especially if they view themselves as deserving of "blame" for them.

LIMITATIONS OF STUDENT CURRICULUM PROGRAMS

Although presenting information to all students regarding suicide is a recommended practice, school personnel should recognize the limitations inherent in this approach. For example, as noted earlier, there are indications that students most likely to be suicidal may benefit from these programs less than their nonsuicidal peers. Moreover, students at risk for a number of mental health problems, including suicide, appear less likely to attend suicide prevention education programs. Finally, youth who are at risk for dropping out of school or being expelled, youth in juvenile detention facilities, runaway and homeless youth, and youth placed in alternative schools have greater risk for suicide than those in mainstream schools (Berman, 2009). As a result, many youth who are most in need of school-based suicide prevention programs may be the least likely to receive them or to benefit from them. School personnel should be aware of this issue and should be proactive in "reaching out" to these youth and to their peers.

It is critically important that *all* students in a given population be exposed to suicide prevention efforts, not because all (or even most) are high risk for suicidal behavior (they typically will not be), but because universal programs can be an important "first step" in the three-tiered model of suicide prevention described in this book. More specifically, it can help to identify students who may require services at the second level (selected/targeted interventions) or third level (tertiary/individualized interventions) of intervention. Finally, school personnel are encouraged to keep this thought in mind: If universal prevention programs do not reach *all* students in a particular population, then by definition they are not really universal programs!

MAXIMIZING UNIVERSAL SUICIDE PREVENTION PROGRAM EFFECTIVENESS: THE IMPORTANCE OF SCHOOL CLIMATE, SCHOOL SATISFACTION, AND SCHOOL CONNECTEDNESS

For school-based universal suicide prevention programs to be maximally effective, they should occur in positive school environments characterized by interpersonal warmth, equity, cooperation, and open communication. The positive and healthy development of children and adolescents depends in part on the degree to which individuals in their key socializing contexts, such as schools, interact with them in ways that are perceived as positive and welcoming. Schools can be designed to promote children's mental health and well-being by creating environments that are enriching, not only educationally, but also emotionally, behaviorally, and socially (Baker & Maupin, 2009).

Three variables of particular interest in this regard are school climate, school satisfaction, and school connectedness. *School climate* refers to the environmental contexts in which students and school personnel interact. A positive school climate is one in which students feel safe and secure, a strong emphasis is placed on student engagement, and the relationships between students and school personnel are highly positive and mutually reinforcing. A positive school climate is also highly associated with students' satisfaction with school.

School satisfaction refers to students' subjective, cognitive appraisal of the quality of their school life (Baker & Maupin, 2009). School satisfaction has consistently been found to be associated with warm, emotionally supportive interpersonal relationships between teachers and students, attitudes of mutual trust and positive peer relationships, and student perceptions that assistance from school personnel will be offered if needed. Classroom environments that are perceived by students to be supportive, positive, and free of harassment and violence are strongly associated with high lev-

> **To maximize the effectiveness of universal suicide prevention programs, school personnel should address issues related to school climate, school satisfaction among students, and school connectedness.**

els of school satisfaction among students (Baker & Maupin, 2009). Schools described by Baker and her colleagues as "caring communities" (Baker, Terry, Bridger, & Winsor, 1997, p. 586) characterized by "psychologically healthy environments" (Baker, Dilly, Aupperlee, & Patil, 2003, p. 206) create optimal conditions for learning in its broadest sense (i.e., academically, socially, emotionally, etc.).

Closely related to school satisfaction, but not identical to it, is the concept of *school connectedness*. This may be defined as "the extent to which students feel personally accepted, respected, included, and supported by others in the school environment" (Goodenow, 1993, p. 80). Referred to by many other names as well, including school engagement, school bonding, and school attachment, there is mounting evidence that school connectedness is an essential protective factor that promotes positive educational, behavioral, and social outcomes in students (Griffiths, Sharkey, & Furlong, 2009). It is also increasingly being recognized as an important parameter in student mental health promotion. For example, in a large sample of over 2,000 students, school connectedness was found to be a significant protective factor against the development of depression and other mental health problems (Shochet, Dadds, Ham, & Montague, 2006). Moreover, given that failed belongingness may be a significant contributor to the development of suicidal behavior (Joiner, 2005, 2009), increasing students' connectedness may be a useful prevention and intervention strategy for potentially suicidal students.

Schools that are characterized by a positive climate are more likely to have students who are highly satisfied with their educational experiences and feel strongly connected to school and school personnel. Students in such schools are less likely to exhibit mental health problems, and even if they have problems they are more likely to seek help for them and to have teachers and others school personnel who are more responsive to effectively treating them. The creation of positive school climates and psychologically healthy classroom environments should therefore be viewed as a universal strategy that can serve as a potential moderating variable in the development and maintenance of student mental health problems, including suicidal behavior.

THE EXAMPLE OF PRAISE AND OTHER UNIVERSAL STRATEGIES FOR IMPROVING SCHOOL CLIMATE

One simple and practical way that schools can improve their climate is for school staff members to increase the amount of positive interactions they have with students. Research suggests that there is initially a high ratio of positive to negative interactions between teachers and students during the early elementary years, but that as children grow older this ratio decreases significantly, to the point where students generally experience a high amount of negative interactions with teachers and other school personnel, particularly in middle school and high school (Maag, 2001). Not surprisingly, there is a usually a corresponding decrease in the level of school satisfaction and school connectedness as children grow older. To counteract this effect, teachers and other school personnel can systematically program for more positive interactions with students by increasing their level of appropriate, contingent verbal praise and prosocial interactions. Students who experience a high rate of contingent teacher praise, as opposed to punishment and reprimands, have higher levels of academic achievement and school engagement and lower levels of disruptive behavior (Flora, 2000; Sawka-Miller & Miller, 2007).

For example, I worked as a school psychologist in an alternative day school for students with severe emotional and behavioral disorders (Centennial School of Lehigh University) where all teachers were taught and trained (through direct instruction and performance feedback) to implement and sustain a high ratio (4:1) of positive to negative or neutral statements directed toward students. Students with emotional and behavioral disorders often find themselves in a continuing spiral of negative interactions with school personnel (Jenson, Olympia, Farley, & Clark, 2004), and this universal intervention strategy was implemented in an attempt to make the school environment more reinforcing for students and to increase the prosocial interactions between students and school staff. For this procedure to be effective, teachers need to self-monitor their behavior, actively seek out examples of appropriate behaviors exhibited by students, and when this is observed immediately, genuinely, appropriately, and enthusiastically reward this behavior with verbal praise (e.g., "John, I really like how you are keeping your eyes on your paper and completing your assignment. Keep up the good work!"). As a result of this intervention, a more positive school environment and better relationships between students and school personnel were achieved.

Other interventions used successfully at Centennial School to increase students' positive experiences in schools included placing students (through the use of curriculum-based assessment) at their appropriate instructional level, incorporating "spirit days" throughout the year (e.g., Crazy Hat Day) in which both faculty and students participated, and creating a School Climate Committee made up of school personnel charged with creatively developing a variety of reinforcing activities and events (e.g., school carnival) designed to enhance the school's positive climate and foster positive relationships and greater connectedness between students and school staff (Miller, George, & Fogt, 2005).

Several interventions were also implemented to strengthen relationships between parents and school personnel. Perhaps the most interesting of these interventions was ensuring that each teacher regularly phoned students' parents when their son or daughter exhibited behaviors worth celebrating (e.g., the student received an A on a spelling test when he had previously struggled with spelling). In most schools, when parents receive phone calls from school personnel it is typically for the purpose of providing negative information about their child (e.g., the student got into a fight with another student; the student was required to stay after school). It is far less common for schools to call parents with good news rather than bad. Although calling parents to inform them of their child's inappropriate or problem behavior is understandable and often necessary, when it is the primary or only kind of interaction between parents and the school it often creates a negative dynamic.

The common element in these interventions is that each one was designed with the intent of increasing connectedness between students and school personnel. Collectively, these and other universal interventions can reduce the "sea of negativity" (Jenson et al., 2004, p. 67) and excessively punitive practices often observed in schools (Maag, 2001), particularly at the secondary level. Although none of these interventions relates specifically to youth suicidal behavior, each of them can potentially contribute to positive youth development and promote behaviors that will hopefully result in students feeling better connected to other adults in the school and to school generally. If this occurs, the risk for suicidal behaviors may decrease.

CONCLUDING COMMENTS

Universal strategies are designed to be used with entire student populations, including all the students in a particular classroom, school, or school district. In the context of school-based suicide prevention, universal strategies typically include information presented to students and staff about risk factors, warning signs, school and community resources, and how to access help. Although universal programs should be considered an essential component of school-based suicide prevention efforts, a challenge school personnel face is providing effective services to those students who often most need suicide prevention programs but fail to benefit from them. Moreover, more intensive interventions will be necessary for at-risk and high-risk students. Finally, for universal suicide prevention programs to be maximally effective, issues related to school climate, school satisfaction, and school connectedness need to be adequately addressed.

Youth Suicide: Myths and Reality

1. **Myth:** Asking questions or talking about suicide with children and adolescents will increase the probability of its occurrence.

   Reality: There is no evidence for this belief. In fact, youth who are able to openly discuss the issue of suicide often have many beneficial outcomes, including decreased risk for suicide.

2. **Myth:** Suicide is caused primarily by stress; with enough of it, anyone can be suicidal.

   Reality: Although a stressful life event can be the final "trigger" to a suicidal crisis, stress by itself is not sufficient to cause suicide. The causes of suicide are complex and there is no simple or single reason why people die by suicide.

3. **Myth:** People who are suicidal are "crazy, " "insane," or "out of their minds."

   Reality: Usually when we think someone is "crazy" it is because they are engaging in bizzare behaviors such as talking to themselves or hearing voices—behaviors largely associated with schizophrenia. The term *insanity* is a legal term, not a psychological one. People who are suicidal are not crazy, insane, or out of their minds, but they typically do suffer from a great deal of emotional pain, caused in part by mental illness, most frequently depression.

4. **Myth:** If someone really wants to die by suicide, there is little or nothing that can be done to to stop it.

   Reality: Often people who are suicidal are in a state of crisis, and when the crisis passes so too does the suicidal behavior. Preventing someone from suicide does not guarantee that the person will not attempt suicide again at a later date. But many people stopped from suicide do not later die from it (providing students with information about Seiden's 1978 study regarding suicide survivors from the Golden Gate Bridge—discussed in Chapter 3—can be useful here).

5. **Myth:** People who talk about killing themselves don't do it; they are just looking for attention, or it is just a "cry for help."

   Reality: For many suicidal people, suicide is more of a "cry of pain" than a "cry for help." People who talk about killing themselves often make suicide attempts; it is not simply a way to get attention.

6. **Myth:** Suicide is an impulsive act that people do "on a whim."

   Reality: Although some suicides may appear as if the person behaved impulsively, this is typically not the case. People who attempt or die by suicide have usually thought about killing themselves for a long time and have made specific plans to do so.

(cont.)

7. Myth: The number of suicides increases in December because people feel their loneliness more acutely because of the many family holidays during that month.

Reality: The number of suicides actually *decreases* in December. Spring is the season in which most suicides occur.

8. Myth: Listening to certain music, or watching certain movies, videogames, or television shows, can make someone suicidal.

Reality: Doing these things can have a potentially negative impact on individuals who are *already vulnerable* to suicidal thoughts or behaviors. If an individual is not already suicidal, however, listening to certain music or watching particular movies will not lead a person to become suicidal.

9. Myth: Suicide can be a rational solution to one's problems.

Reality: Young people who are suicidal are often very sad and depressed and feeling hopeless. Their pain is very real, but they may not understand that it will get better and even go away.

10. Myth: Antidepressant medication causes suicides.

Reality: Despite media reports to the contrary, this is not true. There is some evidence to suggest that the use of antidepressant medication may have caused some individuals to have increased suicidal ideation, but the use of antidepressants has not been found to lead to greater suicide attempts or suicides. In fact, it is probably more dangerous *not* to make use of antidepressants under certain situations (more information is provided on this issue in Chapter 7).

11. Myth: Suicide is "contagious."

Reality: Under certain circumstances, suicide can occur in clusters. This is not as typical as some believe, however.

Stressful Events That May Trigger
or Precipitate Suicidal Behavior

- Romantic breakup.
- Bullying or victimization.
- Death of a loved one or significant other.
- Unwanted pregnancy; abortion.
- Relational, social, work, or financial loss.
- Serious injury that may alter the individual's life course.
- A personal experience involving extreme disappointment or rejection.
- Getting into trouble with adult authority figures, such as school officials or the police.
- Conflict with family; family dysfunction.
- Parental divorce.
- High demands placed on the student at home or at school.
- Increased caretaking responsibilities on the student in the home environment.
- Increased community violence in the area in which the student lives.
- Severe or terminal physical illness.
- The sudden emergence of mental or physical health problems.
- School failure or other problems at school.

Based on Kalafat and Lazarus (2002); Miller and McConaughy (2005).

CHAPTER 5

Identifying At-Risk
and High-Risk Students and
Linking Assessment to Intervention

No problem facing clinicians is more urgent than suicidal behavior.
And yet, clinicians are surprisingly ill-equipped to deal with this most
profound of all human problems.

—DAVID H. BARLOW

The answers you get depend upon the questions you ask.

—THOMAS KUHN

The only good assessment is one that results in an effective intervention.

—FRANK M. GRESHAM

The previous chapter described some possible and recommended components of a universal
suicide prevention program. Although universal programs should be considered essential and
necessary in a comprehensive approach to suicide prevention in the schools, they will not by
themselves be sufficient. Also needed are procedures for identifying those students who might
be at risk for suicidal behavior, as well as those students who are at high risk. How to go about
making that distinction, including the specific procedures involved in doing so, is the subject
of this chapter.

This chapter provides a model for how schools can effectively identify students who are at
risk and high risk for subsequent suicidal behavior. Identification and assessment is an important first step in determining which particular students will require a level of intervention more
intensive than the universal level provided to all students described in Chapter 4. Determining
whether students are at risk or high risk for suicidal behavior is also important for determining the level of intervention that will be required to meet these students' unique needs; that is,
whether these students should receive selected interventions (at risk students) or more individualized tertiary-level interventions (high-risk students).

Three models of identification and assessment will be reviewed: (1) a universal screening approach; (2) selected assessment approaches for identifying potentially at-risk students based on demographic information and other known risk factors, or via referrals from students or school personnel; and (3) individual suicide risk assessments of students identified as being at risk for suicide either through universal screening or selected assessment procedures. Procedures for how to distinguish students who may be suicidal from those who may initially *appear* to be suicidal, but are actually engaging in nonsuicidal self-injury (NSSI), will also be provided. Many school professionals are reporting significant increases in student NSSI, and it is critical that school personnel, particularly school-based mental health practitioners, understand the similarities and the differences between these two different but related problems. Finally, the issue of assessing student suicide and homicide is addressed in this chapter, particularly in regards to school shootings.

UNIVERSAL SCREENING APPROACHES

Historically, both educational and mental health professionals have been reactive rather than proactive in the use of prevention, early identification, and remediation practices in assisting children and adolescents with academic, behavioral, and/or emotional problems (Albers, Glover, & Kratochwill, 2007). In particular, school classrooms are typically organized to promote the acquisition of academic knowledge and skills among "typical" learners rather than to serve and support those with special needs, including those with mental health needs (Kratochwill, Albers, & Shernoff, 2004). Although universal screening for the prevention, early identification, and treatment of medical problems has a long history within the field of public health, educators and schools have only recently begun to discover the many benefits of this approach.

Screening is a process of identifying students, often through the use of self-reports, who may be at risk for various emotional, behavioral, or academic problems. Within a public health model, screening programs are often used to separate those students who are at risk for particular problems from those who are not, so that additional, more individualized approaches to assessment can be conducted. Based on the results of this assessment, interventions can then be provided to the students who need them.

LINKING SUICIDE RISK ASSESSMENT TO INTERVENTION

Traditionally, most assessment methods and procedures in schools have been designed to make normative comparisons. That is, they have been used to assess students in various areas to see how students compare to other students of a comparable grade or age. These assessment measures are frequently used to make diagnostic or classification decisions, such as eligibility determination for placement in special education. In recent years, however, there has been a growing dissatisfaction with these procedures, largely because they are often not very helpful in suggesting or monitoring interventions. Consequently, there has been a strong interest in assessment methods and procedures such as the curriculum-based measurement (CBM) for assessing academic problems (Shinn, 2008) and functional behavioral assessment (FBA) for assessing behavior problems (Steege & Watson, 2008).

The purpose of these assessment methods is not to provide normative comparisons between students or to classify them, but rather to identify particular areas or skills that are targets for needed intervention as part of a data-based, problem-solving model of service delivery. In other words, such procedures link assessment to intervention (Batsche, Castillo, Dixon, & Forde, 2008). In the context of youth suicide prevention, the primary purpose of student suicide screening programs is to identify students in need of additional assessment or intervention.

> **The primary purpose of student suicide screening programs is to identify students in need of additional assessment or intervention.**

AN OVERVIEW OF SUICIDE SCREENING PROGRAMS

Many contend that directly screening students for the possible presence of suicidal behavior is an important, if not critical, component of comprehensive school-based suicide prevention programs (e.g., Gutierrez, Watkins, & Collura, 2004; Kalafat, 2003; Mazza, 1997; Miller & DuPaul, 1996). Their use has been widely advocated because universal prevention programs may not (and often do not)

> **Many contend that directly screening students for the possible presence of suicidal behavior is an important, if not critical, component of comprehensive school-based suicide prevention programs.**

lead to the identification of students who are at highest risk for suicidal behavior. Although screening is a universal process in the sense that its intent is to assess an entire population of students (e.g., students in an entire district, school, or classroom), because its primary purpose is to identify and intervene with students considered at risk for suicide, screening programs should be viewed as a selected prevention procedure rather than as a universal one (Miller, Eckert, & Mazza, 2009).

Several options exist for school personnel interested in using screening procedures to identify potentially suicidal youth. For example, Reynolds (1991) devised a two-phase procedure that has been widely emulated (Shaffer & Craft, 1999). The first phase typically involves a universal (i.e., districtwide, schoolwide, or classwide) administration of a brief, self-report measure designed to identify youth who meet a predetermined set of suicide risk criteria or cutoff point (the self-report measures usually indicate the cutoff point of clinical significance). In the second phase, all students who score above the predetermined cutoff points on the self-report instrument are then individually interviewed by a mental health professional for a more comprehensive assessment of suicide risk. Students who are identified as being at risk for suicide based on their individual interviews are then categorized in terms of their suicide risk (e.g., low, moderate, high) and provided with interventions to meet their particular level of need.

In Reynolds's model, all students in a particular population are administered the *Suicide Ideation Questionnaire* (SIQ; Reynolds, 1988), a brief self-report measure designed to assess the level of suicidal ideation among high school students (a middle school version of the SIQ, known as the SIQ-JR, is also available). The SIQ appears to be a reliable and valid measure as a screening device (Gutierrez & Osman, 2009) and has been used successfully to

> **Useful screening programs that have been used in schools include the Columbia TeenScreen and the Signs of Suicide (SOS) programs.**

identify students who would otherwise not have been targeted for intervention (Reynolds, 1991). Students who score at clinically significant levels on the SIQ are then individually interviewed by a school-based mental health professional for a more precise assessment of suicide risk.

Variations on this procedure can be seen in more recent student suicide screening programs, including the Columbia TeenScreen (2007) and Signs of Suicide (SOS; Aseltine & DeMartino, 2004) programs. TeenScreen requires supplies (including laptop computers), postage, and three staff members to administer it. Additional (free) training, consultation, and technical assistance are available if requested. The SOS program must be purchased and includes a manual and training video for school staff. In-person training is also offered, although costs for this service appear to vary. The SOS also includes a brief screening for depression and other risk factors associated with suicidal behavior. Both programs have been evaluated by the Substance Abuse and Mental Health Services Administration (SAMHSA) and are listed in their national registry of Evidence-based Programs and Practices. In addition, both programs are standardized, making their use in schools generally simple and convenient (Gutierrez & Osman, 2009).

> Research conducted on screening programs indicates that they can accurately identify students at risk for suicide and that they can identify youth who would not otherwise be known to be at risk for suicidal behavior.

Research conducted on screening programs indicates that they can accurately identify students at risk for suicide and that they can identify youth who would not otherwise be known to be at risk for suicidal behavior. However, there is currently no conclusive evidence that student screening programs for suicide are effective in actually reducing youth suicide or suicide attempts (Peña & Caine, 2006).

ADVANTAGES OF SCREENING PROGRAMS

Student suicide screening programs have many advantages. For example, although many students will not make a self-referral to a school professional if they are feeling suicidal, when directly asked about whether or not they have suicidal thoughts, or whether they have made previous suicide attempts, many youth will self-disclose in an honest manner if the individual asking them is someone they trust (Miller & DuPaul, 1996). Furthermore, self-report screening is the only school-based suicide prevention procedure that directly assesses students. In addition, good screening programs are commercially available, and can be administered and scored fairly quickly. Their use can lead to the identification of youth who likely would not come to the attention of school personnel using alternative suicide prevention programs. These advantages are significant and provide a strong rationale for the use of suicide screening programs in schools.

CHALLENGES IN IMPLEMENTING
SCHOOL-BASED SUICIDE SCREENING PROGRAMS

Unfortunately, there are also several challenges associated with screening programs that school personnel need to carefully consider prior to implementing them. For example, some school administrators, teachers, and/or parents may object to a schoolwide or classwide screening on the grounds that it might inadvertently increase suicidal ideation and distress among those who participate in the screening (Peña & Caine, 2006). This fear is a common one but has no basis in fact. As mentioned earlier, Gould and colleagues (2005) found that a group of students who were screened for suicide did not result in an increase either in suicidal ideation or emotional distress among the students. This finding remained consistent even among high-risk youth who had a history of depression or a previous suicide attempt. In fact, additional analyses indicated that the high-risk youth in the group that received the screening reported *lower distress* than youth in a control group who did not receive the screening. Nevertheless, because this myth is so pervasive, it can be a challenge to convince school administrators and parents to conduct schoolwide and classwide screenings.

Perhaps related to this issue is the level of acceptability of screening procedures among relevant consumers. My colleagues and I have conducted a series of studies looking at the acceptability of various school-based suicide prevention programs, including student self-report screenings, curriculum-based/informational programs presented to students, and staff in-service training. Our research has consistently found that student screening is less acceptable than these other approaches among high school principals (Miller, Eckert, DuPaul, & White, 1999), school psychologists (Eckert, Miller, DuPaul, & Riley-Tillman, 2003), school superintendents (Scherff, Eckert, & Miller, 2005), and students (Eckert, Miller, Riley-Tillman, & DuPaul, 2006).

Other challenges to screenings include their cost, both financially (SOS kits need to be purchased, as would self-report forms such as the SIQ) and more importantly in terms of the time and effort required of students and school staff. The use of screening procedures would likely be a particularly time- and labor-intensive process for school mental health professionals, who would need to assist in conducting and coordinating assessments, possibly score protocols (although many screening programs can quickly be machine scored), and conduct follow-up suicide risk assessments with identified students. Furthermore, because student screenings typically have a high rate of false positives (i.e., falsely identifying a student as being at risk for suicide when he or she is not), school-based mental health professionals could be conducting dozens or even hundreds of individual interviews after each screening. Although overidentifying students at risk for suicide is preferable to underidentifying them, it does create certain logistical challenges for school personnel. A related issue is when, and how often, screenings would be conducted. The timing of when screenings are conducted may affect which students are identified as being at risk. For example, if a schoolwide screening for suicide was conducted in September, some students who were not suicidal at that time but *were* suicidal sometime later during the school year would be missed by the screening.

A final challenge facing those who want to implement screening programs is the need for schools to be prepared to effectively respond to those students who are identified as potentially suicidal (Gutierrez & Osman, 2009). In particular, "large scale screenings are only practical if the resources exist to provide every identified high-risk student with adequate follow-up services within a few days of identification" (Gutierrez & Osman, 2008, p. 135). Minimally, these researchers suggest that this would require that each identified student be individually assessed by a qualified school psychologist, counselor, social worker, or other mental health professional.

ETHICAL AND LEGAL ISSUES IN STUDENT SCREENING

Jacob (2009) raises several ethical issues involved in the use of suicide screening procedures in schools. For example, although she agrees with Gutierrez and Osman (2009) that schools must have the necessary resources available to conduct large-scale screenings, she views this not just as a logistical issue but as an ethical one as well. In particular, Jacob (2009) suggests that "it is unethical to screen for suicidal behaviors but then fail to provide individualized follow-up evaluation and intervention" (p. 241).

Jacob (2009) also cites a variety of other ethical issues regarding screening procedures. For example, she indicates that parents must be notified about the use of such screening measures and give their consent to them. School personnel are also ethically required to ensure that students are adequately informed about the purpose of the screening and about who will be informed of and have access to the results. She also suggests that because the screening may not result in any direct benefits to an individual student, the students who are targeted for the screening should be given a choice as to whether they would like to participate in it. Jacob also expresses concern about the ethical issue involved in incorrectly identifying a student as being at risk for suicide based on a screening measure. Specifically, she recommends that school personnel conduct a "risk-benefit analysis of large-scale screenings" and that they "must take into account the possibility that such screenings will result in harm to those students who are false positives (i.e., inaccurately identified as being at risk for suicidal behavior), including the stigma and embarrassment of being subjected to an unnecessary follow-up mental health evaluation and . . . worry to their parents" (Jacob, 2009, p. 241). Jacob's point is an understandable one, although one could also argue that inaccurately identifying students who are in fact not suicidal is preferable to failing to identify students who are suicidal.

Jacob (2009) also indicates that school personnel have an ethical responsibility to "minimize possible stigmatization of students if large-scale screenings are conducted" by ensuring that the names of students who are identified as being potentially suicidal "solely on the basis of screening results are not disclosed to instructional staff. Furthermore, if school mental health professionals have concerns about a student following an individualized suicide risk assessment, these concerns should be shared only on a *need to know basis*" (p. 241).

There is also the issue of legal liability in student screenings. As mentioned in Chapter 2, school personnel may be held liable if they fail to prevent a foreseeable suicide from occurring. However, to date the courts have not required that school personnel take active measures to identify suicidal youth (such as via a screening). Conducting screenings would likely result in more students being identified for interventions, and school-based mental health professionals as well as others concerned about the need to better identify suicidal youth who might otherwise "slip through the cracks" would likely welcome this development. It would probably not be enthusiastically embraced by school administrators, however, who might view the increase in the number of students identified as also increasing the probability that mistakes will be made in providing services for them, and that more potential lawsuits will occur as a result.

Given the many logistical, ethical, and legal

> **Although there are many advantages to large-scale student screenings for suicidal behavior, there are also many challenges associated with their implementations, including ethical and legal ones.**

challenges confronting schools considering using large-scale suicide screening programs, it is not surprising that their use is not widespread, despite some clear advantages they have over other suicide prevention programs. Although school personnel who are willing and able to provide large-scale screenings are encouraged to do so, they should be aware of the many challenges involved in using them prior to their implementation.

OTHER PROCEDURES FOR IDENTIFYING POTENTIALLY AT-RISK YOUTH

Identification Based on Demographics and Risk Factors

Universal suicide screening procedures present many logistical difficulties. As a result, many school personnel may be reluctant to use them. Though not a better procedure, an easier and less challenging one for identifying potentially at-risk students is to do so based on demographic information and known risk factors. For example, students who meet one or more of the following criteria might be considered for additional assessment and/or intervention:

- Male high school students.
- Native American youth.
- Lesbian, gay, bisexual, or transgender youth.
- Students known to have made a previous suicide attempt.
- Youth with clinical depression, substance abuse problems, and/or acting-out behavior problems.
- Students who engage in self-injury.
- Youth known to engage in reckless or dangerous behavior.
- Students who have access to guns.
- Youth who recently had a family member or friend die by suicide.
- Students who have a family history of suicide or depression.

School personnel, particularly school-based mental health professionals, should be aware that students who can be placed in any of these categories may be at increased risk for suicidal behavior. Furthermore, the risk for suicidal behavior may increase depending on the number of risk factors students possess. It is particularly important that mental health professionals in the schools carefully and continually monitor those students who are known to have made a previous suicide attempt, as these students are at especially high risk for future suicidal behavior, including additional suicide attempts.

Being mindful of these risk factors does not mean that school-based mental health professionals should necessarily conduct an individual suicide risk assessment for each student in their schools that meet one or more of these criteria. For example, individually assessing every male high school student for suicide risk would be a time-consuming and often unnecessary task. Nevertheless, students who exhibit one or more of these demographic variables and/or risk factors, particularly if they also exhibit the possible warning signs for suicide that were discussed in Chapter 4, should be carefully monitored. Individualized suicide risk assessments should be conducted if there is any reason to even suspect a student might be suicidal or potentially suicidal.

Identification Based on Referrals from Students or School Staff

A final procedure for identifying potentially suicidal youth, and the one most commonly used in schools, is through referrals made to school-based mental health professionals from students or school staff. For this procedure to be effective, all students and school staff need to receive accurate information regarding the possible warning signs of suicide as well as procedures for how and to whom suspected cases of student suicidal behavior should be reported.

CONDUCTING INDIVIDUAL STUDENT SUICIDE RISK ASSESSMENTS

If schools elect to conduct large-scale screenings, those students who are identified as potentially suicidal as a result of the screenings will require individualized suicide risk assessments. Similarly, those schools that use selected identification procedures, whether based on demographic information and risk factor status or on referrals from students or school staff, will also require that follow-up risk assessments be conducted. Of course, many schools may not elect to make use of universal screenings, and some may also decide not to implement the less challenging procedure for identifying potentially at-risk youth based on demographic and risk factor information. In truth, although both of these procedures offer significant benefits, most school districts in the United States currently implement neither of them.

Regardless of whether or not these procedures are implemented, it is clear that every school, at least at the middle school and high school level, has likely been confronted at one time or another with the need for school-based professionals to conduct individual suicide risk assessments. Conducting individual student suicide risk assessments has been, is now, and will continue to be an important and necessary skill for all mental health professionals working in the schools. Unfortunately, as indicated in earlier chapters, many school-based mental health practitioners do not perceive themselves as having received adequate training in this area (e.g., Miller & Jome, 2008). Although no book can substitute for practical and supervised experience, the information provided in the following section is intended to assist mental health professionals in the schools to more effectively conduct suicide risk assessments.

THE PURPOSE OF SCHOOL-BASED SUICIDE RISK ASSESSMENT

School-based suicide risk assessments have two primary purposes. The first is to determine if a student is potentially suicidal and, if so, to what extent. One useful way to make this determination is to classify students into one of several groups, depending on their degree of risk. How many categories of risk should be considered, and how can school professionals determine in which category students should be placed? There are no clear and absolute answers to these questions, and to some extent clinical judgment is involved. That said, school personnel will need some criteria on which to base their decisions regarding students' risk for suicide.

> **One of the primary purposes of school-based suicide risk assessment is to determine if the student in question is suicidal and, if so, to what extent.**

Rudd (2006) identifies five possible risk levels based on a continuum from "minimal risk" to "extreme risk." Here is a listing of each risk level he suggests using, along with a brief description of the behavioral markers for each category:

1. *Minimal risk level:* No identifiable suicidal ideation.
2. *Mild risk level:* Suicidal ideation of limited frequency, intensity, duration, and specificity.
3. *Moderate risk level:* Frequent suicidal ideation with limited intensity and duration; some specificity in terms of plan; no associated intent.
4. *Severe risk level:* Frequent, intense, and enduring suicidal ideation; specific plans; no subjective intent but some objective markers of intent (e.g., choice of lethal methods).
5. *Extreme risk level:* Frequent, intense, and enduring suicidal ideation; specific plans; clear subjective and objective intent.

The first three risk levels in Rudd's categorization system are generally considered to be in the lower range of suicide risk because, although suicidal ideation may be present, more severe forms of suicidal behavior typically are not. Rudd (2006) suggests that several things occur as an individual's risk level moves from moderate to severe and extreme risk for suicide. First, the issue of actual suicide intent emerges. Second, the number and intensity of symptoms will escalate, in conjunction with a deterioration of protective factors.

The second purpose of school-based suicide risk assessment is to link assessment results with interventions that will best meet that student's needs. Assessment is linked to intervention in the sense that the level of suicide risk will help determine the level of intervention that is required. For example, if the risk assessment indicates that the

> **A second primary purpose of school-based suicide risk assessment is to link the assessment results with interventions that will best meet the student's individual needs.**

student should be considered a severe or an extreme risk for suicide, the intervention will typically involve keeping the student safe until the student can be transported elsewhere, either to the student's home or to another location (e.g., psychiatric hospital) for further assessment or needed intervention. Regardless of what level of risk in which the student is ultimately categorized, each time a suicide risk assessment is conducted the student's parent or guardian should be immediately notified and informed of the results. Moreover, even if it is determined that a student is considered to be at low risk for suicide, that student should not be left alone at any time. If possible, school personnel should also recommend to the parents that they come to the school to pick the student up.

MULTIMETHOD RISK ASSESSMENT

To accomplish the two primary goals of school-based suicide risk assessment, the school mental health practitioner is encouraged to take a multimethod approach. This can include a number of assessment methods and measures, but should *always* include an individual interview conducted with the identified student. Some recommendations for conducting multimethod suicide risk assessments are provided in the following section.

Interviewing Children and Adolescents

The single most important component of an effective student suicide risk assessment is meeting with and individually interviewing the identified student. Given the extreme importance and sensitivity of this issue, it is not surprising that conducting these assessments can be an extremely stressful and anxiety-producing experience, for both the student and the interviewer. Although easier said than done, it is very important that interviewers not become so intimidated or anxious by the process of conducting suicide risk assessments that they become immobilized

The single most important component of a suicide risk assessment is an individual interview with the identified student.

(Miller & McConaughy, 2005). Having a standard protocol in place for conducting risk assessment interviews, as well as gaining clinical experience in doing them, can often reduce nervousness and increase confidence on the part of the interviewer (Miller & McConaughy, 2005). Additional questions can be added to the protocol and others deleted, depending on the particular case and the information desired.

Developmental issues become an issue when interviewing children, particularly younger students (McConaughy, 2005). For example, children under the age of 12 may have difficulty articulating or verbalizing their suicide intent (Pfeffer, 2003), which is why interviewing other adults in younger students' environments (e.g., parents, teachers) is particularly important. Moreover, children under the age of 8 (and older children or adolescents with cognitive impairments) often have significant difficulty reflecting on and reporting on their subjective experience. Consequently, the interviewer is challenged by both the age of the student and his or her cognitive level when conducting suicide risk assessments. Both variables need to be taken into account when interviewing children.

When conducting an interview with a potentially suicidal student, it is important to appear concerned about the student but to conduct the interview in a calm and relaxed manner. Barrett (1985) identified three important issues that individuals conducting suicide risk assessments must consider to effectively assess and respond to potentially suicidal youth. According to Barrett, interviewers (1) must not let their attitudes toward death in general, and suicide in particular, interfere with their ability to be reasonably comfortable with the topic; (2) they must be careful not to exhibit anxiety or irritation to interviewees; and (3) they must deal with feelings of insecurity or lack of confidence and seek out additional training and support on an as-needed basis. School-based mental health professionals are encouraged to keep this helpful advice in mind when conducting suicide risk assessments.

When meeting with the student to conduct the suicide risk assessment, it is helpful if there is already a positive, preestablished relationship between the school professional and the student for purposes of rapport. If there is no such history, the assessor should ensure that he or she behaves in a manner designed to make the student feel as comfortable as possible. Giving the student the opportunity to have a preferred school staff member present during the suicide risk assessment can be beneficial in this regard, for it sends the clear message of wanting the student to feel comfortable and supported.

Several structured and semistructured interviews have been developed that focus specifically on child and adolescent suicidal behavior (Goldston, 2003). Unfortunately, many of these interviews are expensive, difficult to obtain, and vary widely in their degree of reliability and validity (Goldston, 2003). Nevertheless, it is critical that all school-based mental health professionals have a general list of questions that can quickly and accurately lead to the acquisition of needed information.

When conducting a suicide risk assessment, it is important to be very specific and direct in one's language and in one's approach (Miller & McConaughy, 2005; Rudd, 2006). When the interview begins, the student should be informed as to why the assessment is being conducted. It should be clearly communicated to the student that many people care about him or her, and want him or her to be safe. The assessor is encouraged to document exactly what the student says in response to questions; directly quoting the student is preferred and recommended (Rudd, 2006).

The school-based mental health professional should assess the student in a variety of areas, including:

- How the student currently feels.
- Past and current level of depression.
- Past and current level of hopelessness.
- Past and current level of suicidal ideation.
- Perceptions of burdensomeness.
- Perceptions of belongingness.
- History of drug abuse (students may be less willing to answer this question).
- Current problems/stressors at home.
- Current problems/stressors at school.
- History of any previous suicide attempts.
- Method used in any previous attempt(s).
- Presence or absence of suicide plan.
- Specificity and lethality of method in suicide plan.
- Availability of lethal means.
- Possibility of rescue.
- Current support systems.
- Reasons to live.

Handout 5.1 (at the end of the chapter) provides examples of several questions that can be helpful in assessing suicide risk.

Rudd (2006) points out that is it important in a suicide risk assessment to distinguish between what an individual *says* and what an individual *does*—that is, the differences and similarities between an individual's words and his or her behavior. What an individual says in a suicide risk assessment may be described as subjective or *expressed intent*. What an individual does (i.e., concrete behavior that is observed during the interview) is known as objective or *observed intent* (Rudd, 2006). Behavior observed during a risk assessment interview should be described in simple and direct terms. For example:

- Did the student prepare for suicide (e.g., write letters to parents and/or friends and/or significant others)?
- Did the student take actions to prevent discovery and/or rescue?
- Was the suicide attempt in an isolated, secluded, or protected area?

- Was the suicide attempt timed in such a way as to prevent discovery (e.g., when the student knew no one would be home for hours of days)?
- Was rescue and intervention only possible by random chance? (Rudd, 2006)

Markers of objective intent include behaviors that demonstrate (1) a desire to die; (2) preparation for death (e.g., letters to loved ones); and (3) efforts to prevent discovery or rescue (Rudd, 2006).

According to Rudd (2006), there will usually be a high degree of consistency between what a suicidal person says and what a suicidal person does. However, there may be some instances in which a child or adolescent will say one thing but do another. For example, the person may deny any suicidal thoughts but display behavior that suggests the contrary (e.g., he or she made multiple suicide attempts; he or she is known to have made highly detailed suicidal plans of high lethality with little possibility of rescue). Clarifying and resolving such discrepancies is one of the most important tasks in the risk assessment process, and gently but firmly challenging the youth when such discrepancies are present is very important (Rudd, 2006). Rudd (2006) presents an example of one such response involving the hypothetical suicide risk assessment of an adolescent female high school student:

> "You've told me that you really don't want to die, but all of your behavior over the last few weeks suggests otherwise. You've been drinking heavily, you've written a letter to your [boyfriend] saying you wanted to die, and several weeks ago you took an overdose when you knew no one would be home and waited 3 days to tell me about it. I need for you to help me make some sense of this contradiction. It almost seems like you're telling me one thing and doing another. Frankly, I'm more inclined to consider your behavior as the most important variable here, especially because I'm very concerned about your safety and well-being." (p. 10)

Interviewing Teachers, Other School Personnel, and Parents

As was previously discussed, research suggests that parents and other adults are often unaware of the degree to which particular youth may be exhibiting suicidal behavior. In crisis situations in which the risk for suicidal behavior in a student is very high, interviewing other teachers or school staff members may not be viable or necessary, at least not initially. However, because this information is provided by multiple informants who interact with the identified student in different contexts, it can often be useful for treatment planning and other purposes. Questions to teachers should focus primarily on any possible warning signs they may have observed. Parent interviews can be useful for getting a better sense if there is a family history of depression, substance abuse, suicide, or other mental health problems. Handout 5.2 (at the end of the chapter) provides examples of sample questions that can be used with teachers and parents.

Projective Techniques

Some practitioners, especially those whose theoretical orientation includes a psychodynamic perspective on human behavior, may elect to use projective techniques (e.g., Rorschach, figure drawings, apperception tests) for assessing potentially suicidal youth. However, these assessment techniques have not demonstrated adequate reliability or validity for identifying suicidal children and adolescents (Miller & McConaughy, 2005). The use of projective techniques in the context of suicide risk assessment is problematic for other reasons as well. Even if an assessment procedure is both reliable and valid, this should not be the only considerations for determining whether the procedure should be used. For example, what information does the assessment methods provide above that which is already known? Or what information can the assessment method provide that cannot be gained in some other, easier way? This added bit of information is referred to as incremental validity, and projective techniques typically lack this as well (Miller & Nickerson, 2006). Consequently, for these and other reasons, projective techniques are not recommended for conducting suicide risk assessments (Miller & McConaughy, 2005).

SUICIDE AND NONSUICIDAL SELF-INJURY

Nonsuicidal self-injury (NSSI) refers to "intentional, self-effected, low-lethality bodily harm of a socially unacceptable nature, performed to reduce psychological distress" (Walsh, 2006, p. 4). The relationship between suicide and NSSI is complex and nuanced (Jacobson & Gould, 2007; Klonsky & Muehlenkamp, 2007). For example, suicide was found to be the psychiatric condition most highly associated with NSSI in both outpatient and community-based samples, and to be second only to depression in inpatient samples (Lofthouse, Muehlenkamp, & Adler, et al., 2009). A significant portion (50% in community samples; 70% of inpatient samples) of self-injurers report having attempted suicide at least once (Muehlenkamp & Gutierrez, 2007; Nock, Joiner, Gordon, Lloyd-Richardson, & Prinstein, 2006). However, although students who self-injure are at increased risk for suicide (Laye-Gindhu & Schonert-Reichl, 2005; Lloyd-Richardson, Perrine, Dierker, & Kelley, 2007), many are not suicidal and the functions of NSSI and suicide are frequently quite different (Miller & McConaughy, 2005). NSSI is in many ways counterintentional to suicide; the suicidal individual typically wants to end all feelings, whereas the individual engaging in NSSI typically wants to feel better (D'Onofrio, 2007). Consequently, most students who engage in NSSI appear to do so as a morbid, but effective, form of coping and self-help (Miller & Brock, 2010).

Nevertheless, engaging in NSSI clearly places individuals at risk for a variety of suicidal behaviors, including suicidal ideation and suicide attempts (Jacobson & Gould, 2007). In particular, research indicates that individuals who engage in self-injury are more likely to attempt suicide if they report being repulsed by life, have greater apathy and self-criticism, fewer connections to family members, and less fear about suicide (Muehlenkamp & Gutierrez, 2004, 2007). Moreover, individuals who engage in NSSI to escape or avoid the experience of highly distressful emotions are at increased risk for attempting suicide (Miller & Brock, 2010).

As noted in Chapter 1, Joiner (2005, 2009) has suggested that engaging in NSSI may essentially serve as "practice" for engaging in other potentially lethal behaviors such as suicide by desensitizing individuals to pain and habituating them to self-inflicted violence. Gratz (2003) has theorized that individuals who engage in NSSI may become isolated, hopeless, and despairing as a result of it, which may lead them to become potentially suicidal. There is also some evidence to suggest that adolescents who engage in both NSSI and suicide attempts are more impaired than those who do one or the other, and that these individuals may require more intensive treatment (Jacobson & Gould, 2007). Finally, Walsh (2006) has suggested that individuals who frequently engage in NSSI may eventually turn to suicide if and when their self-injury stops functioning as an effective emotional management technique.

AN ASSESSMENT CHALLENGE: DIFFERENTIATING SELF-INJURY FROM SUICIDAL BEHAVIOR

Although NSSI and suicidal behavior overlap considerably, these two problem behaviors should be understood and treated differently (Walsh, 2006). Guidelines containing nine points of distinction for determining whether a self-destructive behavior is suicidal or self-injurious is provided by Walsh (2006) and summarized as follows.

Intent

Walsh (2006) suggests that assessing the individual's intent is a fundamental place to begin in differentiating youth suicidal behavior from NSSI. Essentially, when considering intent, the school mental health practitioner needs to assess what the individual intends to accomplish by engaging in the self-destructive behavior. In other words, what is the goal of the behavior? For example, if during an interview an adolescent girl is asked why she cuts herself and she responds, "I cut myself to feel better" and denies any suicidal intent, this would suggest the student does engage in NSSI but is not currently suicidal. In contrast, a statement such as "No one cares about me and no one ever will—life just isn't worth living anymore" clearly suggests a certain degree of potential suicidality. Unfortunately, mental health professionals often find it difficult to elicit a clear articulation of intent from the individuals they are assessing. Youth who engage in self-destructive behavior are frequently emotionally overwhelmed, as well as very confused about their own behavior (Walsh, 2006). As a result, they often provide answers to the question of intent that are ambiguous (e.g., "It seemed like the right thing to do at the time") or simply not very helpful (e.g., "I don't know").

Assessing intent can be a relatively simple matter, but it is frequently complex and requires a combination of compassion and investigative persistence (Walsh, 2006). Both individuals who are suicidal and individuals who engage in NSSI are typically experiencing a significant amount of psychological and emotional suffering. The suicidal individual will do whatever it takes to make this suffering go away permanently. In contrast, "the intent of the self-injuring person is not to *terminate* consciousness, but to *modify* it" (Walsh, 2006, p. 7). That is, in most instances youth who engage in NSSI do so not to die, but rather to relieve painful emotions. In most cases, these individuals appear to be hurting themselves in order to relieve the presence of too *much* emotion, such as anger, shame, sadness, frustration, contempt, anxiety, tension, or panic. Others, who appear to be in the minority, appear to hurt themselves to relieve too *little* emotion or states of dissociation (Walsh, 2006).

Level of Physical Damage and Potential Lethality

The chosen method of self-harm by an individual often communicates a great deal about the intent of the behavior. The most common form of self-harm among youth who engage in NSSI is skin cutting. Among youth who die by suicide, however, only a very small percentage (less than 1%) die as result of cutting themselves. Consequently, when assessing whether a student intends suicide or NSSI, the method or methods these students use to engage in self-destructive behavior will often provide critical information. School-based mental health professional should understand that the type of cutting that is most likely to result in death is severing the carotid artery or jugular veins in the neck. It is not the cutting of the arms or legs, the most common bodily locations for those who engage in NSSI (Walsh, 2006).

Frequency of the Behavior

In general, NSSI in youth occurs at a much higher rate than suicide attempts. Most youth who attempt suicide do so infrequently, whereas youth who engage in NSSI often do so at a high rate. Although a small percentage of youth attempt suicide on a fairly regular basis, these individuals most often appear to ingest pills (a low-lethality method) and frequently disclose their suicide attempts to others, typically resulting in preventative measures being undertaken. However, even compared to youth who engage in recurrent suicide attempts, many if not most youth who engage in NSSI do so at a much higher rate (Walsh, 2006).

Multiple Methods

More research is needed in this area, but there are some indications that, in comparison with youth who make suicide attempts, youth who engage in NSSI are more likely to use multiple methods (Walsh, 2006). The reasons for this are unclear, although they may be related to issues related to preference and circumstances. For example, many youth engaging in NSSI report their preference for using multiple methods. However, adolescents who are placed in more restricted settings, such as a hospital or group home, may have greater difficulty accessing particular devices (e.g., razors) for cutting or burning themselves, and may then have to use other methods of self-injury (e.g., hitting themselves) to achieve their desired effects (Walsh, 2006).

Level of Psychological Suffering

Some youth may view suicide as their only means of escape from a level of psychological and emotional suffering they may perceive as unendurable. In contrast, although the emotional pain of an individual engaging in NSSI is intense and often extremely uncomfortable, it typically does not reach the level of a suicidal crisis.

Constriction of Cognition

Shneidman (1985, 1996) often pointed out that suicidal individuals frequently exhibit cognitive constrictions or "tunnel vision," in which they engage in a dichotomous, "either-or" type of thinking. For example, a suicidal youth may think to himself, "if my girlfriend dumps me, I can't bear to live." The suicidal individual often engages in an "all or nothing" style of thinking, and these cognitive distortions can have deadly consequences. In contrast, individuals who engage in NSSI are characterized less by constrictive thinking than by disorganized thinking (Walsh, 2006). Unlike many people who are suicidal, people who engage in NSSI do not see their choices as limited; they simply make bad choices (e.g., cutting themselves to reduce emotional stress rather than to deal with this problem in a more appropriate, constructive, and socially acceptable manner).

Hopelessness and Helplessness

Both hopelessness (Beck et al., 1979) and helplessness (Seligman, 1992) are associated with suicidal behavior. In contrast, individuals who engage in NSSI frequently do not exhibit these forms of cognitive distortion (Walsh, 2006). Unlike people who are suicidal, who often perceive themselves as having no control over their psychological suffering, for many individuals the option of self-injury provides a needed sense of control. Many students engaging in NSSI may find it reassuring that cutting, burning, or some other form of self-harm is most likely quickly available when needed (Walsh, 2006).

Psychological Aftermath of the Self-Harm Incident

For the individual who engages in NSSI, the aftermath of the self-harm is often experienced as quite positive because in many cases the behavior relieves emotional distress. Moreover, not only is the NSSI effective in relieving distressful emotions, it frequently does so immediately. In contrast, most individuals who survive suicide often report feeling no better after their attempt, and many may feel worse (Walsh, 2006). When a student engaging in NSSI reports that it is no longer effective for achieving desired outcomes such as reduced tension, the school-based mental health professional should monitor the situation carefully, as the probability of suicidal behavior may increase.

NSSI is an emerging issue of great concern, and school-based mental health professionals are encouraged to enhance their knowledge and skills in assessing and treating youth who exhibit it. For a comprehensive overview of assessment and treatment issues in NSSI generally, the reader is referred to Walsh (2006). An excellent and broad overview of issues in the assessment and treatment of youth engaging in NSSI can be found in Nixon and Heath (2009). Individuals interested specifically in the school-based assessment and treatment of youth who engage in NSSI are encouraged to review Lieberman and Poland (2006), Lieberman, Toste, and Heath (2009), and especially Miller and Brock (2010), which discusses the assessment and treatment of NSSI exclusively within a school context.

SUICIDE AND HOMICIDE: YOUTH SUICIDAL BEHAVIOR AND SCHOOL SHOOTINGS

Mental health professionals working in the schools should also pay attention to the relationship between suicide and homicide, particularly as they relate to school shootings. The issue of students killing other students and school personnel in schools has received significant media attention in recent years. When considering this issue, however, it should first be clearly understood that school shootings are extremely rare events. Students are actually *safer* in schools than in most any other place they could be, and the odds of a student being injured or killed as a result of a school shooting is literally millions to one. Nevertheless, the numerous multiple-victim shootings that occurred during the late 1990s, particularly the 1999 school shootings at Columbine High School in Colorado (Cullen, 2009), dramatically changed public opinion about the safety of America's schools (Van Dyke & Schroeder, 2006).

Suicide and violence prevention efforts have generally occurred in relative isolation from one another (Lubell & Vetter, 2006), although recent tragic events have highlighted the occasional relationship between suicidal behavior and violent behavior toward others, particularly in the context of school shootings (Nickerson & Slater, 2009). For example, the U.S. Secret Service and U.S. Department of Education's study of school shootings found that 78% of school shooters exhibited suicidal ideation to a significant degree (Vossekuil, Fein, Reddy, Borum, & Modzeleski, 2002).

The most infamous school shootings to date occurred at Columbine High School on April 20, 1999. High school seniors Eric Harris and Dylan Klebold shot and killed 12 students and one teacher, and wounded 21 other students (three additional students were wounded attempting to escape the massacre). Harris and Klebold then died by suicide. The school shootings at Columbine High School is the deadliest to date for an American high school and the fourth-deadliest school massacre in U.S. history, after the 1927 Bath incident (which involved the bombing of a school in Bath Township, Michigan, by a disgruntled adult school board member), the 2007 massacre on the college campus of Virgina Tech, and the 1966 shootings at the University of Texas. Of the five perpetrators involved in these incidents, two were high school students and one was a college student. Four of the five perpetrators died by suicide (Charles Whitman, the adult shooter at the University of Texas, was killed by police gunfire).

The extensive media coverage given to school shootings has made this a topic of intense interest in the United States, particularly among parents, policymakers, and school administrators. Although attempts have been made to "profile" school shooters for purposes of identification and prediction, the FBI has cautioned against the use of student profiling to identify potential school shooters (Cornell & Williams, 2006; O'Toole, 2000). Instead, the FBI has recommended that schools adopt a *threat assessment approach*, which is consistent with subsequent recommendations made by both the Secret Service and the Department of Education (Fein et al., 2002; National Institute of Justice, 2002). Some common characteristics of school shooters have been identified, including (1) being male, (2) having a history of peer mistreatment and bullying; (3) demonstrating a preoccupation with violent games and fantasies, and (4) exhibiting symptoms of depression and suicidality (Fein et al., 2002; National Institute of Justice, 2002).

A listing of these characteristics is not particularly helpful, however, because it does not provide sufficient specificity for practical use—far too many students would be falsely identified as potentially violent (Sewell & Mendelsohn, 2000). For example, the observation that several school shooters wore black trench coats to school to hide their firearms prompted some school administrators to view *any* student wearing a trench coat (particularly a black one) with suspicion, and even to ban the wearing of trench coats at school. Members of the FBI's National Center for the Analysis of Violent Crime even began using the term *black trench coat problem* to refer to all such well-intentioned but misguided efforts at profiling potentially dangerous students (Cornell & Williams, 2006). As with predicting precisely which students are most likely to engage in suicidal behavior (Pokorny, 1992), predicting which students will engage in school violence based on particular risk factors has inherent limitations (Mulvey & Cauffman, 2001) because it is a low base-rate behavior. However, although we cannot reliably predict which students will become school shooters any more than we can predict which students will attempt suicide or die by suicide, we can determine periods of heightened risk for both.

For example, the most promising finding from the FBI's study of school shootings was that the student perpetrators almost always made threats or communicated their intentions to harm someone before the shooting occurred (Cornell & Williams, 2006). The FBI also identified a number of cases where school shootings were prevented because authorities investigated a student's threatening statement and found that the student was engaged in plans to carry out the threat. These observations suggested that schools should focus their efforts on the identification and investigation of student threats rather than on the presence of particular risk factors (Cornell & Williams, 2006).

It is critical that this discussion of youth suicide and homicide be viewed in appropriate perspective. The overwhelming majority of youth who engage in suicidal behavior do not engage in homicidal behavior, either at school or outside of it. This is true for adults as well. For example, murder-suicides account for only about 1.5% of all annual suicides in the United States (Holinger, Offer, Barter, & Bell, 1994). That said, there does seem to be a relationship between suicidal behavior and other forms of violence. For example, a study involving over 11,000 students who completed the Youth Risk Behavior Survey in 2005 found that predictors of suicidal behavior for both male and female adolescents included carrying a weapon, being threatened or injured at school, having property stolen or damaged at school, and getting in a fight (Nickerson & Slater, 2009). Consequently, when youth are suspected of engaging in or being capable of violence toward others or of suicidal behavior, it would be prudent to conduct both a threat assessment and a suicide risk assessment. For more information on conducting a comprehensive student threat assessment in schools, the reader is referred to Cornell and Williams (2006), Delizonna, Alan, and Steiner (2006), Van Dyke and Schroeder (2006), and the summary of the report on school shootings made by the U.S Secret Service (National Institute of Justice, 2002).

> **When conducting suicide risk assessments, it is also useful to assess for the possible presence of self-injury and/or to conduct a student threat assessment when appropriate.**

Finally, several protective factors have been identified for both suicidal behavior and violent behavior toward others, including problem-solving and coping skills (Lubell & Vetter, 2006), availability of parent support (Overstreet, Dempsey, Graham, & Moely, 1999), and connectedness to parents (Borowski, Ireland, & Resnick, 2001; Lubell & Vetter, 2006). School personnel are therefore encouraged to design intervention programs in schools that target these behaviors.

ENHANCING PROFESSIONAL SKILLS IN SUICIDE RISK ASSESSMENT

Because of space limitations, a more comprehensive review of suicide risk assessment cannot be provided. Many outstanding resources designed to improve the clinical skills and decision making among mental health professionals conducting suicide risk assessments are available, and interested readers are encouraged to review them. Some of these suicide risk assessment approaches include the Chronological Assessment of Suicide Events developed by Shea (2002), the Collaborative Assessment and Management of Suicidality (CAMS) developed by Jobes (2006), and the Suicide Risk Assessment Decision Tree developed by Joiner and his colleagues (Joiner, Walker, Rudd, & Jobes, 1999; Joiner et al., 2009). Although these risk assessment models were not developed specifically for youth, they can be effectively used with this population. Interested school-based mental health professionals are encouraged to enhance their professional skills in suicide risk assessment by reviewing these sources.

CONCLUDING COMMENTS

Conducting student suicide risk assessments is one of the most critical tasks for school-based mental health professionals. The primary purpose of a risk assessment is to determine a student's level of suicide risk and, based on that assessment, to provide the student with interventions to best meet his or her needs. In this chapter, a number of different approaches to identifying students at risk for suicidal behavior were identified and reviewed, including large-scale screening measures, identifying at-risk students based on particular risk factors, and conducting individual suicide risk assessments for referred youth. Accurate assessment is a critical "first step" in providing adequate treatment and is a very important part of the school-based mental health professional's role.

Possible Questions
in a Student Suicide Risk Assessment

- Have you been feeling more sad or down lately?

- Are you having trouble sleeping? Has your appetite changed recently? Do you feel like you have less energy than you used to?

- Does life seem less fun?

- How long have you been feeling this way?

- Sometimes people feel like hurting themselves, or even killing themselves. Do you ever have any thoughts about killing yourself?

- Have you had any thoughts about killing yourself lately? How about in the last month? The last 6 months?

- How often have you had these thoughts? (daily, a few times a week, a few times a month, etc.)

- What have you thought about doing to yourself?

- Have you actually tried to kill yourself or hurt yourself on purpose in the last month? In the last 6 months?

- Does anyone know what you've done to yourself?

Sample Questions
for Teachers and Parents/Caregivers

Sample Questions for Teachers

- Have you noticed any major changes in your student's schoolwork lately, or in the student's behavior? What kind of changes?

- Have you noticed any kind of emotional or social changes in the student?

- Has the student experienced any trouble in school, especially recently? What kind of trouble?

- Does the student appear depressed? What has the student done or said that would lead you to believe the student is depressed?

- Has the student either verbally, behaviorally, or symbolically (in an essay or a story) threatened suicide? Has the student exhibited any behaviors or made any statements associated with self-destructiveness or death?

- Does the student have a substance abuse problem that you have observed? A problem with self-injury?

Sample Questions for Parents/Caregivers

- Have there been any major changes occurring in your family or in your child's life recently?

- If there have been changes, how did your child respond to them?

- Is there a history in your family of suicidal behavior? Depression? Substance abuse? Other mental health problems?

- Has your child experienced a loss recently?

- Have you observed any recent changes in your child's behavior recently?

- Has your child ever communicated to you or someone else a desire to die? Has your child ever made a suicide attempt? If so, what method did your child use to attempt suicide?

- Do you keep guns in your house? Are they safely stored in a locked cabinet? Does your child have access to that cabinet?

- Has your child been depressed? Does your child have a substance abuse problem? Conduct problems?

- Does your child seem hopeless about the future, or optimistic about the future?

CHAPTER 6

Selected and Tertiary Interventions for At-Risk and High-Risk Students

The most fortunate of us frequently meet with calamities which may greatly affect us, and to fortify our minds against the attacks of these misfortunes should be one of the principal studies and endeavors of our lives.

—THOMAS JEFFERSON

The need to belong and to contribute in some way to society seems to be an essential part of what it means to be human.

—THOMAS JOINER

The primary goal of the crisis intervention response is to help re-establish immediate coping.

—STEPHEN E. BROCK

Selected suicide intervention programs focus on the subpopulation of students who are potentially at risk for suicidal behavior. For example, these may include students who have mental health problems (e.g., clinical depression), Native American youth, students with substance abuse problems, students who engage in self-injury, students who have access to firearms, and/or students who have family members with an affective disorder.

Tertiary suicide prevention and intervention programs target youth who have already engaged in or have exhibited suicidal behavior, such as students who have through written or spoken communication indicated a desire or wish to die, students who have explicitly expressed the desire to kill themselves, and students who have made one or more suicide attempt. The focus of tertiary programs is to reduce the current crisis or conflict, as well as the risk for further suicidal behavior—particularly escalating suicidal behavior. In school settings, these interventions are typically provided in crisis situations, in which the primary goal is to help the student reestablish immediate coping (Brock, 2002).

This chapter provides information regarding possible selected interventions for students identified as being potentially at risk for suicide, as well as tertiary interventions for those students who have been identified as being at high risk for suicide and therefore requiring more immediate interventions.

SCHOOL-BASED SELECTED INTERVENTIONS FOR AT-RISK STUDENTS

School personnel have several options for providing prevention and intervention services to students who may be at risk for suicide. In general, interventions provided at this level will often be provided by school-based mental health practitioners, perhaps in conjunction with other school personnel. Moreover, in many cases these interventions may be provided in a group format, or at least to several different students with similarly identified risk factors. For example, school personnel could provide selected-level interventions for students exhibiting self-injury, or training in gun safety and management. In the next section I summarize some possible examples of selected interventions that could be used with at-risk students, depending on the particular nature of their problems. The interventions I am recommending are all evidence-based in that they have been demonstrated through research to be effective to at least some degree. Because of space limitations, this review is by necessity a brief one, but I encourage readers interested in any of these programs to review the references provided in each section for additional information.

> **Interventions at the selected level for at-risk students include cognitive-behavioral interventions for depression and hopelessness, as well as interventions for substance abuse problems and conduct problems.**

Selected Interventions for Depression and Hopelessness

Evidence-based interventions for depression include a variety of cognitive-behavioral strategies such as cognitive restructuring, disputing irrational thoughts, attribution retraining, self-monitoring and self-control training, and increasing engagement in pleasant activities (Merrell, 2008b). Cognitive-behavioral strategies can also be used for enhancing students' hope and optimism. For example, the Penn Resiliency Program (PRP) is a 12-session, structured program that can be used with groups of students (Gillham, Brunwasser, & Freres, 2008). It includes instruction and guided practice in topics such as decatastrophizing, cognitive explanatory style, procrastination and social skills, problem solving, and relaxation and coping strategies. A cognitive-behavioral approach can also be useful in promoting hope in children and adolescents by systematically teaching students how to (1) clearly conceptualize their goals; (2) develop specific strategies for meeting those goals; and (3) initiate and sustain the motivation for using these strategies (Lopez, Rose, Robinson, Marques, & Pais-Ribeiro, 2009).

A central characteristic of cognitive-behavioral therapy (CBT) is having youth come to the understanding that the emotional consequences we experience often have less to do with what happens to us than with how we cognitively interpret them. Assisting students in actively questioning some of their underlying (and often irrational) assumptions about themselves and then to cognitively reframe them in a more realistic (and positive) light can be helpful, especially for students whose depression or hopelessness is exacerbated by cognitive distortions that may contribute to the development of perceived burdensomeness of failed belongingness. Merrell's (2008b) text provides a useful overview of how CBT can be used to treat internalizing problems associated with suicidal behavior, including depression and anxiety.

Selected Interventions for Conduct Problems

Although the two most popular interventions for students who exhibit antisocial and aggressive behavior are counseling and punishment procedures (Maag, 2001; Stage & Quiroz, 1997), research suggests that both counseling (Stage & Quiroz, 1997) and punishment (Maag, 2001) are frequently ineffective in ameliorating students' antisocial behaviors. Although some forms of cognitive-behavioral therapy may be useful with some students exhibiting disruptive behavior problems (Polsgrove & Smith, 2004), effective school-based intervention typically involves the modification of environmental variables within classrooms and schools (Furlong, Morrison, & Jimerson, 2004). Moreover, punishment procedures, particularly in the form of suspension or expulsion, are actually associated with increases in disruptive behavior (Maag, 2001).

One of the few proven and effective treatments for students exhibiting conduct problems is parent management training (PMT). PMT is designed to promote more positive interactions between parents and children in an effort to strengthen prosocial child behavior and prevent the development or escalation of disruptive and deviant behavior (Kazdin, 2005). The central focus of PMT is on alleviating the coercive communication patterns between parents and their children by teaching and training parents/caregivers a specific set of skills to address child noncompliance, one of the core ingredients of antisocial behavior. For a more complete description of PMT, the reader is referred to Kazdin (2005). For a discussion of how PMT can be applied in low-income urban schools, the reader is referred to Sawka-Miller & McCurdy (2009).

Selected Interventions for Substance Abuse Problems

Substance abuse among children and youth remains a serious problem, and billions of dollars are spent annually in school-based substance abuse prevention programs (Brown, 2001). Although the Drug Abuse Resistance Education (D.A.R.E.) program has been the most widely implemented drug prevention program in the United States (Burke, 2002), research has consistently demonstrated that D.A.R.E.'s effectiveness with regard to student knowledge and attitudes is neither sustained nor leads to lower use of drugs or alcohol (Weiss, Murphy-Graham, & Birkeland, 2005). Moreover, despite the availability of other empirically supported school-based substance abuse programs, the adoption and implementation integrity of such programs appears to be low (St. Pierre & Kaltreider, 2004).

Burrow-Sanchez and Hawken (2007) provide an excellent resource for helping students overcome substance abuse. They describe various kinds of group-format interventions that can be used in schools, including psychoeducational groups, support groups, self-help groups, and therapy groups. They also provide useful information on developing screening programs, prevention programs, and individual interventions for students who need them.

Selected Interventions for Increasing Connectedness

Students who do not feel connected to school or to other people are at risk for a host of mental health problems, including suicidal behavior, and are at increased risk for dropping out of school entirely. Although Chapter 3 described some possible universal interventions for students (e.g., increasing the use of contingent praise), at-risk students may require more intensive interventions designed to foster positive relationships and connectedness. A focus on creating school climates that students experience as caring and supportive is a common component of interventions designed to decrease school dropout and increase school connectedness (Jimerson, Reschly, & Hess, 2008).

> **Students who do not feel connected to school or to other people are at risk for a host of mental health problems, including suicidal behavior, and are at increased risk for dropping out of school entirely.**

One intervention that has been successfully used to forge stronger and more positive connections between students and schools is *check and connect* (Sinclair, Christenson, Hurley, & Evelo, 1998). This intervention is designed to promote engagement with school and with learning. Students receiving the intervention are assigned a mentor from the school staff who monitors the student, routinely "checks in" with him or her, and helps the student with any problems that might develop. Mentors work to create a relationship with students characterized by mutual trust and open communication. Mentors make a commitment to work with students in check and connect for at least 2 years, which emphasizes to students the school personnel's commitment to their development. They also help students become solution-focused and teach them conflict resolution skills. The program also provides more intensive services if necessary, including increased academic interventions and greater student participation in extracurricular activities. For more information on check and connect, the reader is referred to this website: http://ici.umn.edu/checkandconnect.

Another intervention, *structured extracurricular activities* (SEAs), also can enhance school connectedness and engagement. When students are not in school, most of their leisure time is spent in unstructured activities with little or no adult supervision. An overreliance on unstructured, sedentary activities can lead to many unhealthy consequences, including increased suicidal behavior (Mazza & Eggert, 2001). Excessive recreational screen time (e.g., watching television or video games; playing on a computer) is also associated with increased numbers of overweight children. Because of these problems, there has recently been greater interest in developing ways in which youth can be more actively engaged and adult supervised during nonschool hours.

> **Check and connect and structured extracurricular activities are two examples of interventions that may be useful in getting students more connected to school and potentially reducing other problems, including suicidal behavior.**

Typically, SEAs are facilitated by one or more adult leaders, contain established standards of performance or work effort, require voluntary and ongoing participation, and foster skill development and growth (Miller, Gilman, & Martens, 2008). The activities require sustained attention and provide clear and consistent feedback from an adult regarding the student's level of performance. Although SEAs are often associated with school sports, that is not the only way students can participate in them; other examples include being in school plays or in the school band. Research indicates that SEAs can produce positive psychological as well as physical benefits. Moreover, SEAs are helpful for establishing and strengthening meaningful connections with others, which has been found to be a key variable in enhancing psychological growth and interpersonal competence (Baumeister & Leary, 1995). For more information on structured extracurricular activities, the reader is referred to articles by Gilman and his colleagues (Gilman, Meyers, & Perez, 2004; Miller, Gilman, & Martens, 2008).

SCHOOL-BASED TERTIARY INTERVENTIONS FOR HIGH-RISK STUDENTS

Students who are identified through a thorough suicide risk assessment as being at high risk for suicide require immediate, individualized, tertiary-level interventions. In such crisis situations, the primary goal is to keep the student safe and to mobilize resources as quickly as possible to provide the student with the necessary supports needed during the crisis.

Removing Access to Lethal Means

If a youth is suspected to be suicidal, the first order of business should be to determine if the student possesses any device or weapon that may be used to inflict physical pain or cause death. If the students does possess a weapon that can be used for such purposes (e.g., gun; knife), the student should be asked to relinquish it. Fortunately, this situation is atypical. Students will not likely have in their possession the means to kill themselves.

Keeping the Student Safe

A student who is suicidal should never, under any circumstances, be left alone. The student should always be accompanied by at least one adult, in close proximity, at all times.

> One of the most important things school personnel can do if a student appears to be imminently suicidal is to not leave the student alone at any time and ensure that the student is safe at all times.

Breaking Confidentiality

Some suicidal students, either during the suicide risk assessment or afterward, may ask that the information they provided be kept confidential and not be shared with their parents. It is very important that it be clearly communicated to students that you *cannot* keep their suicidal behavior secret from their parents. This should be done in a way that emphasizes that many people care about the student, including his or her parents, and want the student to be safe. For example, I would not recommend first saying to the student that you must break confidentiality because ethical codes require it. Rather, I would recommend telling the student something like this: "I know you don't want me to tell your parents about the way you are feeling. But your parents care about you, and they love you, and they want to do everything they can to help you and to show you how much they do care about you. They cannot do that unless they know about these thoughts you've had about killing yourself."

Making Use of Commitment to Treatment Statements Rather Than No-Suicide Contracts

"No-suicide" or "safety" contracts are written or verbal agreements commonly negotiated with suicidal individuals in the hope that it will improve intervention compliance and decrease the probability of further suicidal behavior (Brent, 1997). This procedure appears to be popular among many mental health professionals, particularly in outpatient settings where they often are a major element of treatment (Berman et al., 2006). Although some individuals appear to support the use of no-suicide/safety contracts in risk assessment (e.g., Stanford, Goetz, & Bloom, 1994) and intervention (e.g., Egan, 1997), there is now an increasing belief that such procedures should not be used (e.g., Goin, 2003; Lewis, 2007) because they provide mental health professionals with a false sense of security and decrease clinical vigilance.

For example, Jobes (2003) has suggested that "safety contracts are neither contractual nor do they ensure genuine safety, because they tend to emphasize what patients won't do versus what they will do" (p. 3). A recent literature review on this topic found no empirical support for the use of no-suicide contracts, leading the authors to propose the use of commitment to treatment statements as an alternative (Rudd, Mandrusiak, & Joiner, 2006). Nevertheless, the use of no-suicide contracts continues to be a widespread practice among many mental health professionals (Berman et al., 2006).

Notifying Parents/Caregivers

Parents/caregivers should be notified and apprised of all suicide risk assessments after they have been conducted, regardless of risk level. School-based mental health professionals should routinely contact parents on the same day suicide risk assessments are conducted.

Notifying the Police or Other Community Supports

The police or other community supports may be notified, depending on the severity of suicide risk and possible needs for transportation or other services. If the police or other community supports are notified, they should be clearly informed of the seriousness of the situation, and that it involves a potentially suicidal student.

Documentation

All actions taken by the school should be documented. This documentation should be kept in a secured location. All documentation should be completed on the day the incident occurred to ensure greater accuracy. As much as possible, the responses of the student and others who were interviewed should be recorded verbatim.

Preparing for the Student's Return to School

In providing these services, school personnel are encouraged to use a "wraparound" approach, similar to that used most commonly with students with disruptive, acting-out behavior problems (Quinn & Lee, 2007). As the term implies, a wraparound approach provides comprehensive, multisystemic interventions that encapsulate the different environmental contexts in which the student lives his or her life. A collaborative, multidisciplinary approach in which school personnel work closely with professionals in other fields (e.g., medical, hospital, juvenile justice, etc.), wraparound has been found to improve adaptive behavior and reduce emotional and behavioral problems in youth, as well as the likelihood of their functioning more successfully in schools and in the community (Quinn & Lee, 2007). Although the effectiveness of wraparound has not been evaluated in the context of suicidal youth, this approach is consistent with what is known about effective treatments for a variety of mental health problems in children and adolescents.

OTHER INTERVENTIONS FOR SUICIDAL YOUTH

Psychosocial Interventions

Increasing Contact

Only two interventions to date have been demonstrated to have a significant and positive effect on preventing deaths by suicide in randomized, controlled trials. Both are psychosocial interventions, and both target social connectedness or belongingness, a variable highly associated with suicide (Joiner, 2005, 2009). Although neither study included children or adolescents in their sample, the results of these studies are instructive and have some useful implications for school-based efforts at suicide prevention.

Motto and Bostrom (2001) conducted a large-scale study involving 843 former patients who had been hospitalized in a psychiatric facility after making a suicide attempt. The 843 individuals, all of whom had resisted ongoing patient care, were randomly assigned either to receive short, periodic letters from hospital staff (experimental condition), or to receive no letter at all (control condition). The "caring letters" received by the first group were not lengthy or involved; they simply consisted of brief expressions of concern and reminders that the treatment facility was accessible when the patients needed it. Despite their short length, the letters sent to patients were not standard form letters. Letters to patients were worded differently each time they were sent, and they were personalized to the patients as much as possible. Letters were sent every month for 4 months, bimonthly for 8 months, and every 3 months for 4 years; this resulted in a total of 24 letters over the course of 5 years.

The results of the study indicated that the group of patients who received the letters were significantly less likely to die by suicide after the first two years of the intervention, after which the two groups began to converge to the point of having similar suicide risk levels. The authors speculated that the intervention, a systematic program of contact with individuals at high risk for continued suicidal behavior, was effective because it made the former patients feel as though they were still connected in some way to the larger institution of the hospital.

> **Increasing student connectedness may be a useful and viable strategy for decreasing suicidal behavior in youth.**

Fleischmann and colleagues (2008) also conducted a study that involved increased contact with suicidal individuals. They randomly assigned individuals who had been hospitalized for making a suicide attempt into one of two groups: either a control group that received treatment as usual or treatment as usual plus brief intervention and contact (BIC), which included patient education and follow-up. The study involved over 1,000 individuals who had been hospitalized in emergency units of eight collaborating hospitals across five culturally different sites. Rates of death by suicide were examined at an 18-month follow-up; the results indicated that significantly fewer deaths occurred in the BIC group as compared to the treatment-as-usual control group.

According to Joiner (2009), the emphasis on both of the interventions described above on "interpersonal contact (including, of course, treatment access)—as well as the compelling results regarding the outcome of maximal interest, death by suicide—has the potential to inform future work on school-based prevention" (p. 246). In particular, these studies are notable for suggesting the significant and profound impact even limited contact can have on the well-being of individuals, including potentially reducing risk for suicide. These results support the notion that a key ingredient of school-based suicide prevention efforts should focus on keeping at-risk and high-risk students connected to other individuals, whether they be parents/caregivers, peers, or school personnel.

Dialectical Behavior Therapy

Dialectical behavior therapy (DBT) is a cognitive-behavioral treatment for complex, difficult to treat mental health disorders and problems. Dimeff and Linehan (2001) provide the following description of DBT:

> **Dialectical behavior therapy, or DBT, is a form of cognitive-behavioral therapy that has shown some promise as a psychosocial intervention for suicidal youth.**

> DBT combines the basic strategies of behavior therapy with eastern mindfulness practices, residing within an overarching dialectical worldview that emphasizes the synthesis of opposites. The term dialectical is also meant to convey both the multiple tensions that co-occur in therapy with suicidal clients with [borderline personality disorder] as well as the emphasis in DBT on enhancing dialectical thinking patterns to replace rigid, dichotomous thinking. The fundamental dialectic in DBT is between validation and acceptance of the client as they are within the context of simultaneously helping them to change. Acceptance procedures in DBT include mindfulness (e.g., attention to the present moment, assuming a nonjudgmental stance, focusing on effectiveness) and a variety of validation and acceptance-based stylistic strategies. Change strategies in DBT include behavioral analysis of maladaptive behaviors and problem-solving techniques, including skills training, contingency management (i.e., reinforcers, punishment), cognitive modification, and exposure-based strategies. (p. 10)

Like other so-called third-wave behavior therapies (first-wave behavior therapies emphasized the application of basic behavioral principles to clinical problems; second-wave behavior therapies added a cognitive component via the elimination or replacement of irrational, problematic thoughts; O'Brien, Larson, & Murrell, 2008) such as acceptance and commitment therapy (ACT; Hayes, Strosahl, & Wilson, 1999), functional analytic psychotherapy (FAP; Kohlenberg & Tsai, 1991), and mindfulness-based cognitive therapy (MBCT; Segal, Williams, & Teasdale, 2002), DBT emphasizes two fundamental and related concepts: *acceptance* and *mindfulness* (Greco & Hayes, 2008; Hayes, Follette, & Linehan, 2004).

ACCEPTANCE

DBT and other third-wave therapies focus on both acceptance of problems *and* changing them—ideas that would perhaps initially appear to be mutually exclusive. However, as noted by O'Brien and colleagues (2008):

> The goal of these techniques is not to change problematic thoughts or emotions, but rather to accept them for what they are—just private experiences, not literal truth. In this view, acceptance is accompanied by change, but the change is of a different sort than that seen in traditional cognitive-behavioral therapies: rather than changing the content of their thoughts, clients are changing their relationship to their thoughts. The careful balance of acceptance and change, referred to as the central dialectic in DBT, characterizes a dialectic common to all third-wave therapies. When clients are able to balance acceptance and change, accepting their thoughts as thoughts and thereby changing their relationship to their thoughts, they gain the flexibility to move in valued directions. (p. 16)

DBT therefore differs from traditional cognitive-behavioral therapies in its treatment of private events and internal experiences, such as thoughts, feelings, and bodily/physical sensations. As noted by Greco and Hayes (2008): "Rather than targeting and attempting to change the content, frequency, and form of thoughts and feelings directly, acceptance-based approaches . . . seek to alter the function of internal phenomena so as to diminish their behavioral impact" (p. 3). Consequently, professionals who are familiar and comfortable with traditional cognitive behavioral techniques, particularly those that emphasize cognitive restructuring and the disputation of irrational thoughts and beliefs, may initially find the "mental shift" necessary to understand third-wave approaches (such as DBT) difficult, given that these techniques are so different from the basic premises of cognitive therapy (Merrell, 2008b). In particular, in contrast to the emphasis in traditional cognitive-behavioral therapy on changing the *contents* of the client's thoughts, DBT emphasizes changing the client's *relationship* to their thoughts (O'Brien et al., 2008).

MINDFULNESS

In addition to embracing acceptance, another common element in third-wave behavior therapies such as DBT is their emphasis on *mindfulness*. Mindfulness is "paying attention in a particular way; on purpose, in the present moment, and nonjudgmentally" (Kabat-Zinn, 1994, p. 4). As such, mindfulness entails being present and nonjudgmental even in those situations and moments that are most unpleasant and painful (O'Brien et al., 2008). Engaging in mindfulness requires three different but interrelated elements: observing, describing, and participating. More specifically, "observing entails watching one's own thoughts, feelings, and behaviors without trying to change them; describing refers to the labeling of thoughts, feelings, and behaviors without judgment; and participating requires complete involvement in the present moment, without self-consciousness" (O'Brien et al., 2008, p. 21). Although the application of mindfulness procedures for addressing mental health problems has a relatively recent history (Greco & Hayes, 2008), the practice of mindfulness has been practiced by Buddhists for over 2,500 years (Kabat-Zinn, 2003).

Originally developed by Linehan (1993), DBT grew out of a series of failed attempts to apply standard cognitive-behavioral therapy protocols to chronically suicidal adult clients with comorbid borderline personality disorder (Dimeff & Linehan, 2001). It has since been adapted for a variety of other problems involving emotion dysregulation, such as substance abuse and binge eating (Dimeff & Linehan, 2001), and has emerged as a potentially useful treatment for NSSI (Klonsky & Muehlenkamp, 2007). Moreover, in recent years DBT has been used successfully to treat child and adolescent populations (e.g., Callahan, 2008; Woodberry, Roy, & Indik, 2008), including adolescents exhibiting suicidal behavior (Miller, Rathus, & Linehan, 2007).

As noted earlier, the core dialectic in standard DBT is the balance between acceptance and change (Linehan, 1993). Because DBT was largely developed and implemented initially for adults with borderline personality disorder who exhibited the combination of a biological predisposition toward emotional dysregulation and an invalidating social environment (Linehan, 1993), DBT therapists attempt to provide validation of their clients through acceptance. Under this framework, acceptance refers to "the ability to view previously unacceptable thoughts, emotions, and behaviors as valid given a particular context" (O'Brien et al., 2008, p. 20).

Mindfulness is one of the core skills taught to individuals struggling with this seeming polarity of acceptance and change. Although mindfulness is not the only skill taught in DBT, its teaching and practice provide a base from which other needed skills can be developed, including skills in distress tolerance, emotion regulation, and interpersonal effectiveness (Wagner, Rathus, & Miller, 2006). As noted by O'Brien and colleagues (2008):

> By cultivating a nonjudgmental awareness of the present moment, individuals . . . can better observe and label their emotions without impulsively acting on them; their tolerance for distressing feelings thereby increases, their ability to regulate emotions improves, and they can thus more effectively relate to others, whose emotions are also observed and labeled nonjudgmentally. (p. 20)

Nock, Teper, and Hollander (2007) describe the role and function of the DBT therapist as follows:

- The DBT clinician carefully identifies and operationalizes the target behaviors to be changed in treatment (using a comprehensive assessment of mental disorders, problem behaviors, and client functioning) and continuously measures these over the course of treatment.
- The DBT clinician helps the client to identify the antecedents and consequences of their self-injury and other target behaviors so that they will better understand their behaviors and will be able to modify them.
- Once the clinician and client understand the functions of the client's self-injury, they work together to develop other alternative and incompatible behaviors to replace it.
- As with other forms of behavior therapy, the clinician attempts to modify the client's environment to achieve behavior change, and with adolescents this involves working with the (student's) family throughout the course of treatment.
- In addition to sharing the treatment philosophy and plan with the family, the clinician works to modify their interactions with the adolescent when necessary, such as by teaching parent management skills. (p. 1084)

DBT therapists working with students who are potentially suicidal should first work with them to commit to treatment and then focus on the main targets of DBT, which include (1) decreasing life-threatening behaviors, (2) decreasing therapy-interfering behaviors, (3) decreasing quality of life-interfering behaviors, and (4) increasing behavioral skills. The main skills taught to students during DBT sessions should include mindfulness, emotional regulation, interpersonal effectiveness, distress tolerance, and "walking the middle path" skills (Nock et al., 2007). This last skill module is a unique aspect of adolescent DBT and involves teaching several family-focused skills, including validation of self and others, the use of behavioral principles, and common adolescent-family dilemmas (Nock et al., 2007). Although DBT therapy for adults is recommended to occur for at least one year, an outpatient version of DBT for adolescents developed by Miller and colleagues (2007) is significantly shorter and can be completed within a 16-week period.

A more comprehensive discussion of DBT is beyond the scope of this book. Although most school-based mental health professionals would probably not be providing direct psychosocial interventions like DBT in the schools, these professionals should at least be aware of the basic principles of DBT and why it is hypothesized to be a potentially useful treatment for suicidal youth. More research on DBT with this population is clearly needed, but initial work in this area has been promising. School-based mental health practitioners interested in more information on DBT are encouraged to review other sources, including Linehan (1993), Callahan (2008), and especially Miller, Rathus, and Linehan (2007).

Hospitalization

> **Hospitalization may at times be necessary, but school personnel should not confuse it with comprehensive or effective treatment. It is currently unclear if hospitalization is beneficial to suicidal youth.**

Many people seem to be relieved when suicidal youth are hospitalized, largely because they believe that being in a hospital will be helpful. That can certainly be the case, but school personnel should not equate hospitalization with treatment or be under the impression that hospitalization will solve all the problems of suicidal youth. Most individuals who are hospitalized for making a suicide attempt or for engaging in some other form of suicidal behavior do not stay hospitalized for long—often only a day or two. The purpose of hospitalizing suicidal youth (and suicidal adults, for that matter) is primarily for reasons of containment and stabilization rather than extended and intensive treatment.

Moreover, as noted by Joiner (2010), "thousands of people die by suicide in the U.S. every year either while hospitalized for psychiatric conditions or days after being discharged from the hospital. There is an association, therefore, between being hospitalized and dying by suicide" (p. 181). This statement should not be interpreted as stating that hospitalization *causes* suicide. Rather, the two conditions are understandably highly correlated because the underlying severity of mental illness increases the likelihood of both hospitalization and suicide. Although hospitalization can be beneficial, and is clearly recommended if a student is at high-risk for suicide, it is important to realize that we do not currently know with any degree of certainty whether hospitalization is an effective treatment (Joiner, 2010), regardless of whether hospitalization is voluntary or involuntary, and regardless of length of stay in the hospital.

Hospital staff will endeavor to keep hospitalized youth safe; they will not have access to anything that may be used to hurt themselves. Assuming they are not released from the hospital the same day they are admitted, they will also be fed, be given a bed, and be kept as comfortable as possible during their stay. They may be visited by a psychiatrist, psychologist, social worker, and/or other hospital-based mental health professionals, but given the typically short stay of patients hospitalized for suicide there will be no sustained efforts at inpatient psychotherapy. Given that hospitals are medical facilities, youth who are admitted to them may well be prescribed medications, such as antidepressants for unipolar or major depression, or lithium if they are diagnosed by hospital staff as having bipolar disorder.

Medication Issues and Controversies

A significant controversy involves the use of antidepressant medication with children and adolescents and its possible relationship to suicidal behavior. This controversy began when research suggested that Paroxetine, a selective serotonin reuptake inhibitor (SSRI), demonstrated a slight increase in suicidal ideation and behavior in children and adolescents with major depressive disorder. This finding led to public concerns voiced by the Food and Drug Administration (FDA) and other regulatory agencies (Kratoch-

> **There is significant controversy about the use of antidepressant medication, particularly in regards to whether it can increase suicidal behavior in youth. The use of antidepressants has not led to increased suicide attempts or suicide among students taking these medications.**

vil et al., 2006). In 2004, the results of a meta-analysis including 24 controlled clinical trials (approximately 4,400 pediatric patients) of nine antidepressant medications were presented at a public hearing. There were no suicides within any of the trials, and the cumulative risk of spontaneously reported suicidal ideation was 4% for active medication and 2% for placebo (Hammad, Laughren, & Racoosin, 2006). There was no evidence that antidepressants increased suicidal behavior among adults; actually, the opposite was found (Joiner, 2010).

The precise reason for the higher rates of suicidal ideation (though not suicide) among those receiving antidepressant medication versus those receiving placebo is not clear. A leading explanation has been noted by Joiner (2010):

> Many people find antidepressant medicines activating—they can help with energy problems and can alter flat moods into more positive ones. In most instances, this represents welcome relief from fatigue, lack of energy and focus, and low mood. But can there be too much activation? The answer is yes, and when this occurs, it can lead to agitation, restlessness, anxiety, and insomnia. These can comprise acute risk factors for suicidal ideation and behavior, as agitation and insomnia are ranked among the most serious suicide warning signs. The upshot of all this is that medicines which prevailingly lead to relief from depression can, in a small subset of people, potentially lead to overactivation and thus to increased suicidality. (p. 250)

Following this hearing and recommendations from various public health and psychopharmacological organizations, in October 2004 the FDA issued its "black box" warning for all antidepressants. This warning, the strongest measure the FDA takes short of actually withdrawing its approval of a drug (Joiner, 2010), essentially stated that an increased risk of suicidality may accompany the use of antidepressants with pediatric populations (Hammad et al., 2006). Following this warning, the number of antidepressant prescriptions written for pediatric populations has decreased significantly (Bhatia et al., 2008). Ironically, there is now speculation that the decreased numbers of youth taking antidepressant medication due to fears about its possible relationship to suicidality may be at least partially responsible for more suicidality in youth (Gibbons et al., 2007). For example, as the number of SSRI prescriptions for youth decreased in the United States, the number of deaths by suicide increased (Joiner, 2010). Libby and colleagues (2007) have also found that physicians have been diagnosing child and adolescent depression to a lesser degree than would be predicted, presumably owing to the fears generated by antidepressants.

In a comprehensive literature review, Bostwick (2006) found the evidence for a link between antidepressants and youth suicide to be "underwhelming." He suggested that, if vulnerability to suicide due to medication use exists, it is most likely to develop in the first few weeks after beginning medication, and that the more time an individual is medicated, the less likely suicidal behavior will occur. Pierson (2009), while acknowledging possible increases in suicidal ideation in youth as a result of antidepressant medication, observed that there is no evidence that other, more serious forms of suicidal behavior have been affected. Moreover, Joiner (2010) indicates that "the overwhelming majority of the evidence indicates that these medicines [i.e., antidepressants], although imperfect, have prevented and reduced enormous amounts of human suffering" (p. 245) and have led to less, rather than more, suicidal behavior in children and adolescents.

This issue remains a highly controversial one in the media (though not among knowledgeable scientists and researchers), and there are vocal critics of antidepressant medication, particularly members of the Church of Scientology (Joiner, 2010). However, school personnel should understand that although antidepressant medication should be prescribed on an individual, case-by-case basis and should always be carefully monitored, no compelling evidence exists that when used appropriately it will have the unintended and counterintuitive effect of increasing suicidality. When used appropriately and judiciously, antidepressant medication can be an important treatment component in preventing future incidents of suicidal behavior in youth who exhibit comorbid depression.

School personnel, particularly school-based mental health professionals, can play an important role in monitoring antidepressant medications in youth, particularly for those students with a history of or a potential for engaging in suicidal behavior (Miller & Eckert, 2009). For example, youth who will be prescribed this medication can be individually administered self-report measures, such as the Reynolds's Adolescent Depression Scale, second edition (RADS-2) or the Suicidal Ideation Questionnaire (SIQ), before, during, and after medication. Monitoring medication is an appropriate role for health professionals such as school nurses and mental health professionals such as school psychologists, and it is one that research suggests they are willing and able to perform (Gureasko-Moore, DuPaul, & Power, 2005).

For medication monitoring to be most effective in schools, practitioners are encouraged to take a flexible approach and include an assessment of the acceptability and feasibility of evaluation components (Volpe, Heick, & Gureasko-Moore, 2005). Prior to becoming an active participants in medication monitoring, school personnel should ensure that they have (1) an awareness of legal, ethical, and training issues regarding medications; (2) knowledge of psychotropic medication treatments; and (3) knowledge of behavioral assessment techniques (Carlson, 2008). For more information on medication monitoring in the classroom, as well as psychopharmacological interventions in the schools, the reader is referred to Anderson, Walcott, Reck, and Landau (2009), Carlson (2008), DuPaul and Carlson (2005), and Volpe, Heick, and Gureasko-Moore (2005).

CONCLUDING COMMENTS

This chapter provided an overview of interventions that can be used in schools for students at risk for suicidal behavior (selected interventions) as well as interventions for high-risk students (tertiary interventions). It is particularly important that school personnel know how to effectively respond to a student who is experiencing a suicidal crisis. Pertinent issues related to school-based psychosocial interventions for suicidal youth were reviewed, as well as issues involved in the hospitalization of suicidal youth and medication controversies involving the use of antidepressants. School-based mental health professionals who are knowledgeable about these areas will be more likely to prevent youth suicidal behavior and respond more effectively to it when it occurs.

CHAPTER 7

School-Based Suicide Postvention

Suicide carries in its aftermath a level of confusion and
devastation that is, for the most part, beyond description.
—KAY REDFIELD JAMISON

What we least expect generally happens.
—BENJAMIN DISRAELI

Be prepared.

—BOY SCOUT MOTTO

Unfortunately, even when schools implement suicide prevention programs, some students may still take their own lives. In such situations, the school the student attended often becomes a focal point of attention and scrutiny—from other students, from school staff, from parents, and from the media (Poland, 1989). Too frequently, when a student suicide (or the suicide of a school staff member) does occur, schools are unprepared for it. There is often a sense of shock and disbelief in the school community, as well as confusion about what should be done, who should do what, and how to most effectively respond to students and staff experiencing the loss of one of their own. Poland (1989), who for years directed and coordinated crisis intervention services at a large, urban school district where he dealt with hundreds of suicidal youth, stated that "the one question school personnel are probably the least trained to deal with and the most apprehensive about is what to do in the aftermath of a suicide" (p. 122).

The term *postvention* refers to a series of preplanned activities that are put in place after a suicide occurs. A primary purpose of postvention is to assist other students and school staff in coping with the many complex feelings that often accompany a student's suicide, such as shock, sadness, grief, and confusion (Brock, 2002; Lieberman, Poland, & Cassel, 2008). Another

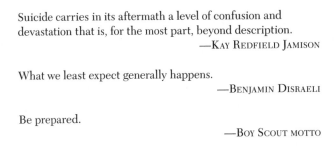

The term *postvention* refers to a series of preplanned activities that are put in place after a suicide occurs.

important postvention activity is to take appropriate steps to prevent any further incidents of suicide or suicidal behavior, a phenomenon often referred to as "suicide contagion," and to carefully monitor those students who might be at highest risk (Brock, 2002).

114

Although they may have the best of intentions, school administrators (e.g., superintendents, principals, vice-principals) will often fail to provide needed leadership in the aftermath of a student's suicide because they typically have not received training in suicide prevention, let alone postvention, and at times their most frequent strategy seems to be "to pretend that the suicide did not happen and hope that no other suicides will occur" (Poland, 1989, p. 135). Given this situation, it is incumbent upon school-based mental health professionals to develop, implement, and train postvention procedures to all school staff in case a student suicide occurs. How this can be accomplished is the subject of this chapter.

GOALS OF SCHOOL-BASED POSTVENTION

As was discussed in Chapter 2, all schools should have a detailed description of their policies and procedures regarding how the issue of youth suicidal behavior will be addressed. These should include a detailed and specific description of postvention procedures as well, including identifying who is serving on the postvention team and what their duties entail. *Preparedness* is an essential component of effective suicide postvention, and these procedures should be developed and in place *before* a suicide occurs. In addition, those serving on the school's postvention crisis team should ensure that postvention procedures are in fact needed before implementing them (Brock, 2002).

> **Preparedness is an essential component of effective suicide postvention, and these procedures should be developed and in place *before* a suicide occurs.**

Although there is no decision rule regarding which school professionals should or should not be on school crisis teams, in my view it makes the most sense to have all mental health professionals employed at the school included as members of the team, including the school psychologist, school counselor, and school social worker. In those situations in which one or more of these professionals is assigned to multiple schools within the district, those individuals should be assigned to multiple school crisis teams. It would also appear sensible to have the school nurse as a member of the crisis team, as well as at least one administrator, perhaps the principal or assistant principal. These individuals may be all that is needed, although if responsible, reliable, and reputable teachers are willing to serve as members of the crisis team they should be welcomed to become members as well.

The primary goal of any crisis intervention response, including postvention, is to help individuals reestablish immediate coping skills (Brock, 2002). A key question that should be immediately addressed following a student suicide is the degree to which the death will present coping challenges for other students. For example, if the decedent was well known (e.g., a popular student or teacher) and/or the suicide was public (e.g., it occurred at school), postvention procedures will likely be needed. However, if a death occurred but students are unaware (and will remain unaware) that it was the result of suicide, postvention (for suicide) would not occur (although providing grief counseling would likely still be needed for at least some students). As noted by Ruof and Harris (1988): "Suicidal behavior is only contagious if other people know about

> **The primary goal of any crisis intervention response, including postvention, is to help individuals reestablish immediate coping skills.**

it . . . if you can keep knowledge of [suicide] attempts out of a school building it is probably wise to do so" (p. 8). The rationale for this recommendation is that "if a postvention is provided when it is not required it will bring undue attention to the suicide and may send the message that suicide is a way to be noticed" (Brock, 2002, pp. 557–558).

> A key question that should be immediately addressed following a student suicide is the degree to which the death will present coping challenges for other students.

In many if not most cases, however, if a suicide does occur, students will obtain this information one way or another. When students are aware that a student suicide has occurred, the absolute worst thing schools can do is to have school personnel pretend it did not (Brock, 2002). Unfortunately, this is not an uncommon practice. For example, I know of one medium-sized urban school district that experienced four student suicides during the 2008–2009 school year. All of the suicide victims were high school students, and two of the suicides occurred in the span of a week. The district apparently had no postvention procedures in place until after the third suicide (a fourth student suicide then occurred less than 2 months later). Why did the

> When students are aware that a student suicide has occurred, the absolute worst thing schools can do is to have school personnel pretend it did not.

district not have any postvention procedures in place? According to newspaper reports, the school district superintendent stated that the district typically did not discuss the matter of suicides with students for fear of glorifying it and subsequently increasing the probability of other suicides occurring. The irony of this statement should not go unnoticed.

A SCHOOL-BASED SUICIDE POSTVENTION PROTOCOL

In the following section is a protocol developed by Brock (2002) providing school personnel with a prioritized list of procedures to implement when a student dies by suicide. Although these tasks are listed in their order of importance, different crisis response team leaders will likely work on many of them simultaneously. The timeline for completion of this protocol will vary, but the school's crisis response team should initiate it immediately upon learning of a student's death. School personnel should plan to complete all but the final three procedures within 24 hours (Brock, 2002). A summary of these procedures is provided in Handout 7.1 (at the end of the chapter).

> School personnel are encouraged to make use of a school-based suicide postvention protocol to effectively mobilize an effective response.

Verify That a Death Has Occurred

Immediately after reports that a student's death has occurred, the crisis team leader should attempt to verify the death and determine whether the cause of that death was suicide. The legal classification of a death as suicide is complex and is typically made by medical examiners working in a coroner's office. A death should not be considered as resulting from suicide unless it is confirmed by reputable, and ideally multiple, sources. These can include the family of the suicide victim, the coroner's office, hospitals, or police or sheriff departments. Statements from students, teachers, or other school personnel should *not* be accepted without first verifying the facts (Brock, 2002).

School personnel should not alert other students that a suicide occurred until reputable sources provide this information, regardless of any rumors that may be circulating. For example, I am aware of a situation in which school personnel felt pressured to reveal information about a student's possible suicide because several students in the school were text-messaging each other, spreading rumors about the alleged incident. Though understandable, school personnel should resist the temptation to move too quickly if they do not have the necessary information to proceed.

In many cases, a student's death will be verified, but the specific cause of death may not be, at least not for several days after the death. In these circumstances, many postvention interventions would still be implemented, although given an unknown cause of death it would likely focus more on grief-related issues.

Mobilize the Crisis Response Team

Once a death has been verified, the crisis team leader should immediately mobilize the school's crisis response team. This team will collectively take primary leadership roles in completing all remaining postvention tasks. Although these efforts require a team approach, members of the crisis team will likely be assigned specific roles in this process (Brock, 2002).

Assess the Impact of the Suicide on the School and Estimate Required Level of Postvention Response

Once assembled, the crisis team should immediately begin to assess the potential impact of the death on the school and the level of postvention response required (Brock, 2002). The level of response may range from simply focusing on a few selected students to an entire school. Accurately determining the appropriate response is important because there are potential problems involved in both underestimating and overestimating the needed level of support. An underestimation may result in not providing enough postvention services for the students and staff who need them. An overestimation runs the risk of potentially sensationalizing the death by giving it greater attention than was warranted under the circumstances (Brock, 2002).

The assessment of a suicide's impact on a school primarily involves estimating the number of students affected by the death (Brock, 2002). Several factors need to be considered in this decision, including temporal proximity of the suicide (e.g., if other traumatic events recently occurred as well, such as prior suicidal crises) and the time in which it occurs (e.g., suicides that occur during a school vacation, especially an extended one, may have less of an impact on other students than a suicide that occurs during times school is normally in session). School personnel also need to know the number (and the names) of the students personally affected by the suicide. For example, if the suicide occurred in school, those students who discovered the body should certainly be considered in this calculation. These students may often require interventions for trauma, posttraumatic stress, and/or grief (Brock, 2002).

An additional aspect of effective postvention is to accurately identify the close friends of the suicide victim (Brock, 2002). Research suggests that a friend's suicide during adolescence is associated with an increased probability of suicidal thoughts and suicide attempts, as well

> **Monitoring close friends of suicide victims is essential, and conducting individualized suicide risk assessments with these youth is strongly recommended.**

as increased levels of depression, during the first year after the suicide (Feigelman & Gorman, 2008). Consequently, monitoring close friends of suicide victims is essential, and conducting individualized suicide risk assessments with these youth is strongly recommended (Miller & Eckert, 2009).

Notify Other Involved School Personnel

The crisis team should next contact other school personnel who will likely be affected by the death and/or will be involved in the school's postvention response (Brock, 2002). These notifications of school personnel should be made as soon as possible, ideally within the first hour after the verification of death. This information should be provided to appropriate school staff members before the suicide is publicly announced. Notification and updates regarding the suicide should also be shared with the district office (where many concerned parents will call), other potentially affected school sites, and staff members at the school(s) affected by the death (Brock, 2002).

Contact the Family of the Suicide Victim to Express Condolences and Offer Assistance

Contact with the family of the suicide victim will often be one of the first postvention tasks, as the crisis team attempts to verify the facts of the death. It is recommended that this contact be made by appropriate school personnel in person, within 24 hours of the death (Brock, 2002). Visits to parents under such circumstances are obviously somber occasions and may make school personnel feel uncomfortable and awkward. This is understandable, but it is useful to remember that any awkwardness school personnel may feel is insignificant in comparison to the emotional devastation experienced by the family of the student. When meeting with families soon after the suicide death of their son or daughter, it is important to sensitively communicate condolences for their loss and to sincerely offer to assist the family in any way possible. For example, looking directly into the eyes of parents and making a statement such as, "Mr. Jones, I am so, so sorry about what happened to Adam. You and your family are in our thoughts, and we wanted you to know if there is anything you need, to please let us know. We don't want to bother you in any way, but we do want to help you in any way we can."

Efforts at expressing condolences and support to parents and families should not be undermined by making certain well-intentioned but unhelpful statements, such as indicating that the suicide was "God's will," that their son or daughter is now "in a better place," or that the parents will "get over" their loss in time and obtain eventual "closure." Use of such words or phrases will very possibly, and quite understandably, result in parental anger and contempt. Gordon Livingston (2004), a psychiatrist who lost one son to suicide and another to leukemia, has stated that he learned "an abiding hatred for the word *closure* with its comforting implications that grief is a time-limited process from which we all recover. The idea that I could reach a point when I would no longer miss my children was obscene to me and I dismissed it" (p. 116).

Livingston also recounted an anecdote about the late actor Gregory Peck, perhaps best known for his Oscar-winning portrayal of Atticus Finch in the classic film *To Kill a Mockingbird*, based on the Harper Lee novel. In an interview conducted many years after his son's death by suicide, Peck was asked how often he thought about him. "I don't think of him every day," he said, "I think of him every hour of every day" (quoted in Livingston, 2004, p. 116). Similarly, Joiner relates an anecdote about a man who was being "comforted" by someone who said that his son's death by suicide was "God's will." In responding to this perhaps well-meaning but inept attempt at providing some measure of consolation, the man angrily replied, "It was NOT God's will that my precious son shot himself in the head!" (quoted in Joiner, 2010, p. 3). These brief examples provide some clear object lessons about what *not* to say to grieving family members following a suicide.

Discuss with Parents and Family Members Issues Related to the Suicide and the School's Response

At this meeting with the parents, it is recommended that a crisis team member discuss with the parents which details about the death can be shared with outsiders, including school personnel and students. It should be clearly communicated to family members that school staff will neither discuss nor speculate on any possible reasons for the suicide (Brock, 2002). However, it is typically inappropriate to keep secret the fact that the cause of death was suicide, even if the parents request that this information not be shared. When sharing information about the suicide with school personnel and students, however, the need to be honest and truthful about what occurred should not take precedence over the need not to violate the privacy of the student suicide victim or the student's family (Poland, 2003). The family may also be helpful for identifying any friends of the decedent who might need assistance. If and when appropriate, the school's postvention response to the suicide might be discussed with the family, although this may be delayed if the team has not yet precisely determined what the procedures will be (Brock, 2002).

Determine What Information to Share about the Death

After meeting with the family, the crisis team will have to make decisions as to what to tell school staff members, students, parents, and the media about the death (Brock, 2002). As soon as the death is verified, the team should announce it as quickly as possible. The longer the school delays in sharing with other students and staff what it knows, the more likely rumors (often inaccurate) are likely to start.

Before a Death Is Certified as a Suicide

In many cases, a death will be verified, but the cause of death will not be, at least not immediately. As a result, public acknowledgment of the student death will often occur before it is revealed that the death was caused by suicide. Until the death is confirmed and verified as being caused by suicide, the school should simply and truthfully treat it as a death in which the cause is currently unknown. Communication between the crisis team and students and school personnel should be conducted in such a way that the team sticks to the facts, avoids speculation, and encourages students and staff to do the same. As more information becomes available (e.g., it is later verified that the cause of the student's death was suicide), the crisis team will need to evaluate it and determine what information to share (Brock, 2002).

After a Death Is Certified as a Suicide

As soon as a death is acknowledged as a suicide, the school should announce this information to students and staff. School personnel should be informed before students. A school phone tree could be used to contact all school personnel and have them report one-half hour early given the occurrence of a crisis situation. School personnel could then be briefed on the incident prior to students' arrival at school. The statement presented to students should be truthful, but brief.

Provide Facts and Dispel Rumors

Avoid excessive detail about the suicide, but do provide students with basic facts. Not providing information, or even giving the appearance of not providing information, will typically lead to rumors spreading. Because rumors are often inaccurate as well as frequently more anxiety-provoking than the facts, it is important that any rumors be dispelled. Here are some recommendations regarding the statement that should be provided to students:

- It should clearly state that the student's cause of death was suicide. There should be no mention of the method used or other unnecessary details.
- The announcement should make clear that this is obviously a very sad and terrible situation and that it may be difficult for some students and staff members.
- The announcement should let students clearly know that counselors and other professionals are available to speak with them if they choose to do so, and should let students know where to go to access these services. These services should be made available throughout the day, for as long as necessary, and teachers should freely allow students to access them.
- Information should be avoided that either glorifies or vilifies the victim.
- The focus of the message should be on grieving and seeking to learn from the tragedy.
- Emphasize to students that suicide is a preventable, treatable problem. Review the warning signs, and let students know where to get help for themselves or others.
- Students should also be informed that mental health professionals will be available to answer any questions they may have.
- If students ask if they can attend the funeral if it is held during the school day, they should be told that they can, if the funeral is open to the public and if the student receives permission from his parents to attend. The school should not set up an organized event to do this, however, nor should the district make buses available for students.
- After the statement is read to students in their classes, teachers should then begin instruction as it would normally occur. Some students may not be ready to engage in schoolwork and may ask to leave the room to go talk to a counselor. If this occurs (and it likely will for some if not several students), they should be given permission to do so. Others, especially those students

who perhaps did not know the student well, may not be as emotionally affected by it and may be able to concentrate on schoolwork with little difficulty. Proceeding in this way sends the clear message that anyone who wants help can get it, but that the school will also be continuing in its normal academic routine.

Determine How to Share Information about the Death

After creating the message regarding the death, the next step will be to determine how the information will be reported, particularly how it will be reported to students. Possible options include phone calls, classroom presentations and discussion, written letters or announcements, and individual conferences (Davis & Sandoval, 1991). The message should be disseminated to students as soon as possible, but not before information has first been shared with school personnel (Brock, 2002).

Reporting the Death to Students

The *process* by which information about the suicide is provided is as important as the *content*. For example, using large auditoriums or loudspeakers to provide this information is not recommended. Having teachers or other staff members make the announcement to students in their own classrooms is a more preferable option. To keep the message to students as consistent as possible, the crisis team may wish to prepare a statement that all school personnel can read (verbatim) to their students (Brock, 2002).

After being provided with information about the suicide, which may well be the first students have directly experienced, it is not uncommon for them to have questions for school personnel. Members of the school crisis team should anticipate many of these questions, and provide classroom teachers with the appropriate answers or have them direct these questions to other school personnel. Poland (2003) has identified some common questions by students following a suicide, including the following:

- Why did the person die by suicide?
- What method did the person use?
- Why didn't someone (e.g., a person; God) stop the person?
- Isn't someone or something to blame for this?
- Didn't this person make a poor choice and, because of that, is it OK to be angry at him or her?

Identify Students Significantly Affected by the Suicide and Initiate a Referral Mechanism

This process should have already been begun by the crisis response team. From their assessment of the impact of the death on the school, the crisis team will now want to begin to contact those individuals identified as possibly being most affected by the suicide. Crisis team members should actively "reach out" to these individuals, whether they be students or school staff members, and to monitor these individuals over time (Brock, 2002).

Conduct a Faculty Planning Session

Following the initial communication/debriefing with faculty, a faculty planning session should be held. Goals for this session include reviewing suicide warning signs, discussing how the school has responded thus far, and identifying what actions will follow. Meeting with faculty will also provide an opportunity for school staff to express their own emotions about the suicide, and school personnel should be permitted to feel uncomfortable in dealing with this topic with their students and to be candid about this if it is the case. In such situations, some teachers may not be able to offer students their full support and guidance, and should be provided with other opportunities to contribute to postvention efforts (Brock, 2002).

Initiate Crisis Intervention Services

As individuals in need of services are identified, these services should be provided, preferably within 24 hours of the death. The crisis team should ensure that team members (a) walk through the suicide victim's class schedule and (b) meet separately with students who were physically and/or emotionally proximal to the suicide (Brock, 2002).

Conduct Daily Planning Sessions

After initiating postvention procedures, the crisis team should plan to meet at least once each day, typically at the end of the school day, for as long a period as is deemed appropriate and necessary. The purpose of these meetings will be to review the day's events and to make additional plans (Brock, 2002).

Plan Memorial Activities and Actions

Many individuals may wish to memorialize the suicide victim in some tangible way. Although this is an understandable impulse, school personnel need to be cautious about the use of memorials because of possible "contagion" effects (discussed below). In general, tangible, physical memorials should be avoided in favor of so-called living memorials, such as a student assistance fund to promote suicide awareness named in honor of the suicide victim, or donations to a national organization devoted to suicide prevention made in the name of the decedent. Students who wish to attend the funeral, as already noted, should be given permission to do so with parent permission, but organized trips by the school are discouraged, as is flying the flag at half-mast (Brock, 2002).

Debrief Personnel Involved in Postvention Response

At the conclusion of postvention, a debriefing should be provided for all those who contributed to postvention efforts. Goals for this meeting should include a review and follow-up of crisis intervention activities, an evaluation of the strategies employed, and plans for any additional steps that may be required or desirable. Perhaps most important, the debriefing gives crisis responders an opportunity to discuss their own reactions to the crisis and share their own emotional experiences—an activity that prior to the debriefing they likely had little or no time to do

(Brock, 2002). Handout 7.1 provides a summary of the major postvention activities that should be implemented following the suicide of a student.

SUICIDE "CONTAGION"

A primary purpose of postvention procedures is to prevent any further instances of suicidal behavior, a phenomenon known as suicide contagion. This concern developed from research supporting the notion that suicide can be "contagious" in the sense that exposure to suicidal behaviors can influence others to copy them. Exposure to suicidal behaviors may occur either through students' personal experience (e.g, someone they know at school dies by suicide) or through media exposure of a celebrity's suicide. Adolescents appear to be particularly susceptible to possible contagion effects, so school personnel should be aware of this issue and how to best address it.

If a student dies by suicide, school personnel can follow the steps already described to reduce the likelihood of suicide contagion occurring. In regards to suicide contagion and the media, research suggests that the extent of media contagion is modest, although the media can play a crucial role in the decision-making process of vulnerable individuals (Hawton & Williams, 2001), especially in cases of nonfictional presentations of suicide on television or in books or newspapers (Pirkis & Blood, 2001).

Media-related suicide contagion appears more likely to occur when members of the audience identify with the suicide victim (e.g., age, gender, nationality), when the method of suicide is specified in a story, when a story is reported or displayed prominently or dramatically, and when suicides of celebrities are reported (Hawton & Williams, 2001; Pirkis & Blood, 2001; Pirkis, Blood, Beautrais, Burgess, & Skehan, 2007; Stack, 2003). Listening to or viewing certain kinds of rock music or music videos may also increase suicidal ideation in certain vulnerable individuals (Rustad, Small, Jobes, Safer, & Peterson, 2003).

Given that children and adolescents may be especially vulnerable to media influences (Hawton & Williams, 2001), providing guidelines to the media about the appropriate portrayal of suicide is critical. Unfortunately, Pirkis and her colleagues (2007) suggested that there is currently inconclusive evidence regarding whether media guidelines have had an impact on the behavior of media professionals or on suicide rates.

GUIDELINES FOR WORKING WITH THE MEDIA

When a student suicide occurs, there is likely to be at least some media coverage of it. School personnel should carefully choose how information is shared with the media. Although media coverage in such cases is often understandably perceived by school personnel as an unwelcome intrusion, it can and should be viewed as an opportunity for public education and community outreach as well. The media can play a powerful role in educating the public about suicide, including its warning signs, how to reduce the stigma associated with suicidal people, and what individuals can do to help. It is not media coverage of suicide per se that is problematic; it is the way in which suicide is presented that is the real issue. The tragic loss of life that results from a student's suicide cannot be changed, but one positive result of this tragedy can be the increased opportunity for communicating to people that suicide is a very preventable problem and that we all can play a role in it.

Several national organizations devoted to suicide prevention and public health, including the American Association of Suicidology (AAS), the American Foundation for Suicide Prevention (AFSP), and the Annenberg Public Policy Center (APPC), collaboratively developed recommended guidelines for the media following a suicide. These recommendations, which apply to media coverage generally and not just youth suicides, cover a variety of different topics, notably (1) suicide contagion; (2) suicide and mental illness; (3) interviews of surviving relatives and friends; (4) appropriate language to use when reporting information; (5) special situations; and (6) stories to consider covering. Some of these recommendations are as follows.

Suicide Contagion

- Research suggests that inadvertently romanticizing suicide or idealizing those who take their own lives by portraying suicide as a heroic or romantic act may encourage others to identify with the victim.
- Exposure to suicide method through media reports can encourage vulnerable individuals to imitate it. Clinicians believe the danger is even greater if there is a detailed description of the method. Research indicates that detailed descriptions or pictures of the location or site of suicide encourages imitation.
- Presenting suicide as the inexplicable act of an otherwise healthy or high-achieving person may encourage identification with the victim.

Suicide and Mental Illness

- Conveying the information that effective treatments for most of these conditions are available (but underutilized) may encourage those with such problems to seek help.
- Acknowledging the deceased person's problems and struggles as well as the positive aspects of his/her life or character contributes to a more balanced picture.
- Questions to ask in covering suicides should include: Had the victim ever received treatment for depression or any other mental disorder? Did the victim have a problem with substance abuse?

Interviews of Surviving Relatives and Friends

- Thorough investigation generally reveals underlying problems unrecognized even by close friends and family members. Most victims do, however, give warning signs of their risk for suicide.
- Some informants are inclined to suggest that a particular individual, for instance a family member, a school, or a health service provider, in some ways played a role in the victim's death by suicide. Thorough investigation almost always finds multiple causes for suicide and fails to corroborate a simple attribution of responsibility.
- Dramatizing the impact of suicide through descriptions and pictures of grieving relatives, teachers, or classmates, or community expressions of grief, may encourage potential victims to see suicide as a way of getting attention or as a form of retaliation against others.

Other Media Guidelines

- Using adolescents on TV or in print media to tell the stories of their suicide attempts may be harmful to the adolescents themselves or may encourage other vulnerable people to seek attention in this way.

- Whenever possible, it is preferable to avoid referring to suicide in the headline. Unless the suicide death took place in public, the cause of death should be reported in the body of the story and not in the headline.

- In deaths that will be covered nationally, such as of celebrities, or those apt to be covered locally, such as persons living in small towns, consider phrasing for headlines such as: "Marilyn Monroe dead at 36," or "John Smith dead at 48." Consideration of how they died should be reported in the body of the article.

- In the tone of the story, it is preferable to describe the deceased as "having died by suicide," rather than as "a suicide," or having "committed suicide." The latter two expressions reduce the person to the mode of death, or connote criminal or sinful behavior.

- Contrasting "suicide deaths" with "nonfatal attempts" is preferable to using terms such as "successful," "unsuccessful," or "failed."

CONCLUDING COMMENTS

Postvention becomes necessary if and when a student dies by suicide. The two fundamental purposes of postvention are to provide crisis intervention services and prevent any further suicides from occurring. Effective preplanning is critical in postvention, but unfortunately many schools do not have an organized crisis response team ready to quickly respond if necessary. There are few if any more shocking and unexpected events in schools than a student's suicide, but school personnel can make the best of a tragic situation by responding to it in a proactive, coordinated, and effective manner. Ultimately, effective postvention is really effective prevention.

General School-Based Postvention Guidelines

- Plan in advance of any crisis and review guidelines from reputable national organizations such as the AAS and the NASP.

- Have the school crisis team meet or communicate as soon as possible following the suicide to make plans and assign duties.

- Verify and confirm that a suicide did occur. This should be accomplished through communicating with the medical examiner, police, and family of the deceased.

- Do not dismiss school or encourage funeral attendance during school hours, but let students know they can attend the funeral (if open to the public) with parental approval.

- Do ensure that school staff members attend the funeral to support the affected students as well as the family of the suicide victim.

- Do not dedicate a physical memorial to the deceased (e.g., yearbook; tree; bench; etc.). However, "living" memorials, such as making a donation to an organization promotiong suicide prevention made in the name of the victim, or engaging in fundraising projects in the student's name to promote suicide awareness, can provide comfort, increase awareness, and create something positive out of a tragic event.

- Contribute to a suicide prevention effort on behalf of the school, school district, or the community.

- Contact the family of the deceased youth and offer condolences, offer support to siblings attending the school, and provide assistance as needed or requested. Apprise the family of how the school is responding to the suicide.

- Do not release information to students announcing the suicide in a large assembly or over intercom systems. Disseminate information to the faculty and students in small groups, preferably in their regular classrooms. Be truthful in verifying that the cause of the student's death was suicide, but avoid explicit details of the method used and focusing on why the suicide happened. Focus instead on general factors in suicide prevention, emphasize coping skills, and let students know the school and community resources available to help them.

- Make available additional mental health professionals, either from within the school district or outside it, for several days after the suicide and have them be "on call" should students or school staff need additional supports.

- Monitor close friends and classmates of the deceased; meet with them individually if possible.

- Arrange for makeshift counseling rooms to be made available in the school building so that mental health professionals can meet with students and staff privately.

- Collaborate with media, law enforcement, and community agencies.

- Emphasize two major points with the media and parents of students in the district: (1) no one thing, event, or person is to blame for the suicide; (2) help is available.

- Provide counseling or discussion opportunities for school faculty and staff.

- Provide follow-up services to those most affected and be aware of anniversary dates, such as the deceased's birthday and the first anniversary of the student's death.

- Evaluate the postvention response.

Compiled from Brock (2002); Brock, Sandoval, and Hart (2006); Poland and Lieberman (2002); Lieberman, Poland, and Cassel (2008).

Epilogue

[Suicide is] a profound and fearsome human tragedy. It is a tragedy because it has tractable causes that can be understood and thus counteracted (but currently are not, at least not enough); it is fearsome because it requires a forsaking of our basic nature as self-preserving creatures, because it kills a million people a year worldwide, and because no one should have to die alone . . . thinking (incorrectly) that the world will be better off.

—THOMAS JOINER

Suicide prevention is everyone's responsibility.

—SCOTT POLAND

Whoever saves a life, it is as if [that person] saved an entire world.

—THE TALMUD

In the Preface to this book, I suggested that one of the primary reasons we as a society have not been as effective as we could be in preventing suicide, including youth suicide, is the level of secrecy and stigma that surrounds it. Like the treatment of people who have experienced serious forms of mental illness (Penney & Stastny, 2008; Whitaker, 2010), the reaction to suicidal individuals has been characterized throughout much of our history by fear, confusion, and mistreatment. This has been further exacerbated by the many myths and misunderstanding that surround suicidal behavior, including what causes it and how best to treat it, as well as an underestimation of its pervasiveness. As noted by Joiner and his colleagues (2009), there is a large "discrepancy between the scope of the public problem [of suicide] and the response of the public at large" to it (p. 168).

As a further illustration of this point, consider the following facts. First, for every two deaths by homicide in the United States, three people die by suicide. Second, for each death due to HIV/AIDS, two people die by suicide (Joiner et al., 2009). Despite many more people dying annually from suicide than from either homicide or HIV/AIDS, national funding efforts to address these two problems far outpace funding efforts for suicide prevention. For example, during the 2006 fiscal year the National Institutes of Health provided $32 million in funding for suicide research, whereas it provided 90 times that amount ($2.9 billion) in funding to research HIV/AIDS. Similarly, $29.5 billion was spent in 2001 to fund adult state correctional facilities, and during that same year $53.6 million was spent on mental health treatment. To put these later figures in context, correctional facilities received 550 times the amount of funding that mental health treatment received. Consequently, although suicide annually causes a significant number of deaths in the United States, it has not received the same degree of attention and financial support as other causes of preventable death (Joiner et al., 2009).

State and national funding for school-based suicide prevention efforts is similarly limited. Fortunately, substantial funding is not necessary for schools to actively engage in comprehensive, school-based suicide prevention efforts. Unfortunately, this is not occurring in too many of our nation's schools. Stigma is one reason, a lack of understanding about the pervasiveness of suicidal behavior is another, and reluctance by some parents and school professionals to provide mental health services in schools is likely an additional factor. All of these issues can be overcome, and they need to be overcome if we really want to prevent suicidal behavior in children and adolescents. And there is no better place to do this than in our nation's schools.

THE DISTINCTION BETWEEN CURING AND HEALING

The field of medical anthropology has proposed a useful distinction between *curing a disease* and *healing an illness*. Kleinman (1980) notes that "disease refers to a malfunctioning of biological processes, while the term *illness* refers to the psychosocial experience and meaning of perceived disease. . . . Viewed from this perspective, illness is the shaping of disease into behavior and experience. It is created by personal, social, and cultural reactions to disease" (p. 72). To illustrate this distinction, Crossan (1994) discussed this issue in the context of HIV/AIDS. Although developing a cure for the disease of HIV/AIDS is clearly desirable, "in its absence we can still heal the illness by refusing to ostracize those who have it, by empathizing with their anguish, and by enveloping their suffering with both respect and love" (p. 81).

The analogy to suicide, and to suicide prevention in the schools, is clear. Like people with HIV/AIDS, young people who are suicidal are not only suffering from the effects of their "disease" (i.e., the emotional suffering that results from the mental disorders, such as depression, that typically underlies suicidal behavior), but also from their "illness" (i.e., the stigma and shame often experienced by suicidal youth). School personnel can play a significant role in addressing both the "disease" of suicide and its corresponding "illness." How? By putting the information presented in this book into practice. In particular, by breaking down barriers— barriers to understanding, and barriers to getting youth the help they need without feeling stigmatized by it.

One of the barriers that I believe keeps us from being more proactive in preventing suicide, including youth suicide, is the common perception that suicide is an individual problem rather than a societal one—or, stated another way, that it is a personal health issue rather than a public health issue. Too often, suicide is viewed as a problem only for those people who directly experience it (whether through suicidal ideation, suicide-related communications, suicide attempts, or suicide), or who are directly affected by it (which is, of course, a much higher number than most people think). As I hope has now become clear, this is simply not the case; suicide is a problem that confronts all of us at some point in our lives. We cannot escape it.

YOUTH SUICIDE: A LARGELY PREVENTABLE PROBLEM AND AN UNNECESSARY TRAGEDY

Youth suicide is a largely preventable problem, which means that it is largely an unnecessary tragedy. Scott Poland, who developed and coordinated a nationally recognized school-based suicide prevention program in the Cypress-Fairbanks Independent School District in Texas, has said that "suicide prevention is everyone's responsibility." I agree, and I hope readers of this book will too. By taking responsibility for suicide prevention, we become accountable for it. If school personnel don't perceive themselves as responsible—and therefore accountable—for youth suicide prevention, it is unlikely others will either. In the words of journalist David K. Shipler (2004), "When accountability is spread so broadly and diffused, it seems to cease to exist. The opposite is true. It may look as if nobody is accountable. In fact, everybody is." (p. 299).

My hope is that readers will take from this book the essential points that youth suicidal behavior is a massive and complex public health problem, that it reflects underlying mental health disorders, that most suicidal youth don't want to die as much as they want their suffering to end, that suicide can be prevented, that all of us have a role to play in that process, and that schools and school personnel can be especially helpful in this regard. For this to occur, we must all accept responsibility for youth suicide. Not for causing it to occur, but rather for not doing everything that we can—which is substantial and more than we are doing now—to prevent it. Preventing youth suicide is everyone's responsibility—including yours.

There is arguably no greater accomplishment in life than saving the life of another, especially if it involves saving a child or an adolescent from an unnecessary, premature, and tragic death by suicide. Given their frequent contact with youth, school-based practitioners have perhaps the best opportunity of anyone to accomplish this worthy goal. An urgent problem demands an urgent response, and there is no better time for making that response than right now. Together, let's make suicide prevention, assessment, and intervention a priority in our schools.

Student Suicide Case Law in Public Schools

RICHARD FOSSEY and PERRY A. ZIRKEL

This appendix reviews the published court decisions in which families have sought to hold school officials liable for a student's suicide. The focus is on the almost two dozen decisions in which plaintiffs sued educators (including school counselors and psychologists) for damages arising from a student's suicide. A review of the cases shows that the vast majority of the decisions were in favor of the school officials. The plaintiffs sought money damages in these cases on two theories of liability: negligence under state common law or Section 1983 constitutional torts.

NEGLIGENCE CASES

Some school-based mental health professionals fear liability for a student's suicide if they were to fail to warn others about the student's suicidal behavior. This concern may be based on the much-publicized California case of *Tarasoff v. Regents of the University of California* (1976), in which the California Supreme Court established a psychotherapist's duty-to-warn if the psychotherapist's patient presents a serious danger of violence to another. However, *Tarasoff* has not been universally adopted by other courts, and California's highest court itself refused to extend Tarasoff's duty-to-warn to cases involving suicide (*Nally v. Grace Community Church*, 1988).

It was not until 1991 that the first appellate court recognized a cause of action against a school district or school-based mental health professional for a student's suicide. In *Eisel v. Board of Education of Montgomery County* (1991), Nicole Eisel, 13 years old, died in an apparent murder-suicide pact with another student. Nicole's father sued the Montgomery County Board of Education and two of its school counselors, arguing that a special relationship existed between Nicole and school

Richard Fossey, JD, EdD, is Professor in the Department of Teacher Education and Administration, Program Coordinator for the Educational Administration Program, Senior Research Associate at the Center for the Study of Education Reform, and Director of the Texas Higher Education Law Institute at the University of North Texas.

Perry A. Zirkel, PhD, JD, LLM, is University Professor of Education and Law at Lehigh University.

authorities, which imposed a duty on the counselors to report Nicole's suicidal ideation to her parents. According to the father's complaint, Nicole had expressed a desire to kill herself to classmates, who passed this information on to school counselors. The counselors allegedly questioned Nicole about these statements, but Nicole denied having any suicidal feelings. The counselors denied receiving any communication that Nicole had expressed a desire to kill herself.

The trial court dismissed the father's lawsuit, ruling that school employees had no legal duty to attempt to prevent Nicole from committing suicide. On appeal, however, Maryland's highest court reversed this decision, sending the case back to the lower court for a trial. The appellate court listed six factors for determining whether school employees had a duty to warn Nicole's parents that she was suicidal: (1) foreseeability of harm, (2) public policy considerations about the value of preventing future harm, (3) the close proximity in time between the actions of the school defendants and the suicide, (4) moral blame, (5) the burden on defendants that would be imposed if they assumed a duty to prevent Nicole's suicide, and (6) the defendants' ability to obtain insurance to cover the risk of liability for a student's suicide.

In the *Eisel* court's view, foreseeability was the most important variable in determining whether the school defendants had a legal duty to try to prevent Nicole from committing suicide. Unless Nicole's suicide was foreseeable to the defendants, they had no duty to attempt to prevent her from killing herself. In this case, the court pointed out that despite their denial to the contrary, school counselors allegedly had actual knowledge that Nicole had expressed a desire to commit suicide. Even if Nicole denied having any suicidal feelings, the counselors were not relieved of their duty to Nicole if her action was foreseeable. The court pointed to guidance from a Maryland social service agency, which recommended that school authorities give serious consideration to peer reports about a student's suicidal feelings even when the student denies having suicidal thoughts.

As a second major factor in the appellate court's view, public policy considerations favored the imposition of a duty on schools to prevent student suicides. Maryland had adopted a law entitled the Suicide Prevention School Programs Act, which authorized the state education agency to develop a student suicide prevention program in cooperation with local school districts. At Nicole's own school, the suicide prevention program contained this advice to school staff members: "Tell others— as quickly as possible, share your knowledge with parents, friends, teachers, or other people who might be able to help. Don't worry about breaking a confidence if someone reveals suicidal plans to you. You may have to betray a secret to save a life" (p. 454). In light of an explicit state-level public policy aimed at preventing student suicides, the court had little trouble imposing a duty of care on school counselors to take action to prevent a student from committing suicide. Specifically, the court concluded: "Holding counselors to a common-law duty of reasonable care to prevent suicides when they have evidence of a suicidal intent comports with the policy underlying this Act" (p. 454).

Although this *Tarasoff*-type decision has received substantial publicity, it is much less well known that upon remand to the trial court, the jury determined that the defendant counselors were not liable for Nicole's death (Fossey & Zirkel, 2004). Although the record does not indicate why the jury found in favor of the counselors, it may well be that the jury members decided that the school counselors did not know or have reason to know of Nicole's suicidal intent.

Since the *Eisel* decision in 1991, parents have sued schools, universities, and their employees a number of times concerning the suicide death of a student. The plaintiff-parents have brought some of these cases, akin to *Eisel*, under the common law theory of negligence. In others they have filed a Section 1983 federal civil rights action, claiming a constitutional violation. Regardless of the theory, plaintiffs have rarely prevailed.

In several cases, courts ruled that schools and their employees enjoy governmental and official immunity, respectively, to negligence suits arising from student suicides. For example, in *Killen v.*

Independent School District No. 706, a 1996 Minnesota case, Jill Dibley, a ninth-grade student, killed herself at home with a firearm. A school counselor had warned Jill's parents that Jill had expressed suicidal feelings and recommended that she get counseling. However, the counselor allegedly did not inform the parents when Jill later made a more specific statement about committing suicide.

Jill's parents sued the school district for failing to implement a formal suicide prevention policy and the counselor for not telling them of Jill's specific statements about suicide. The trial court granted the defendants' motion to dismiss the lawsuit, and a Minnesota appellate court affirmed the dismissal. In the appellate court's view, the school district and the school counselors were immune from suit under Minnesota's governmental immunity provisions. These provisions applied to discretionary actions in relation to negligence claims. The court concluded that the employees' acts were discretionary acts and, thus, in the absence of evidence of malice or willful misconduct, the immunity protections applied.

Likewise, in *Grant v. Board of Trustees of Valley View School District* (1997), Jason Grant, a high school senior, had written notes expressing thoughts of suicide and told other students that he was going to kill himself. Several students reported the matter to a school counselor, who called Jason's mother, urging her to take Jason to a hospital for treatment of a drug overdose. The counselor allegedly failed, however, to tell Jason's mother about his suicidal behavior. Later that day, Jason jumped to his death from a highway overpass. Similar to the *Killen* case, Jason's mother sued Jason's school district as well as Jason's counselor for negligence, claiming that the school district should have implemented a suicide prevention plan, and that the counselor should have informed her of Jason's suicidal behavior. In response to the defendants' motion, the trial court dismissed the parent's claims.

Like the *Killen* court, an Illinois appellate court upheld the dismissal on the grounds that state law provided public schools and their employees with immunity from such suits unless their misconduct was willful or wanton. In the appellate court's view, the school counselor had not engaged in willful misconduct in her communication to Jason's mother. Indeed, the court reasoned, "If [the counselor] had failed to take any action upon learning of Jason's statements, her inaction could constitute willful and wanton conduct" (p. 709). The court concluded that the counselor's communication to the parents, even assuming that she failed to mention Jason's suicidal ideations, was not willful or wanton.

Suits in states without applicable governmental immunity protections have similarly been largely unsuccessful. For example, in another student suicide case involving a public school counselor, a Wisconsin appellate court concluded that as a matter of law, that is, without a trial, the parents' suit failed for lack of an essential element of a negligence claim—causation. More specifically, the court ruled that suicide is a superseding or intervening force in a negligence action, thus breaking the causal link to third parties, such as school counselors (*McMahon v. St. Croix Falls School District*, 1999). In this case, Andrew McMahon, a high school freshman, had skipped school, gone to a friend's home, doused himself with gasoline in the home's garage, and died by self-immolation. Prior to his suicide, Andrew had apparently become despondent about his failing grades, which caused him to be removed from the school's basketball team. One of Andrew's classmates alleged that she told a school counselor that Andrew planned to cut school and that he had said something about being "sick and tired of life" (p. 878). School authorities, however, denied having received any information about Andrew's suicidal ideation.

The parents' negligence suit was based on two claims. First, they contended that school authorities should have told them about Andrew's failing grades, his removal from the basketball team, his purported depression, and his absence from school on the day he committed suicide. Second, they claimed that the school counselor should have taken some sort of action after receiving information that Andrew was despondent. A Wisconsin intermediate case ruled in favor of the school defendants because under Wisconsin law suicide is an intervening or superseding force, "which breaks the line of causation from the wrongful act and does not render the defendant civilly liable" (p. 879). Thus, the court concluded that it was unnecessary to decide whether "the district had a duty to notify the McMahons or follow up on the student's report to a school counselor that Andrew was despondent" (p. 882).

In a 2009 case, *Corales v. Bennett*, the Ninth Circuit Court of Appeals ruled in a similar fashion, applying California law to a case in which Anthony Soltero, a middle school student, shot himself after being severely admonished by a school administrator for participating in a student walkout to protest a federal immigration reform bill. Anthony's parents sued the school administrator on a variety of federal constitutional theories as well as negligence, but the Ninth Circuit approved the dismissal of all claims.

Regarding the allegation of negligence, the Ninth Circuit concluded that a defendant can only be held liable for another's suicide if the defendant's acts cause the decedent to have "an uncontrollable impulse to commit suicide" (p. 573). Citing California case law, the Ninth Circuit ruled that a defendant is not liable for a person's suicide "where the negligent wrong only causes a mental condition in which the injured person is able to realize the nature of the act of suicide and has the power to control it if he so desires" (p. 572). The Ninth Circuit pointed out that Anthony attended classes after his meeting with the vice principal, spoke with his mother and a friend, and wrote a detailed suicide note. Thus, in the view of the Ninth Circuit Anthony "had the opportunity to appreciate the nature of his action" and Anthony's parents were unable to show that the vice principal's actions were the proximate cause of Anthony's suicidal act (p. 573).

In harmony with the Wisconsin decision and the Ninth Circuit's decision under California law, the New Hampshire Supreme Court also ruled that school officials cannot be held liable for the suicide of a student absent some type of egregious conduct. In *Mikell v. School Administrative Unit #33*, decided in 2009, Joshua Markiewicz, a middle school student, told a teacher's aide that he "wanted to blow his brains out" (p. 1053). The aide informed the school's counselor, who had Joshua sign a "contract for safety" and informed Joshua's mother about the incident (p. 1053). The counselor took no further action regarding the suicide threat, however, and about two months later Joshua died by suicide.

The New Hampshire Supreme Court ruled that school authorities could only be liable for the student's death if they had custodial care of the student (which they did not) or if they had engaged in "extreme and outrageous" conduct that "resulted in an uncontrollable impulse to commit suicide, or prevented the decedent from realizing the nature of his act" (p. 1054). In the New Hampshire court's view, no school employee had engaged in the requisite outrageous, causal conduct. Joshua's mother argued that the school counselor was in a "special relationship" with Joshua that imposed a duty on her under negligence principles to take action to prevent him from committing suicide. The court rejected this argument, finding that the counselor's relationship with Joshua did not involve the responsibility to "care for" Joshua in the sense of assuming full physical custodial control over him (p. 1057). Citing cases from other jurisdictions, the court declined to impose a special duty on the school counselor to prevent Joshua from killing himself.

Another barrier that has impeded common law liability for student suicide is illustrated by two appellate court decisions, one from Michigan (*Nalepa v. Plymouth-Canton Community School District*, 1994) and the other in Maryland (*Scott v. Montgomery County Board of Education*, 1997). In the Michigan case, a second-grade student committed suicide by hanging after watching a video at school that depicted a boy who twice tried to commit suicide, once by hanging. In both cases, the courts summarily disposed of the parents' negligence claims as amounting to educational malpractice, which these states and most other jurisdictions do not recognize.

The decedent's parents argued that teachers had a duty not to show the film to second graders. In other words, the teachers had "utilized improper materials in teaching their child" (p. 594). The appellate court characterized this allegation as a teacher malpractice claim, which the court refused to recognize. The court based its decision not to recognize an educational malpractice claim on three public policy considerations. "First," the court said, "we conclude that the injury to Stephen is out of proportion to any culpability of the teachers, or at least appears too highly extraordinary in relation to the alleged negligence" (p. 595). Second, the court feared that recognition of an educational malpractice claim "could lead to a flood of litigation that would be detrimental to our already overburdened educational system" (p 595). Third, the court expressed a strong reluctance "to embroil our courts into overseeing the day-to-day operations of our schools" (p. 595).

Similarly, in the Maryland case, a federal appellate court upheld the dismissal of a lawsuit brought by the mother of Aaron Scott, an eighth-grade student who died by suicide. Allegedly, the school psychologist had met with Aaron about 2 months before his death and—after conducting a suicide risk assessment and noting Aaron's remark that he would someday kill himself—determined that he was not in immediate danger of harming himself and failed to inform Aaron's parents about Aaron's comment threatening suicide. As a preliminary matter, the Fourth Circuit concluded that the alleged causal linkage to the school psychologist was insufficient as a matter of law. More specifically, the court reasoned that "from the record, which contains evidence of numerous stressors in Aaron's life, it is impossible to discern why Aaron tragically took his own life, and to conclude that the (school's) failures were causally related to Aaron's suicide is conjecture" (p. 17). Second, the court concluded that even if the parents' could prove causation, the mother's negligence claims could be categorized as educational malpractice, a cause of action not recognized in the state of Maryland.

In contrast, as of 2009 only one published court decision has held a district liable for negligence in the wake of a student's suicide. In *Wyke v. Polk County School Board* (1997), Shawn Wyke, a 13-year-old boy, committed suicide at home. However, the evidence revealed that he had first tried twice to kill himself by hanging while at school. Shawn's mother sued Shawn's school district for both common-law negligence and a Section 1983 constitutional tort. The trial court dismissed the constitutional claims, but allowed the negligence claim to go before the jury.

After hearing the evidence, the jury found the damages to total $500,000. However, the jury awarded Shawn's mother only about one-third of that amount, deciding that she and Shawn's caretaker at the time of his death were contributorily negligent for two-thirds of the total damages. On appeal, the Eleventh Circuit upheld the award, ruling that "when a child attempts suicide at school, and the school knows of the attempt, the school can be found negligent in failing to notify the child's parents or guardian" (p. 571). However, no school mental health professional or educator was liable or even implicated in this case.

CONSTITUTIONAL CLAIMS

Faced with such uphill judicial odds in state law negligence cases, parents of students who have committed suicide have sometimes sought to establish liability of school personnel via Section 1983 claims based on alleged violations of the federal Constitution. With one limited exception, the published federal court decisions have rejected such Section 1983 suicide claims (Fossey & Zirkel, 2004; Zirkel & Fossey, 2005). More specifically, in their pair of articles, Fossey and Zirkel analyzed all the published cases brought against school districts and their employees arising from student suicide that had been decided at the time. Their conclusion was that public school educators had little to fear from lawsuits arising from a student's suicide under the theory of constitutional liability, just as under the theory of common law negligence liability. Only one of the constitutional theory cases, *Scott v. Board of Education* (1997), involved school employees with counseling responsibilities (school psychologists); and the court in that case ruled that the decedent's parents had not provided enough evidence to show that school authorities' conduct proximately caused the student's suicide

Armijo v. Wagon Mound Public Schools, a 1998 case, is the only case to recognize a cause of action against school authorities based on a student's suicide. In that case, a New Mexico school principal suspended Philadelphio Armijo, a 16-year-old special-education student, after he allegedly threatened violence toward a teacher who had reported him for harassing an elementary school child. The principal directed a school counselor to drive Armijo home without attempting to contact Philadelphio's parents. His parents returned home later in the day and found Philadelphio dead from a self-inflicted gunshot wound. On the day of his death, Philadelphio reportedly told a school aide that he might be "better off dead" (p. 1256). In the view of the Tenth Circuit Court of Appeals, evidence had been submitted that arguably showed that the principal and counselor left Philadelphio at home alone, with access to a firearm, when they knew he was suicidal.

Several student-suicide cases alleging constitutional violations were decided in federal courts after *Armijo*, but none led to liability for any school employee. For example, in *Sanford v. Stiles* (2006), Michael Sanford, a 16-year-old high school student, gave Karen Martin, a high school girl Michael had once dated, a troubling note in which Michael mentioned suicide (p. 301). Apparently, Karen did not believe that Michael would actually kill himself. Nevertheless, she told her school counselor about the note's contents. This counselor gave a copy of the note to Michael's counselor, Pamela Stiles. According to the court:

> Stiles immediately called Michael into her office. She told Michael that some of his friends were worried about him, and that therefore she was worried about him. Stiles asked Michael if he was upset about some sort of situation with a girl, and he replied: "that was two months ago when I was upset about that. I'm not upset about that now." According to Stiles, Michael responded in a "very straightforward" manner." (p. 302)

During this conversation, Stiles asked Michael if he ever had plans to hurt himself or if he would do such a thing. He answered "'definitely not'" (p. 302). Stiles also asked Michael what she described as some "forward-thinking" questions, and she concluded in her view that Michael was not suicidal.

A few days later, Michael visited the guidance office again. On this occasion, Michael asked Stiles who had given her his note. Stiles declined to share that information with him, citing confidentiality considerations. Michael reportedly said, "Thanks, I thought that's what you would say. That's all I needed" (p. 302). According to Stiles, Michael "did not seem upset" during their interaction. That evening, Michael committed suicide. According to the court, Michael and his mother had an argument immediately before his death. Later, Michael's mother went looking for him and found that he had hanged himself from a door in the basement of the family's home.

Michael's mother sued Stiles on a constitutional theory, alleging that Stiles had increased the danger that Michael would kill himself. She also sued Stiles for negligence under Pennsylvania law. A federal trial court dismissed the suit, finding insufficient evidence for a jury to find that Stiles was liable. On appeal, the Third Circuit affirmed the trial court's decision. Under precedents of the Third Circuit, the appellate court explained, a plaintiff could only prevail on a constitutional claim under a state-created danger theory if the plaintiff could prove four elements:

(1) the harm ultimately caused was foreseeable and fairly direct;

(2) a state actor acted with a degree of culpability that shocks the conscience;

(3) a relationship between the state and the plaintiff existed such that the plaintiff was a foreseeable victim of the defendant's acts, or a member of a discrete class of persons subjected to the potential harm brought about by the state's actions, as opposed to a member of the public in general; and

(4) a state actor affirmatively used his or her authority in a way that created a danger to the citizen or that rendered the citizen more vulnerable to danger than had the state not acted at all. (pp. 304–305)

In the Third Court's view, Michael's mother could not prove at least two of the four required elements to establish a constitutional violation under a state-created danger theory. "Specifically, no reasonable jury could find (1) that Stiles acted with the requisite degree of culpability, or (2) that she "create [d] an opportunity that otherwise would not have existed for [harm] to occur" (p. 305). Furthermore, Michael's mother could not prevail on a common-law negligence claim because Stiles was immune from a negligence suit under Pennsylvania law. A key part of the Third Circuit's ruling was its conclusion that the language in Michael's note was not "a clear cry for help" (p. 311). The court pointed out that Michael's note referred to suicidal thoughts as having occurred in the past and that Karen Martin, the high school girl who received the note, "testified that the expression 'I want to kill myself' was used 'all the time' by her friends" (p. 311). In short, the Court concluded, "the link between the Defendants' conduct and Michael Sanford's untimely death is far too attenuated to justify imposition of liability" (p. 312). In making its decision, the court pointed out that Stiles had not ignored Michael's note. On the contrary, she promptly spoke with Michael and made a conscious decision that he was not suicidal.

CONCLUSION

In sum, parents/caregivers have succeeded in establishing liability for student suicide only rarely in the published case law under both common law and constitutional claims, and none of these decisions has resulted in a school-based mental health professional or other school employee being responsible for a damages award. There may be unpublished cases or settlements to the contrary, and the case law is subject to change in the future (this review runs only through 2009). However, the precedents to date strongly undercut any undue fear of school personnel liability at the K–12 level arising from student suicide.

Although a few courts have recognized a cause of action against school personnel for breaching a duty to prevent a student from committing suicide, a survey of all the cases on this topic shows that courts have to date been reluctant to hold school practitioners liable for these tragedies. Courts have ruled against plaintiffs in these cases on a variety of grounds: statutory immunity, the doctrine that suicide is an intervening cause of death for which third parties cannot be held liable, a refusal to recognize a claim that appears to be based in educational malpractice, or simply on lack of evidence showing that school employees were a contributing cause of the student's suicidal act. Moreover, in the wake of these tragic events, none of the published decisions has awarded monetary damages against a K–12 school counselor, school psychologist, or similarly situated professional staff member. In short, published cases decided at the time of this writing (i.e., through 2009) do not indicate a judicial trend toward finding educational institutions or their employees liable for student suicides..

Recommended Resources

SUICIDE PREVENTION ORGANIZATIONS

American Association of Suicidology
www.suicidology.org

American Foundation for Suicide Prevention
www.afsp.org

Columbia University Teen Screen Program
www.teenscreen.org

Iris Alliance Fund
www.irisfund.org

Jason Foundation
www.jasonfoundation.com

Jed Foundation
www.jedfoundation.org

Kristin Brooks Hope Center
www.hopeline.com

Link Counseling Center's National Resource Center for Suicide Prevention
www.thelink.org

National Council for Suicide Prevention
www.ncsp.org

National Organization for People of Color Against Suicide
www.nopcas.com

National Suicide Prevention Lifeline
www.suicidepreventionlifeline.org

Samaritans, Inc.
www.samaritansofboston.org

SOS Signs of Suicide
www.mentalhealthscreening.org

Suicide Awareness Voices of Education
www.save.org

Suicide Prevention Action Network USA
www.spanusa.org

Suicide Prevention Resource Center
www.sprc.org

Yellow Ribbon Suicide Prevention Program
www.yellowribbon.org

HEALTH, MENTAL HEALTH, AND EDUCATIONAL ORGANIZATIONS

American Academy on Child and Adolescent Psychiatry
www.aacap.org

American Counseling Association
www.counseling.org

American Psychological Association
www.apa.org

American School Counselors Association
www.schoolcounselor.org

American School Health Association
www.ashaweb.org

National Alliance for Mental Illness
www.nami.org

National Assembly on School-Based Health Care
www.nasbhc.org

National Association of School Nurses
www.nasn.org

National Association of School Psychologists
www.nasponline.org

National Association of Social Workers
www.naswdc.org

School Social Work Association of America
www.sswaa.org

JOURNAL

Suicide and Life-Threatening Behavior, official journal of the American Association of Suicidology (AAS), is published six times per year and is widely considered to be the premier journal in the United States devoted to the study of suicide and suicide prevention.

JOURNAL SPECIAL ISSUE

Miller, D. N., & Eckert, T. L. (Eds.). (2009). School-based suicide prevention: Research advances and practice implications [Special issue]. *School Psychology Review, 38*(2).

TRAINING OPPORTUNITY

The School Suicide Prevention Specialist Certification Program in an online training program provided by the American Association of Suicidology (AAS). For more details on this training opportunity, go to *www.suicidology.org.*

BOOKS

General Overviews of Suicide

Colt, G. H. (2006). *November of the soul: The enigma of suicide.* New York: Scribner.

This book provides a broad overview of suicide for the general reader, with sections on adolescent suicide, the history of suicide, the range of self-destructive suicidal behaviors, suicide prevention, the right to die movement, and suicide survivors. It is an excellent "starting point" for better understanding the many facets of suicide.

Hawton, K., & van Heeringen, K. (Eds.). (2000). *The international handbook of suicide and attempted suicide.* New York: Wiley.

This edited book by a wide range of international contributors includes chapters on a variety of topics related to suicide, including suicidal behavior in children and adolescents.

Jamison, K. R. (1999). *Night falls fast: Understanding suicide.* New York: Knopf.

Jamison is a professor of psychiatry at Johns Hopkins University and is one of the leading figures in the study of bipolar disorder. This book, written for the general reader, provides a useful and compelling introduction to understanding suicide.

Joiner, T. (2005). *Why people die by suicide.* Cambridge, MA: Harvard University Press.

Joiner is one of the leading figures in contemporary suicidology, and here he provides his theory as to why people die by suicide as well as the empirical and anecdotal evidence that supports it. Written for the general reader, this is one of the best introductions to suicide currently available.

Joiner, T. (2010). *Myths about suicide*. Cambridge, MA: Harvard University Press.

As its title indicates, this book discusses the many myths that surround suicide. It can be viewed as a companion volume to the earlier *Why People Die by Suicide*.

Shneidman, E. S. (1996). *The suicidal mind*. New York: Oxford University Press.

This book provides an overview of Shneidman's "psychache" theory of suicidal behavior, includes many case histories and is written in a compelling style for the general reader.

Shneidman, E. S. (Ed.). (2001). *Comprehending suicide: Landmarks in 20th-century suicidology*. Washington, DC: American Psychological Association.

This edited volume includes landmark papers related to study of suicide in the 20th century. It provides a useful historical overview of how thinking in the field has changed over time.

Suicidal Behavior in Children and Adolescents

Berman, A. L., Jobes, D. A., & Silverman, M. M. (2006). *Adolescent suicide: Assessment and intervention* (2nd ed.). Washington, DC: American Psychological Association.

Written by three highly influential suicidologists, this book provides the most comprehensive overview of adolescent suicide assessment and intervention currently available.

Gutierrez, P. M., & Osman, A. (2008). *Adolescent suicide: An integrated approach to the assessment of risk and protective factors*. DeKalb: Northern Illinois University Press.

This excellent book provides a wealth of useful information, including a thorough review of prominent risk and protective factors for youth suicide, empirically based self-report instruments, and a guide to the assessment of suicide risk in adolescents.

King, R. A., & Apter, A. (Eds.). (2003). *Suicide in children and adolescents*. New York: Cambridge University Press.

This edited volume includes 10 chapters by prominent suicidologists and covers a wide variety of topics in youth suicide.

Runyon, B. (2004). *The burn journals*. New York: Vintage.

This is a memoir by Brett Runyon, who at age 14 attempted suicide by lighting himself on fire. The book describes how he spent the next year recovering in hospitals and rehabilitation facilities, and provides a rare glimpse into youthful male desolation.

Wagner, B. M. (2009). *Suicidal behavior in children and adolescents*. New Haven, CT: Yale University Press.

This book provides an excellent overview of suicidal behavior in children and adolescents, including particularly helpful information on developmental issues, social relationships, and emotional regulation among suicidal youth.

Clinical Interviewing, Suicide Risk Assessment, and Managing Suicidal Risk

Goldston, D. B. (2003). *Measuring suicidal behavior and risk in children and adolescents*. Washington, DC: American Psychological Association.

This is a highly useful reference guide that provides psychometric data as well as other information on a wide assortment of suicide risk assessment measures for children and adolescents.

Jobes, D. A. (2006). *Managing suicidal risk: A collaborative approach*. New York: Guilford Press.

The book provides a detailed description of the Collaborative Assessment and Management of Suicidality (CAMS) approach. It provides step-by-step instructions and reproducible forms for evaluating suicide risk, treatment planning, and progress monitoring.

Joiner, T. E., Van Orden, K. A., Witte, T. K., & Rudd, M. D. (2009). *The interpersonal theory of suicide: Guidance for working with suicidal clients*. Washington, DC: American Psychological Association.

Written for mental health professionals, this book describes Joiner's interpersonal-psychological theory of suicidal behavior, as well as its practical implications for suicide risk assessment and intervention.

McConaughy, S. H. (2005). *Clinical interviews for children and adolescents: Assessment to intervention*. New York: Guilford Press.

This is the best book currently available on conducting clinical interviews with children and adolescents in school settings. It also contains a useful chapter on conducting suicide risk assessments. A second edition of the book is in preparation.

Rudd, M. D. (2006). *The assessment and management of suicidality*. Sarasota, FL: Professional Resource Press.

This thin (less than 100 pages) but compelling volume by one of the nation's leading suicidologists is a highly practical and useful guide to conducting suicide risk assessments and managing potentially suicidal clients.

Shea, C. S. (2002). *The practical art of suicide assessment: A guide for mental health professionals and substance abuse counselors*. New York: Wiley.

Providing an overview of how to conduct effective suicide risk assessments, this is one of the most comprehensive books currently available on the topic.

Assessment and Intervention for Youth Suicidal Behavior and Related Problems

Merrell, K. W. (2008). *Helping students overcome depression and anxiety: A practical guide* (2nd ed.). New York: Guilford Press.

This is the single best resource currently available for treating child and adolescent depression in school settings.

Miller, A. L., Rathus, J. H., & Linehan, M. M. (2007). *Dialectical behavior therapy with suicidal adolescents*. New York: Guilford Press.

This text provides an excellent overview of dialectical behavior therapy and how it can be used effectively with suicidal adolescents.

Miller, D. N., & Brock, S. E. (2010). *Identifying, assessing, and treating self-injury at school*. New York: Springer.

This is the first book to focus specifically on school-based assessment and intervention for non-suicidal self-injury, and provides a comprehensive overview of the topic.

Promoting Child and Adolescent Mental Health, Competence, and Wellness at School

Doll, B., & Cummings, J. A. (Eds.). (2008). *Transforming school mental health services: Population-based approaches to promoting competency and wellness of children*. Thousand Oaks, CA: Corwin Press.

This book takes a public health approach to mental health services in the schools, including a useful chapter on the schoolwide prevention and treatment of youth depression and suicidal behavior.

Gilman, R., Huebner, E. S., & Furlong, M. J. (Eds.). (2009). *Handbook of positive psychology in schools*. New York: Routledge.

This edited book is the first to apply the emerging science of positive psychology to schools. It contains many chapters that may be useful for preventing potentially suicidal behavior, including chapters on promoting gratitude, hope and optimism, and school connectedness.

Merrell, K. W., & Gueldner, B. A. (2010). *Social and emotional learning in the classroom: Promoting mental health and academic success*. New York: Guilford Press.

The book describes social and emotional learning programs in classrooms, including how to implement these programs and the benefits they provide for promoting mental health and academic achievement.

References

Adelman, H. S., & Taylor, L. (2006). *The school leader's guide to student learning supports: New directions to addressing barriers to learning.* Thousand Oaks, CA: Corwin Press.

Albers, C. A., Glover, T. A., & Kratochwill, T. R. (2007). Where are we, and where do we go now? Universal screening for enhanced educational and mental health outcomes. *Journal of School Psychology, 45,* 257–263.

Alvarez, A. (1971). *The savage god: A study of suicide.* New York: Norton.

Ambrose, S. E. (1990). *Eisenhower: Soldier and president.* New York: Simon & Schuster.

American Association of Suicidology. (2006). Youth suicide fact sheet. Retrieved May 13, 2008, from *www.suicidology.org.*

American Association of Suicidology. (2008). *Suicide postvention guidelines: Suggestions for dealing with the aftermath of suicide in the schools.* Washington, DC: Author.

Anderson, L., Walcott, C. M., Reck, S. G., & Landau, S. (2009). Issues in monitoring medication effects in the classroom. *Psychology in the Schools, 46,* 820–826.

Armijo v. Wagon Mound Public Schools, 159 F.3d 1253 (10th Cir. 1998).

Aseltine, R. H., & DeMartino, R. (2004). An outcome evaluation of the SOS suicide prevention program. *American Journal of Public Health, 94,* 446–451.

Ashworth, S., Spirito, A., Colella, A., & Benedict-Drew, C. (1986). A pilot suicidal awareness, identification, and prevention program. *Rhode Island Medical Journal, 69,* 457–461.

Bageant, J. (2007). *Deer hunting with Jesus: Dispatches from America's class war.* New York: Three Rivers Press.

Baker, J. A., Dilly, L., Aupperlee, J., & Patil, S. (2003). The developmental context of school satisfaction: Schools as psychologically healthy environments. *School Psychology Quarterly, 18,* 206–222.

Baker, J. A., & Maupin, A. M. (2009). School satisfaction and children's positive school adjustment. In R. Gilman, E. S. Huebner, & M. J. Furlong (Eds.), *Handbook of positive psychology* (pp. 189–196). New York: Routledge.

Baker, J., Terry, T., Bridger, R., & Winsor, A. (1997). Schools as caring communities. *School Psychology Review, 26,* 586–602.

Ballantine, H. T. (1979). The crisis in ethics, anno domini 1979. *New England Journal of Medicine, 301,* 634–638.

Barrett, T. (1985). *Youth in crisis: Seeking solutions to self-destructive behavior.* Longmont, CO: Sopris West.

Batsche, G. M., Castillo, J. M., Dixon, D. N., & Forde, S. (2008). Best practices in linking assessment to intervention. In A. Thomas & J. Grimes (Eds.), *Best practices in school psychology V* (pp. 177–194). Bethesda, MD: National Association of School Psychologists.

Baumeister, R. F. (1990). Suicide as escape from self. *Psychological Review, 97,* 90–113.

Baumeister, R. F., & Leary, M. R. (1995). The need to belong: Desire for interpersonal attachments as a fundamental human motivator. *Psychological Bulletin, 117,* 497–529.

Beautrais, A. (2007). Suicide by jumping: A review of research and prevention strategies. *Crisis: The Journal of Crisis Intervention and Suicide Prevention, 28*(Suppl. 1), 58–63.

Beck, A. T. (1996). Beyond belief: A theory of modes, personality, and psychopathology. In P. Salkovskis (Ed.), *Frontiers of cognitive therapy: The state of the art and beyond* (pp. 1–25). New York: Guilford Press.

Beck, A. T., Brown, G., & Street, R. A. (1989). Prediction of eventual suicide in psychiatric inpatients by clinical rating of hopelessness. *Journal of Consulting and Clinical Psychology, 57,* 309–310.

Beck, A. T., Kovacs, M., & Weissman, A. (1975). Hopelessness and suicidal behavior. *Journal of the American Medical Association, 234,* 1146–1149.

Beck, A. T., Rush, A. J., Shaw, B. F., & Emery, G. (1979). *Cognitive therapy of depression.* New York: Guilford Press.

Benneworth, O., Nowers, M., & Gunnell, D. (2007). Effects of barriers on the Clifton suspension bridge, England, on local patterns of suicide: Implications for prevention. *British Journal of Psychiatry, 190,* 266–267.

Berman, A. L. (2009). School-based suicide prevention: Research advances and practice implications. *School Psychology Review, 38,* 233–238.

Berman, A. L., Jobes, D. A., & Silverman, M. M. (2006). *Adolescent suicide: Assessment and intervention.* Washington, DC: American Psychological Association.

Berman, A. L., Litman, R. E., & Diller, J. (1989). *Equivocal death casebook.* Unpublished manuscript, American University, Washington, DC.

Berninger, V. W. (2006). Research-supported ideas for implementing reauthorized IDEA with intelligent professional psychological services. *Psychology in the Schools, 43,* 781–796.

Bhatia, S. K., Rezac, A. J., Vitello, B., Sitorius, M. A., Buehler, B. A., & Kratochvil, C. J. (2008). Antidepressant prescribing practices for the treatment of children and adolescents. *Journal of Child and Adolescent Psychopharmacology, 18,* 70–80.

Blachly, P. H., & Fairley, N. (1989). Market analysis for suicide prevention: Relationship of age to suicide on holidays, day of the week and month. *Northwest Medicine, 68,* 232–238.

Blaustein, M., & Fleming, A. (2009). Suicide from the Golden Gate Bridge. *American Journal of Psychiatry, 166,* 1111–1116.

Bond, L. A., & Carmola Hauf, A. (2004). Taking stock and putting stock in primary prevention: Characteristics of effective programs. *Journal of Primary Prevention, 24,* 199–221.

Borowski, I. W., Ireland, M., & Resnick, M. D. (2001). Adolescent suicide attempts: Risks and protectors. *Pediatrics, 107,* 485–493.

Bostwick, J. M. (2006). Do SSRIs cause suicide in children? The evidence is underwhelming. *Journal of Clinical Psychology, 62,* 235–241.

Bradvik, L., & Berglund, M. (2003). A suicide peak after weekends and holidays in patients with alcohol dependence. *Suicide and Life-Threatening Behavior, 33,* 186–191.

Brent, D. A. (1997). The aftercare of adolescents with deliberate self-harm. *Journal of Child Psychology and Psychiatry, 38,* 277–286.

Brent, D. A., Johnson, S., Bartle, S., Bridge, J., Rather, C., Matta, J., et al. (1993). Personality disorder, tendency to impulsive violence, and suicidal behavior in adolescents. *Journal of the American Academy of Child and Adolescent Psychiatry, 32,* 69–75.

Bridge, J. A., Goldstein, T. R., & Brent, D. A. (2006). Adolescent suicide and suicidal behavior. *Journal of Psychology and Psychiatry, 47*, 372–394.

Brock, S. E. (2002). School suicide postvention. In S. E. Brock, P. J. Lazarus, & S. R. Jimerson (Eds.), *Best practices in school crisis prevention and intervention* (pp. 211–223). Bethesda, MD: National Association of School Psychologists.

Brock, S. E., Sandoval, J., & Hart, S. (2006). Suicidal ideation and behaviors. In G. G. Bear & K. M. Minke (Eds.), *Children's needs III: Development, prevention, and intervention* (pp. 225–238). Bethesda, MD: National Association of School Psychologists.

Brown, J. H. (2001). Youth, drugs, and resilience education. *Journal of Drug Education, 31*, 83–122.

Brunstein Klomek, A., Marrocco, F., Kleinman, M., Schonfield, I. S., & Gould, M. S. (2008). Peer victimization, depression, and suicidality in adolescents. *Suicide and Life-Threatening Behavior, 38*, 166–180.

Burke, M. R. (2002). School-based substance abuse prevention: Political finger-pointing does not work. *Federal Probation, 66*, 66–71.

Burns, M. K., & Gibbons, K. A. (2008). *Implementing response-to-intervention in elementary and secondary schools*. New York: Routledge.

Burrow-Sanchez, J. J., & Hawken, L. S. (2007). *Helping students overcome substance abuse: Effective practices for prevention and intervention*. New York: Guilford Press.

Callahan, C. (2008). *Dialectical behavior therapy: Children and adolescents*. Eau Claire, WI: Pesi.

Callahan, V. J., & Davis, M. S. (2009). A comparison of suicide note writers with suicides who did not leave notes. *Suicide and Life-Threatening Behavior, 39*, 558–568.

Canetto, S. S., & Sakinofsky, I. (1998). The gender paradox in suicide. *Suicide and Life-Threatening Behavior, 28*, 1–23.

Carlson, J. S. (2008). Best practices in assessing the effects of psychotropic medications on student performance. In A. Thomas & J. Grimes (Eds.), *Best practices in school psychology V* (pp. 1377–1388). Bethesda, MD: National Association of School Psychologists.

Carlton, P. A., & Deane, F. P. (2000). Impact of attitudes and suicidal ideation on adolescents' intentions to seek professional psychological help. *Journal of Adolescence, 23*, 35–45.

Caron, J., Julien, M., & Huang, J. H. (2008). Changes in suicide methods in Quebec between 1987 and 2000: The possible impact of Bill C-17 requiring safe storage of firearms. *Suicide and Life-Threatening Behavior, 38*, 195–208.

Centers for Disease Control and Prevention. (2006). Suicide prevention scientific information: Consequences. Retrieved March 27, 2008, from *www.cdc.gov/ncipc/dvp/Suicide/Suicide-conque.htm*.

Centers for Disease Control and Prevention. (2007). Suicide trends among youths and young adults aged 10–24 years—United States—1990–2004. *Morbidity and Mortality Weekly Review, 56*, 905–908.

Ciffone, J. (1993). Suicide prevention: A classroom presentation to adolescents. *Social Work, 38*, 196–203.

Ciffone, J. (2007). Suicide prevention: An analysis and replication of a curriculum-based high school program. *Social Work, 52*, 43.

Cigularov, K., Chen, P. Y., Thurber, B. W., & Stallones, L. (2008). What prevents adolescents from seeking help after a suicide education program? *Suicide and Life-Threatening Behavior, 38*, 74–86.

Colt, G. H. (2006). *November of the soul: The enigma of suicide*. New York: Scribner.

Consensus Statement on Youth Suicide by Firearms. (1998). *Archives of Suicide Research, 4*, 89–94.

Corales v. Bennett, 567 F.2d 554 (9th Cir. 2009).

Cornell, D., & Williams, F. (2006). Student threat assessment as a strategy to reduce school violence. In S. R. Jimerson & M. J. Furlong (Eds.), *Handbook of school violence and school safety: From research to practice* (pp. 587–601). Mahwah, NJ: Erlbaum.

Crossan, J. D. (1994). *Jesus: A revolutionary biography*. New York: HarperCollins.

Cullen, D. (2009). *Columbine*. New York: Twelve.

Daniel, S. S., Walsh, A. K., Goldston, D. B., Arnold, E. M., Reboussin, B. A., & Wood, F. B. (2006). Suicidality, school dropout, and reading problems among adolescents. *Journal of Learning Disabilities, 39*, 507–514.

Darius-Anderson, K., & Miller, D. N. (2010). *School-based suicide prevention: Roles, functions, and level of involvement of school psychologists*. Unpublished manuscript.

Davis, J. M., & Sandoval, J. (1991). *Suicidal youth: School-based intervention and prevention*. San Francisco: Jossey-Bass.

Deane, F. P., Wilson, C. J., & Ciarrochi, J. (2001). Suicidal ideation and help negation: Not just hopelessness or prior help. *Journal of Clinical Psychology, 57*, 901–914.

Debski, J., Spadafore, C. D., Jacob, S., Poole, D. A., & Hixson, M. D. (2007). Suicide intervention: Training, roles, and knowledge of school psychologists. *Psychology in the Schools, 44*, 157–170.

De Leo, D., Dwyer, J., Firman, D., & Nellinger, K. (2003). Trends in hanging and firearm suicide rates in Australia: Substitution of method? *Suicide and Life-Threatening Behavior, 33*, 151–164.

Delizonna, L., Alan, I., & Steiner, H. (2006). A case example of a schoot shooting: Lessons learned in the wake of tragedy. In S. R. Jimerson & M. J. Furlong (Eds.), *Handbook of school violence and school safety: Research to practice* (pp. 617–629). Mahwah, NJ: Erlbaum.

DeMello, A. (1998). *Walking on water*. New York: Crossroad.

Dimeff, L., & Linehan, M. M. (2001). Dialectical behavior therapy in a nutshell. *The California Psychologist, 34*, 10–13.

Doll, B., & Cummings, J. A. (Eds.). (2008a). *Transforming school mental health services: Population-based approaches to promoting the competency and wellness of children*. Thousand Oaks, CA: Corwin Press.

Doll, B., & Cummings, J. A. (2008b). Why population-based services are essential for school mental health, and how to make them happen in your school. In B. Doll & J. A. Cummings (Eds.), *Transforming school mental health services: Population-based approaches to promoting the competency and wellness of children* (pp. 1–20). Thousand Oaks, CA: Corwin Press.

Domitrovich, C. E., Bradshaw, C. P., Greenberg, M. T., Embry, D., Poduska, J. M., & Ialongo, N. S. (2010). Integrated models of school-based prevention: Logic and theory. *Psychology in the Schools, 47*, 71–88.

D'Onofrio, A. A. (2007). *Adolescent self injury: A comprehensive guide for counselors and health care professionals*. New York: Springer.

DuPaul, G. J., & Carlson, J. S. (2005). Child psychopharmacology : How school psychologists can contribute to effective outcomes. *School Psychology Quarterly, 20*, 206–221.

Durkheim, E. (1897). *Le suicide: Etude de socologie*. Paris: F. Alcan.

Durlak, J. A. (2009). Prevention programs. In T. B. Gutkin & C. R. Reynolds (Eds.), *The handbook of school psychology, 4th ed.* (pp. 905–920). New York: Wiley.

Eckert, T. L., Miller, D. N., DuPaul, G. J., & Riley-Tillman, T. C. (2003). Adolescent suicide prevention: School psychologists' acceptability of school based programs. *School Psychology Review, 32*, 57–76.

Eckert, T. L., Miller, D. N., Riley-Tillman, T. C., & DuPaul, G. J. (2006). Adolescent suicide prevention: Gender differences in students' perceptions of the acceptability and intrusiveness of school-based screening programs. *Journal of School Psychology, 44*, 271–285.

Egan, M. P. (1997). Contracting for safety: A concept analysis. *Crisis, 18*, 17–23.

Eggert, L. L., Thompson, E. A., Herring, J. R., & Nicholas, L. J. (1995). Reducing suicide potential among high-risk youth: Tests of school-based prevention program. *Suicide and Life-Threatening Behavior, 25*, 276–296.

Eisel v. Board of Education of Montgomery County, 597 A.2d 447 (Md. 1991).

Emery, P. E. (1983). Adolescent depression and suicide. *Adolescence, 18,* 245–258.

Feigelman, W., & Gorman, B. S. (2008). Assessing the effects of peer suicide on youth suicide. *Suicide and Life-Threatening Behavior, 38,* 181–194.

Fein, R., Vossekuil, B., Pollack, W., Borum, R., Modzeleski, W., & Reddy, M. (2002). *Threat assessment in schools: A guide to managing threatening situations and to create safe school climates.* Washington, DC: U.S. Secret Service and Department of Education.

Fleishchman, A., Bertolote, J. M., Belfer, M., & Beautrais, A. (2005). Completed suicide and psychiatric diagnoses in young people: Examination of the evidence. *American Journal of Orthopsychiatry, 75,* 676–683.

Fleischmann, A., Bertolote, J. M., Wasserman, D., DeLeo, D., Bolhari, J., Botega, N. J., et al. (2008). Effectiveness of brief intervention and contact for suicide attempters: A randomized controlled trail in five countries. *Bulletin of the World Health Organization, 86,* 703–709.

Flora, S. R. (2000). Praise's magic ratio: Five to one gets the job done. *Behavior Analyst Today, 1,* 64–69.

Fossey, R., & Zirkel, P. A. (2004). Liability for a student suicide in the wake of *Eisel. Texas Wesleyan Law Review, 10,* 403–439.

Freedenthal, S. (2007). Racial disparities in mental health service use by adolescents who thought about or attempted suicide. *Suicide and Life-Threatening Behavior, 37,* 22–34.

Friend, T. (2003, October 13). Letters from California—Jumpers: The fatal grandeur of the Golden Gate Bridge. *The New Yorker,* 48–59.

Furlong, M. J., Morrison, G. M., & Jimerson, S. R. (2004). Externalizing behaviors of aggression and violence and the school context. In R. B. Rutherford, Jr., M. M. Quinn, & S. R. Mathur (Eds.), *Handbook of research in emotional and behavioral disorders* (pp. 243–261). New York: Guilford Press.

Garfinkel, B. D., Froese, A., & Hood, J. (1982). Suicide attempts in children and adolescents. *American Journal of Psychiatry, 139,* 1257–1261.

Garland, A. F., Shaffer, D., & Whittle, B. A. (1989). A national survey of school-based adolescent suicide prevention programs. *Journal of the American Academy of Child and Adolescent Psychiatry, 28,* 931–934.

Garland, A. F., & Zigler, E. (1993). Adolescent suicide prevention: Current research and social policy implications. *American Psychologist, 48,* 169–182.

Gibbons, R. D., Brown, C. H., Hur, K., Marcus, S. M., Bhaumik, D. K., Erkens, J. A., et al. (2007). Early evidence on the effects of regulators' suicidality warnings on SSRI prescriptions and suicide in children and adolescents. *American Journal of Psychiatry, 164,* 1356–1363.

Gillham, J. E., Brunwasser, S. M., & Freres, D. R. (2008). Preventing depression in early adolescence: The Penn resiliency program. In J. R. Z. Abela & B. L. Hankin (Eds.), *Handbook of depression in children and adolescents* (pp. 309–332). New York: Guilford Press.

Gilman, R., Meyers, J., & Perez, L. (2004). Structured extracurricular activities among adolescents: Findings and implications for school psychologists. *Psychology in the Schools, 41,* 31–41.

Gimpel Peacock, G., Ervin, R. A., Daly, E. J., & Merrell, K. W. (Eds.). (2010). *Practical handbook of school psychology: Effective practices for the 21st century.* New York: Guilford Press.

Goin, M. (2003). The "suicide prevention contract": Dangerous myth. *Psychiatric News, 18,* 3.

Goldney, R. D., & Fisher, L. J. (2008). Have broad-based community and professional education programs influenced mental health literacy and treatment seeking for those with major depression and suicidal ideation? *Suicide and Life-Threatening Behavior, 38,* 129–139.

Goldsmith, S. K., Pellmar, T. C., Kleinman, A. M., & Bunney, W. E. (2002). *Reducing suicide: A national imperative.* Washington, DC: National Academy Press.

Goldston, D. B. (2003). *Measuring suicidal behavior and risk in children and adolescents.* Washington, DC: National Academy Press.

Goldston, D. B., Davis Molock, S., Whitbeck, L. B., Murakami, J. L., Zayas, L. H., & Nagayama Hall, G. C. (2008). Cultural considerations in adolescent suicide prevention and psychosocial treatment. *American Psychologist, 63,* 14–31.

Goodenow, C. (1993). The psychological sense of school membership among adolescents: Scale development and educational correlates. *Psychology in the Schools, 30,* 79–90.

Gould, M. S., Greenberg, T., Munfakh, J. L., Kleinman, M., & Lubell, K. (2006). Teenagers' attitudes about seeking help from telephone crisis services (hotlines). *Suicide and Life-Threatening Behavior, 36,* 601–613.

Gould, M. S., Kalafat, J., Munfakh, J. L., & Kleinman, M. (2007). An evaluation of crisis hotline outcomes part 2: Suicidal callers. *Suicide and Life-Threatening Behavior, 37,* 338–352.

Gould, M. S., & Kramer, R. A. (2001). Youth suicide prevention. *Suicide and Life-Threatening Behavior, 31*(Suppl.), 6–31.

Gould, M. S., Marrocco, F. A., Kleinman, M., Thomas, J. G., Mostkoff, K., Cote, J., & Davies, M. (2005). Evaluating iatrogenic risk of youth suicide screening programs: A randomized control trial. *Journal of the American Medical Association, 293,* 1635–1643.

Gould, M. S., Munfakh, J. L. H., Lubell, K., Kleinman, M., & Parker, S. (2002). Seeking help from the internet during adolescence. *Journal of the American Academy of Child and Adolescent Psychiatry, 41,* 1182–1189.

Gould, M. S., Velting, D., Kleinman, M., Lucas, C., Thomas, J. G., & Chung, M. (2004). Teenagers' attitudes about coping strategies and help-seeking behavior for suicidality. *Journal of the American Academy of Child and Adolescent Psychiatry, 43,* 1124–1133.

Grant v. Board of Trustees of Valley View School District, 676 N. E.2d 705 (Ill. App. Ct. 1997).

Gratz, K. L. (2003). Risk factors for and functions of deliberate self-harm: An empirical and conceptual review. *Clinical Psychology: Science and Practice, 10,* 192–205.

Gray, C. E. (2007). The university-student relationship amidst increasing rates of student suicide. *Law and Psychology Law Review, 31,* 137–153.

Greco, L. A., & Hayes, S. C. (Eds.). (2008). *Acceptance and mindfulness treatments for children and adolescents: A practitioner's guide.* Oakland, CA: New Harbinger.

Greening, L., Stoppelbein, L., Fite, P., Dhossche, D., Erath, S., Brown, J., et al. (2007). Pathways to suicidal behaviors in childhood. *Suicide and Life-Threatening Behavior, 38,* 35–45.

Griffiths, A. J., Sharkey, J. D., & Furlong, M. J. (2009). Student engagement and positive school adaptation. In R. Gilman, E. S. Huebner, & M. J. Furlong (Eds.), *Handbook of positive psychology in schools* (pp. 197–211). New York: Routledge.

Groholt, B., & Ekeberg, O. (2009). Prognosis after adolescent suicide attempt: Mental health, psychiatric treatment, and suicide attempts in a nine-year follow-up study. *Suicide and Life-Threatening Behavior, 39,* 125–136.

Grossman, A. H., & D'Augelli, A. R. (2007). Transgender youth and life-threatening behaviors. *Suicide and Life-Threatening Behavior, 37,* 527–537.

Grossman, D. (1995). *On killing: The psychological cost of learning to kill in war and society.* Boston: Back Bay Books.

Gureasko-Moore, D. P., DuPaul, G. J., & Power, T. J. (2005). Stimulant treatment for attention-deficit/hyperactivity disorder: Medication monitoring practices of school psychologists. *School Psychology Review, 34,* 232–245.

Gutierrez, P. M., & Osman, A. (2008). *Adolescent suicide: An integrated approach to the assessment of risk and protective factors.* DeKalb: Northern Illinois University Press.

Gutierrez, P. M., & Osman, A. (2009). Getting the best return on your screening investment: Maximizing sensitivity and specificity of the Suicidal Ideation Questionnaire and Reynolds Adolescent Depression Scale. *School Psychology Review, 38,* 200–217.

Gutierrez, P. M., Watkins, R., & Collura, D. (2004). Suicide risk screening in an urban high school. *Suicide and Life-Threatening Behavior, 34*, 421–428.

Hammad, T. A., Laughren, T., & Racoosin, J. (2006). Suicidality in pediatric patients treated with antidepressant drugs. *Archives of General Psychology, 63*, 332–339.

Hawton, K. (2002). United Kingdom legislation on pack sizes of analgesics: Background, rationale, and effects on suicide and deliberate self-harm. *Suicide and Life-Threatening Behavior, 32*, 223–229.

Hawton, K., & Williams, K. (2001). The connection between media and suicidal behavior warrants serious attention. *Crisis: The Journal of Crisis Intervention and Suicide Prevention, 22*, 137–140.

Hayes, S. C., Follette, V. M., & Linehan, M. M. (Eds.). (2004). *Mindfulness and acceptance: Expanding the cognitive-behavioral tradition.* New York: Guilford Press.

Hayes, S. C., Strosahl, K. D., & Wilson, K. G. (1999). *Acceptance and commitment therapy: An experiential approach to behavior change.* New York: Guilford Press.

Hendin, H. (1987). Youth suicide: A psychosocial perspective. *Suicide and Life-Threatening Behavior, 17*, 151–165.

Hendin, H. (1991). Psychodynamics of suicide, with particular reference to the young. *American Journal of Psychiatry, 148*, 1150–1158.

Hendin, H., Brent, D. A., Cornelius, J. R., Coyne-Beasley, T., Greenberg, T., Gould, M. et al. (2005). Youth suicide. In D. I. Evans, E. B. Foa, R. E. Gur, H. Hendin, C. P. O'Brien, M. E. P. Seligman, & B. T. Walsh (Eds.), *Treating and preventing adolescent mental health disorders: What we know and what we don't know* (pp. 430–493). New York: Oxford University Press.

Higgins, E. T. (2004). Making a theory useful: Lessons handed down. *Personality and Social Psychology Review, 8*, 138–145.

Hoagwood, K., & Johnson, J. (2003). School psychology: A public health framework I. From evidence-based practices to evidence-based policies. *Journal of School Psychology, 41*, 3–21.

Hoberman, H. M., & Garfinkel, B. D. (1988). Completed suicide in youth. *Canadian Journal of Psychiatry, 33*, 494–502.

Holinger, P. C., Offer, D., Barter, J. T., & Bell, C. C. (1994). *Suicide and homicide among adolescents.* New York: Guilford Press.

Horn, W. F., & Tynan, D. (2001). Time to make special education "special" again. In C. E. Finn, A. Rotherham & C. R. Hokanson (Eds.), *Rethinking special education for a new century.* Washington, DC: Thomas B. Fordham Foundation and the Progressive Policy Institute.

Horner, R. H., Sugai, G., Todd, A. W., & Lewis-Palmer, T. (2005). School-wide positive behavior support. In L. Bambara & L. Kern (Eds.), *Individualized supports for students with problem behaviors: Designing positive behavior support plans* (pp. 359–390). New York: Guilford Press.

Hunt, T. (2006). *Cliffs of despair: A journey to the edge.* New York: Random House.

Institute of Public Health. (1988). *The future of public health.* Washington, DC: National Academy Press.

Jacob, S. (2009). Putting it all together: Implications for school psychology. *School Psychology Review, 38*, 239–243.

Jacob, S., & Hartshorne, T. S. (2007). *Ethics and law for school psychologists, 5th ed..* Hoboken, NJ: Wiley.

Jacobson, C. M., & Gould, M. (2007). The epidemiology and phenomenology of non-suicidal self-injurious behavior among adolescents: A critical review of the literature. *Archives of Suicide Research, 11*, 129–147.

Jamison, K. R. (1999). *Night falls fast: Understanding suicide.* New York: Knopf.

Jensen, P. (2002a). Closing the evidence-based treatment gap for children's mental health services: What we know versus what we do. *Report on Emotional and Behavioral Disorders in Youth, 2*, 43–47.

Jensen, P. (2002b). Nature versus nurture and other misleading dichotomies: Conceptualizing mental health and illness in children. *Report on Emotional and Behavioral Disorders in Youth, 2,* 81–86.

Jenson, W. R., Olympia, D., Farley, M., & Clark, E. (2004). Positive psychology and externalizing students in a sea of negativity. *Psychology in the Schools, 41,* 67–79.

Jimerson, S. R., Reschly, A. L., & Hess, R. S. (2008). Best practices in increasing the likelihood of high school completion. In A. Thomas & J. Grimes (Eds.), *Best practices in school psychology V* (pp. 1085–1097). Bethesda, MD: National Association of School Psychologists.

Jobes, D. A. (2003). Manual for the collaborative assessment and management of suicidality—revised (CAMS-R). Unpublished manuscript.

Jobes, D. A. (2006). *Managing suicidal risk: A collaborative approach.* New York: Guilford Press.

Joe, S., Canetto, S. S., & Romer, D. (2008). Advancing prevention research on the role of culture in suicide prevention. *Suicide and Life-Threatening Behavior, 38,* 354–362.

Joiner, T. E. (2005). *Why people die by suicide.* Cambridge, MA: Harvard University Press.

Joiner, T. E. (2009). Suicide prevention in schools as viewed through the interpersonal-psychological theory of suicidal behavior. *School Psychology Review, 38,* 244–248.

Joiner, T. E. (2010). *Myths about suicide.* Cambridge, MA: Harvard University Press.

Joiner, T. E., Conwell, Y., Fitzpatrick, K. K., Witte, T. K., Schmidt, N. B., Berlim, M. T., et al. (2005). Four studies on how past and current suicidality relate even when "everything but the kitchen sink" is covaried. *Journal of Abnormal Psychology, 114,* 291–303.

Joiner, T., Kalafat, J., Draper, J., Stokes, H., Knudson, M., Berman, A. L., & McKeon, R. (2007). Establishing standards for the assessment of suicide risk among callers to the National Suicide Prevention Lifeline. *Suicide and Life-Threatening Behavior, 37,* 353–365.

Joiner, T., Sachs-Ericsson, N., Wingate, L., Brown, J., Anestis, M., & Selby, E. (2006). Childhood physical and sexual abuse and lifetime number of suicide attempts: A persistent and theoretically important relationship. *Behaviour Research & Therapy, 45,* 539–547.

Joiner, T. E., Van Orden, K. A., Witte, T. K., & Rudd, M. D. (2009). *The interpersonal theory of suicide: Guidance for working with suicidal clients.* Washington, DC: American Psychological Association.

Joiner, T. E., Walker, R. L., Rudd, M. D., & Jobes, D. A. (1999). Scientizing and routinizing the assessment of suicidality in outpatient practice. *Professional Psychology: Research and Practice, 30,* 447–453.

Kabat-Zinn, J. (1990). *Full catastrophe living.* New York: Dell.

Kabat-Zinn, J. (1994). *Wherever you go, there you are: Mindfulness meditation in everyday life.* New York: Hyperion.

Kalafat, J. (2003). School approaches to youth suicide prevention. *American Behavioral Scientist, 46,* 1211–1223.

Kalafat, J., & Elias, M. (1994). An evaluation of a school-based suicide awareness intervention. *Suicide and Life-Threatening Behavior, 24,* 224–233.

Kalafat, J., Gould, M., Munfakh, J. L., & Kleinman, M. (2007). An evaluation of crisis hotline outcomes part 1: Nonsuicidal crisis callers. *Suicide and Life-Threatening Behavior, 37,* 322–337.

Kalafat, J., & Lazarus, P. J. (2002). Suicide prevention in schools. In S. E. Brock, P. J. Lazarus, & S. R. Jimerson (Eds.), *Best practices in crisis prevention and intervention* (pp. 211–223). Bethesda, MD: National Association of School Psychologists.

Kashani, J. H., Goddard, P., & Reid, J. C. (1989). Correlates of suicidal ideation in a community sample of children and adolescents. *Journal of the American Academy of Child and Adolescent Psychiatry, 28,* 912–917.

Kazdin, A. E. (2005). *Parent management training: Treatment for oppositional, aggressive, and antisocial behavior in children and adolescents.* New York: Oxford University Press.

Killen v. Independent School District No. 706, 547 N. W.2d 113 (Minn. Ct. App. 1996).

King, C. A. (1997). Suicidal behavior in adolescence. In R. W. Maris, M. M. Silverman, & S. S. Canettto (Eds.), *Review of suicidology, 1997* (pp. 61–95). New York: Guilford Press.

King, R., Nurcombe, R., Bickman, L., Hides, L., & Reid, W. (2003). Telephone counseling for adolescent suicide prevention: Changes in suicidality and mental state from beginning to end of a counseling session. *Suicide and Life-Threatening Behavior, 33*, 400–411.

King, R. A., & Apter, A. (Eds.). (2003). *Suicide in children and adolescents.* New York: Cambridge University Press.

Kingsbury, S. J. (1993). Clinical components of suicidal intent in adolescent overdoses. *Journal of the American Academy of Child and Adolescent Psychiatry, 32*, 518–520.

Kleck, G. (1988). Miscounting suicides. *Suicide and Life-Threatening Behavior, 18*, 219–236.

Kleck, G., & Delone, M. A. (1993). Victim resistance and offender weapon effects in robbery. *Journal of Quantitative Criminology, 9*, 55–81.

Klingman, A., & Hochdorf, Z. (1993). Coping with distress and self-harm: The impact of a primary prevention program among adolescents. *Journal of Adolescence, 16*, 121–140.

Klonsky, E. D., & Muehlenkamp, J. J. (2007). Self injury: A research review for the practitioner. *Journal of Clinical Psychology: In Session, 63*, 1045–1056.

Knipfel, J. (2000). *Quitting the Nairobi trio.* New York: Penguin Putnam.

Knitzer, J., Steinberg, Z., & Fleisch, B. (1991). Schools, children's mental health, and the advocacy challenge. *Journal of Clinical Child Psychology, 20*, 102–111.

Knox, K. L., Conwell, Y., & Caine, E. D. (2004). If suicide is a public health problem, what are we doing to prevent it? *American Journal of Public Health, 94*, 37–45.

Kohlenberg, R. J., & Tsai, M. (1991). *Functional analytic psychotherapy: Creating intense and curative therapeutic relationships.* New York: Plenum Press.

Kratochvil, C. J., Vitiello, B., Walkup, J., Emslie, G., Waslick, B., Weller, E. B., Burke, W. J., & March, J. S. (2006). Selective serotonin reuptake inhibitors in pediatric depression: Is the balance between benefits and risks favorable? *Journal of Child and Adolescent Psychpharmacology, 16*, 11–24.

Kratochwill, T. R., Albers, C. A., & Shernoff, E. (2004). School-based interventions. *Child and Adolescent Psychiatric Clinics of North America, 13*, 895–903.

Kratochwill, T. R., & Stoiber, K. C. (2002). Evidence-based interventions in school psychology. Conceptual foundations of the Procedural and Coding Manual of Division 16 and the Society for the Study of School Psychology. *School Psychology Quarterly, 17*, 341–389.

Kreitman, N., & Platt, S. (1984). Suicide, unemployment, and domestic gas detoxification in Britain. *Journal of Epidemiology and Community Health, 38*, 1–6.

LaFromboise, T., & Howard-Pitney, B. (1995). The Zuni life skills development curriculum: Description and evaluation of a suicide prevention program. *Journal of Counseling Psychology, 45*, 479–486.

Laye-Gindhu, A., & Schonert-Reichl, K. A. (2005). Non-suicidal self-harm among community adolescents: Understanding the "whats" and "whys" of self-harm. *Journal of Youth and Adolescence, 34*, 447–456.

Leenars, A., Wenckstern, S., Appleby, M., Fiske, H., Grad, O., Kalafat, J., Smith, J., Takahashi, Y. (2001). Current issues in dealing with suicide prevention in schools: Perspectives from some countries. *Journal of Educational and Psychological Consultation, 12*, 365–384.

Lester, D. (1979). Temporal variation in suicide and homicide. *American Journal of Epidemiology, 109*, 517–520.

Lester, D. (1988). One theory of teen-age suicide. *Journal of School Health, 58*, 193–194.

Lewin, K. (1951). *Field theory in social science: Selected theoretical papers.* New York: Harper & Row.

Lewinsohn, P. M., Rohde, P., Seeley, J. R., & Baldwin, C. L. (2001). Gender differences in suicide attempts from adolescence to young adulthood. *Journal of the American Academy of Child and Adolescent Psychiatry, 40*, 427–434.

Lewis, L. M. (2007). No-harm contracts: A review of what we know. *Suicide and Life-Threatening Behavior, 37*, 50–57.

Libby, A. M., Brent, D. A., Morrato, E. J., Orton, H. D., Allen, R., & Valuck, R. J. (2007). Decline in treatment of pediatric depression after FDA advisory on risk of suicidality with SSRIs. *American Journal of Psychiatry, 164,* 884–891.

Lieberman, R., & Poland, S. (2006). Self-mutilation. In G. G. Bear & K. M. Minke (Eds.), *Children's needs III: Development, prevention, and intervention* (pp. 965–976). Bethesda, MD: National Association of School Psychologists.

Lieberman, R., Poland, S., & Cassel, R. (2008). Best practices in suicide intervention. In A. Thomas & J. Grimes (Eds.), *Best practices in school psychology V* (pp. 1457–1472). Bethesda, MD: National Association of School Psychologists.

Lieberman, R. A., Toste, J. R., & Heath, N. L. (2009). Nonsuicidal self-injury in the schools: Prevention and intervention. In M. K. Nixon & N. L. Heath (Eds.), *Self-injury in youth: The essential guide to assessment and intervention* (pp. 195–215). New York: Routledge.

Linehan, M. M. (1993). *Cognitive-behavioral treatment of borderline personality disorder.* New York: Guilford Press.

Linn-Gust, M. (2010). *Rocky roads: The journeys of families through suicide grief.* Albuquerque, NM: Chellehead Works.

Livingston, G. (2004). *Too soon old, too late smart: Thirty true things you need to know now.* New York: Marlow & Company.

Lloyd-Richardson, E. E., Perrine, N., Dierker, L., & Kelley, M. L. (2007). Characteristics and functions of non-suicidal self-injury in a community sample of adolescents. *Psychological Medicine, 37,* 1183–1192.

Lofthouse, N., Muehlenkamp, J. J., & Adler, R. (2009). Non-suicidal self-injury and co-occurrence. In M. K. Nixon & N. L. Heath (Eds.), *Self-injury in youth: The essential guide to assessment and intervention* (pp. 59–78). New York: Routledge.

Lopez, S. J., Rose, S., Robinson, C., Marques, S. C., & Pais-Ribeiro, J. (2009). Measuring and promoting hope in schoolchildren. In R. Gilman, E. S. Huebner, & M. J. Furlong (Eds.), *Handbook of positive psychology in schools* (pp. 37–50). New York: Routledge.

Lubell, K. M., & Vetter, J. B. (2006). Suicide and youth violence prevention: The promise of an integrated approach. *Aggression and Violent Behavior, 11,* 167–175.

Luoma, J. B., Martin, C. E., & Pearson, J. L. (2002). Contact with mental health and primary care providers before suicide: A review of the evidence. *The American Journal of Psychiatry, 159,* 909–916.

Maag, J. W. (2001). Rewarded by punishment: Reflections on the disuse of positive reinforcement in schools. *Exceptional Children, 67,* 173–186.

Mandrusiak, M., Rudd, M. D., Joiner, T. E., Berman, A. L., Van Orden, K. A., & Witte, T. K. (2006). Warning signs for suicide on the Internet: A descriptive study. *Suicide and Life-Threatening Behavior, 36,* 263–271.

Mann, J. J. (1998). The neurobiology of suicide. *Nature Medicine, 4,* 25–30.

Mann, J. J., Apter, A., Bertolote, J., Beautrais, A., Currier, D., Haas, A., et al. (2005). Suicide prevention strategies: A systematic review. *Journal of the American Medical Association, 294,* 2064–2074.

Maris, R. W., Berman, A. L., & Silverman, M. M. (2000). *Comprehensive textbook of suicidology.* New York: Guilford Press.

Martin, G., Richardson, A. S., Bergen, H. A., Roeger, L., & Allison, S. (2005). Perceived academic performance, self-esteem and locus of control as indicators of need for assessment of adolescent suicide risk: Implications for teachers. *Journal of Adolescence, 28,* 75–87.

Martin, N. K., & Dixon, P. N. (1986). Adolescent suicide: Myths, recognition, and evaluation. *The School Counselor, 33,* 265–271.

Martinez, R. S., & Nellis, L. M. (2008). Response to intervention: A school-wide approach for promoting academic success for all students. In B. Doll & J. A. Cummings (Eds.), *Transforming school mental health services: Population-based approaches to promoting the competency and wellness of children* (pp. 143–164). Thousand Oaks, CA: Corwin Press.

Mazza, J. J. (1997). School-based suicide prevention programs: Are they effective? *School Psychology Review, 26,* 382–396.

Mazza, J. J. (2000). The relationship between posttraumatic stress symptomatology and suicidal behavior in school-based adolescents. *Suicide and Life-Threatening Behavior, 30,* 91–103.

Mazza, J. J. (2006). Youth suicidal behavior: A crisis in need of attention. In F. A. Villarruel & T. Luster (Eds.), *Adolescent mental health* (pp. 156–177). Westport, CT: Greenwood Publishing Group.

Mazza, J. J., & Eggert, L. L. (2001). Activity involvement among suicidal and nonsuicidal high-risk and typical adolescents. *Suicide and Life-Threatening Behavior, 31,* 265–281.

Mazza, J. J., & Reynolds, W. M. (2001). An investigation of psychopathology in nonreferred suicidal and nonsuicidal adolescents. *Suicide and Life-Threatening Behavior, 31,* 282–302.

Mazza, J. J., & Reynolds, W. M. (2008). School-wide approaches to prevention of and treatment for depression and suicidal behaviors. In B. Doll & J. A. Cummings (Eds.), *Transforming school mental health services* (pp. 213–241). Thousand Oaks, CA: Corwin.

McConaughy, S. H. (2005). *Clinical interviews for children and adolescents: Assessment to intervention.* New York: Guilford Press.

McCurdy, B. L., Mannella, M. C., & Eldridge, N. (2003). Positive behavior support in urban schools: Can we prevent the escalation of antisocial behavior? *Journal of Positive Behavioral Interventions, 5,* 158–170.

McMahon v. St. Croix Falls School District, 596 N. W.2d 875 (Wis. Ct. App. 1999).

Menninger, K. (1933). Psychoanalytic aspects of suicide. *International Journal of Psychoanalysis, 14,* 376–390.

Menninger, K. (1938). *Man against himself.* New York: Harcourt Brace.

Merrell, K. W. (2008a). *Behavioral, social, and emotional assessment of children and adolescents (third edition).* Mahwah, NJ: Erlbaum.

Merrell, K. W. (2008b). *Helping students overcome depression and anxiety: A practical guide (2nd ed.).* New York: Guilford Press.

Merrell, K. W., & Buchanan, R. (2006). Intervention selection in school-based practice: Using public health models to enhance systems capacity of schools. *School Psychology Review, 35,* 167–180.

Merrell, K. W., Ervin, R. A., & Gimpel, G. A. (2006). *School psychology for the 21st century: Foundations and practices.* New York: Guilford Press.

Merrell, K. W., Gueldner, B. A., & Tran, O. K. (2008). Social and emotional learning: A school-wide approach to intervention for socialization, friendship problems, and more. In B. Doll & J. A. Cummings (Eds), *Transforming school mental health services: Populations-based approaches to promoting the competency and wellness of children* (pp. 165–185). Thousand Oaks, CA: Corwin Press.

Middlebrook, D. L., LeMaster, P. L., Beals, J., Novins, D. K., & Manson, S. (2001). Suicide prevention in American Indian and Alaska Native communities: A critical review of programs. *Suicide and Life-Threatening Behavior, 31*(Suppl.), 132–149.

Mikell v. School Administrative Unit # 33, 972 A.2d 1050 (N. H. 2009).

Miller, A. L., Rathus, J. H., & Linehan, M. M. (2007). *Dialectical behavior therapy with suicidal adolescents.* New York: Guilford Press.

Miller, D. N., & Brock, S. E. (2010). *Identifying, assessing, and treating self-injury at school.* New York: Springer.

Miller, D. N., & DuPaul, G. J. (1996). School-based prevention of adolescent suicide: Issues, obstacles, and recommendations for practice. *Journal of Emotional and Behavioral Disorders, 4,* 221–230.

Miller, D. N., & Eckert, T. L. (2009). Youth suicidal behavior: An introduction and overview. *School Psychology Review, 38,* 153–167.

Miller, D. N., Eckert, T. L., DuPaul, G. J., & White, G. P. (1999). Adolescent suicide prevention: Acceptability of school-based programs among secondary school principals. *Suicide and Life-Threatening Behavior, 29,* 72–85.

Miller, D. N., Eckert, T. L., & Mazza, J. J. (2009). Suicide prevention programs in the schools: A review and public health perspective. *School Psychology Review, 38*, 168–188.

Miller, D. N., George, M. P., & Fogt, J. B. (2005). Establishing and sustaining research-based practices at Centennial School: A descriptive case-study of systemic change. *Psychology in the Schools, 42*, 553–567.

Miller, D. N., Gilman, R., & Martens, M. P. (2008). Wellness promotion in the schools: Enhancing students' mental and physical health. *Psychology in the Schools, 45*, 5–15.

Miller, D. N., & Jome, L. M. (2008). School psychologists and the assessment of childhood internalizing disorders: Perceived knowledge, role preferences, and training needs. *School Psychology International, 29*, 500–510.

Miller, D. N., & Jome, L. M. (in press). School psychologists and the secret illness: Perceived knowledge, role preferences, and training needs in the prevention and treatment of internalizing disorders. *School Psychology International.*

Miller, D. N., & McConaughy, S. H. (2005). Assessing risk for suicide. In S. H. McConaughy, *Clinical interviews for children and adolescents: Assessment to intervention* (pp. 184–199). New York: Guilford Press.

Miller, D. N., & Nickerson, A. B. (2006). Projective assessment and school psychology: Contemporary validity issues and implications for practice. *The California School Psychologist, 11*, 73–84.

Miller, D. N., Nickerson, A. B., & Jimerson, S. R. (2009). Positive psychology and school-based interventions. In R. Gilman, E. S. Huebner, & M. Furlong (Eds.), *Handbook of positive psychology in schools* (pp. 293–304). New York: Routledge.

Miller, D. N., & Sawka-Miller, K. D. (2009). A school-based preferential option for the poor: Child poverty, social justice, and a public health approach to intervention. In J. K. Levine (Ed.), *Low incomes: Social, health, and educational impacts* (pp. 31–56). New York: Nova Science.

Miller, D. N., & Sawka-Miller, K. D. (in press). Beyond unproven trends: Critically evaluating school-wide programs. In T. M. Lionetti, E. Snyder, & R. W. Christner (Eds.), *A practical guide to developing competencies in school psychology.* New York: Springer.

Miller, M., Azrael, D., & Hemenway, D. (2006). Belief in the inevitability of suicide: Results of a national survey. *Suicide and Life-Threatening Behavior, 36*, 1–11.

Miller, T. R., & Taylor, D. M. (2005). Adolescent suicidality: Who will ideate, who will act? *Suicide and Life-Threatening Behavior, 35*, 425–435.

Minois, G. (1999). *History of suicide: Voluntary death in western culture.* Baltimore, MD: Johns Hopkins University Press.

Mishara, B. L., & Daigle, M. (2000). Helplines and crisis intervention services: Challenges for the future. In D. Lester (Ed.), *Suicide prevention: Resources for the millennium* (pp. 153–177). Philadelphia: Brunner-Routledge.

Moskos, M. A., Achilles, J., & Gray, D. (2004). Adolescent suicide myths in the United States. *Crisis, 25*, 176–182.

Moskos, M., Olson, L., Halbern, S., Keller, T., & Gray, D. (2005). Utah youth suicide study: Psychological autopsy. *Suicide and Life-Threatening Behavior, 35*, 536–546.

Motohashi, Y., Kaneko, Y., Sasaki, H., & Yamaji, M. (2007). A decrease in suicide rates in Japanese rural towns after community-based intervention by the health promotion approach. *Suicide and Life-Threatening Behavior, 37*, 593–599.

Motto, J. A., & Bostrom, A. G. (2001). A randomized controlled trial of post-crisis suicide prevention. *Psychiatric Services, 52*, 828–833.

Muehlenkamp, J. J., & Gutierrez, P. M. (2004). An investigation of differences between self-injurious behavior and suicide attempts in a sample of adolescents. *Suicide and Life-Threatening Behavior, 34*, 12–23.

Muehlenkamp, J. J., & Gutierrez, P. M. (2007). Risk for suicide attempts among adolescents who engage in non-suicidal self-injury. *Archives of Suicide Research, 11,* 69–82.

Mulvey, E. P., & Cauffman, E. (2001). The inherent limits of predicting school violence. *American Psychologist, 56,* 797–802.

Nalepa v. Plymouth-Canton Community School District, 525 N. W.2d 897 (Mich. Ct. App. 1994).

Nally v. Grace Community Church, 253 Cal. Rptr. 97 (1988).

Nastasi, B. K., Bernstein-Moore, R., & Varjas, K. M. (2004). *School-based mental health services: Creating comprehensive and culturally specific programs.* Washington, DC: American Psychological Association.

Nation, M., Crusto, C., Wandersman, A., Kumpfer, K. L., Seybolt, D., Morrissey-Kane, E., et al. (2003). What works in prevention: Principles of effective prevention programs. *American Psychologist, 58,* 449–456.

National Institute of Justice. (2002). Preventing school shootings: A summary of a U.S. Secret Service safe school initiative report. *NIJ Journal, 248,* 10–15.

Nelson, C. M., Sprague, J. R., Jolivette, K., Smith, C. R., & Tobin, T. J. (2009). Positive behavior support in alternative education, community-based mental health, and juvenile justice settings. In W. Sailor, G. Dunlap, G. Sugai, & R. Horner (Eds.), *Handbook of positive behavior support* (pp. 465–496). New York: Springer.

Nelson, E. L. (1987). Evaluation of youth suicide prevention school program. *Adolescence, 22,* 813–825.

Nickerson, A. B., & Slater, E. D. (2009). School and community violence and victimization as predictors of adolescent suicidal behavior. *School Psychology Review, 38,* 218–232.

Nixon, M. K., & Heath, N. L. (Eds.). (2009). *Self-injury in youth: The essential guide to assessment and intervention.* New York: Routledge.

Nock, M. K., Joiner, T. E., Gordon, K. H., Lloyd-Richardson, E., & Prinstein, M. J. (2006). Non-suicidal self-injury among adolescents: Diagnostic correlates and relation to suicide attempts. *Psychiatry Research, 144,* 65–72.

Nock, M. K., Teper, R., & Hollander, M. (2007). Psychological treatment of self-injury among adolescents. *Journal of Clinical Psychology: In Session, 63,* 1081–1089.

Nordentoft, M., Qin, P., Helweg-Larsen, K., & Juel, K. (2007). Restrictions in means for suicide: An effective tool in preventing suicide: The Danish experience. *Suicide and Life-Threatening Behavior, 37,* 688–697.

Nuland, S. B. (1993). *How we die: Reflections on life's final chapter.* New York: Vintage Books.

O'Brien, K. M., Larson, C. M., & Murrell, A. R. (2008). Third-wave behavior therapies for children and adolescents: Progress, challenges, and future directions. In L. A. Greco & S. C. Hayes (Eds.), *Acceptance and mindfulness treatments for children and adolescents: A practitioner's guide* (pp. 15–35). Oakland, CA: New Harbinger.

O'Carroll, P. W., & Silverman, M. M. (1994). Community suicide prevention: The effectiveness of bridge barriers. *Suicide and Life-Threatening Behavior, 24,* 89–91.

Orbach, I., & Bar-Joseph, H. (1993). The impact of a suicide prevention program for adolescents on suicidal tendencies, hopelessness, ego identity, and coping. *Suicide and Life-Threatening Behavior, 23,* 120–129.

O'Toole, M. E. (2000). *The school shooter: A threat assessment perspective.* Quantico, VA: National Center for the Analysis of Violent Crime, Federal Bureau of Investigation.

Overholser, J. C., Hemstreet, A. H., Spirito, A., & Vyse, S. (1989). Suicide awareness programs in the schools: Effects of gender and personal experience. *Journal of the American Academy of Child and Adolescent Psychiatry, 28,* 925–930.

Overstreet, S., Dempsey, M., Graham, D., & Moely, B. (1999). Availability of family support as a moderator of exposure to community violence. *Journal of Clinical Child Psychology, 28,* 151–159.

Peña, J. B., & Caine, E. D. (2006). Screening as an approach for adolescent suicide prevention. *Suicide and Life-Threatening Behavior, 36*, 614–637.

Pfeffer, C. R. (1986). *The suicidal child.* New York: Guilford Press.

Pfeffer, C. R. (2003). Assessing suicidal behavior in children and adolescents. In R. A. King & A. Apter (Eds.), *Suicide in children and adolescents* (pp. 211–226). New York: Cambridge University Press.

Penney, D., & Stastny, P. (2008). *The lives they left behind: Suitcases from a state hospital attic.* New York: Bellevue Literary Press.

Phillips, D. P., & Feldman, K. (1973). A dip in deaths before ceremonial occasions. *American Sociological Review, 38*, 678–696.

Pierson, E. E. (2009). Antidepressants and suicidal ideation in adolescence: A paradoxical effect. *Psychology in the Schools, 46*, 910–914.

Pirkis, J., & Blood, R. W. (2001). Suicide and the media: Part II. Portrayal in fictional media. *Crisis: The Journal of Crisis Intervention and Suicide Prevention, 22*, 155–162.

Pirkis, J., Blood, R. W., Beautrais, A., Burgess, P., & Skehan, J. (2007). Media guidelines on the reporting of suicide. *Crisis: The Journal of Crisis Intervention and Suicide Prevention, 27*, 82–87.

Pokorny, A. (1992). Prediction of suicide in psychiatric patients: Report of a prospective study. In R. Maris, A. Berman, J. Maltsberger, & R. Yufit (Eds.), *Assessment and prediction of suicide* (pp. 105–129). New York: Guilford Press.

Poland, S. (1989). *Suicide intervention in the schools.* New York: Guilford Press.

Polsgrove, L., & Smith, S. W. (2004). Informed practice in teaching self-control to children with emotional and behavioral disorders. In R. B. Rutherford, M. M. Quinn, & S. R. Mathur (Eds.), *Handbook of research in emotional and behavioral disorders* (pp. 399425). New York: Guilford Press.

Power, T. J. (2003). Promoting children's mental health: Reform through interdisciplinary and community partnerships. *School Psychology Review, 32*, 3–16.

Power, T. J., DuPaul, G. J., Shapiro, E. S., & Kazak, A. E. (2003). *Promoting children's health: Integrating school, family, and community.* New York: Guilford Press.

Putnam, R., McCart, A., Griggs, P, & Choi, J. H. (2009). Implementation of schoolwide positive behavior support in urban settings. In W. Sailor, G. Dunlap, G. Sugai, & R. Horner (Eds.), *Handbook of positive behavior support* (pp. 443–463). New York: Springer.

Qin, P., Agerbo, E., & Mortenson, P. B. (2003). Suicide risk in relation to socioeconomic, demographic, psychiatric, and familial risk factors: A national register-based study of all suicides in Denmark, 1981–1997. *American Journal of Psychiatry, 160*, 765–772.

Quinn, K. P., & Lee, V. (2007). The wraparound approach for students with emotional and behavioral disorders: Opportunities for school psychologists. *Psychology in the Schools, 44*, 101–111.

Randall, B. P., Eggert, L. L., & Pike, K. C. (2001). Immediate post intervention effects of two brief youth suicide prevention interventions. *Suicide and Life-Threatening Behavior, 31*, 41–61.

Reisch, T., & Michel, K. (2005). Securing a suicide hot spot: Effects of a safety net at the Bern Muenster Terrace. *Suicide and Life-Threatening Behavior, 35*, 460–467.

Reisch, T., Schuster, U., & Michel, K. (2007). Suicide by jumping and accessibility of bridges: Results from a national survey in Switzerland. *Suicide and Life-Threatening Behavior, 37*, 681–687.

Reynolds, W. M. (1988). *Suicide Ideation Questionnaire: Professional Manual.* Odessa, FL: Psychological Assessment Resources.

Reynolds, W. M. (1991). A school-based procedure for the identification of students at-risk for suicidal behavior. *Family and Community Health, 14*, 64–75.

Reynolds, W. M., & Mazza, J. J. (1993). Suicidal behavior in adolescents: Suicide attempts in school-based youngsters. Unpublished manuscript.

Reynolds, W. M., & Mazza, J. J. (1994). Suicide and suicidal behavior. In W. M. Reynolds & H. F. Johnston (Eds.), *Handbook of depression in children and adolescents* (pp. 520–580). New York: Plenum.

Rich, C. L., Young, J. G., Fowler, R. C., Wagner, J., & Black, N. A. (1990). Guns and suicide: Possible effects of some specific legislation. *American Journal of Psychiatry, 147,* 342–346.

Richardson, A. S., Bergen, H. A., Martin, G., Roeger, L., & Allison, S. (2005). Perceived academic performance as an indicator of risk of attempted suicide in young adolescents. *Archives of Suicide Research, 9,* 163–176.

Richman, J. (1986). *Family therapy for suicidal people.* New York: Springer.

Rodgers, P. L., Sudak, H. S., Silverman, M. M., & Litts, D. A. (2007). Evidence-based practices project for suicide prevention. *Suicide and Life-Threatening Behavior, 37,* 154–164.

Rosenthal, P. A., & Rosenthal, S. (1984). Suicidal behavior by pre-school children. *American Journal of Psychiatry, 141,* 520–525.

Ross, C. P. (1980). Mobilizing schools for suicide prevention. *Suicide and Life-Threatening Behavior, 10,* 239–244.

Rudd, M. D. (2006). *The assessment and management of suicidality.* Sarasota, FL: Professional Resource Press.

Rudd, M. D., Berman, A. L., Joiner, T. E., Nock, M. K., Silverman, M., Mandrusiak, M., Van Orden, K., & Witte, T. (2006). Warning signs for suicide: Theory, research, and clinical applications. *Suicide and Life-Threatening Behavior, 36,* 255–262.

Rudd, M. D., Joiner, T. E., & Rajab, M. H. (1995). Help negation after acute suicidal crisis. *Journal of Consulting and Clinical Psychology, 63,* 499–503.

Rudd, M. D., Joiner, T. E., & Rajab, M. H. (2001). *Treating suicidal behavior: An effective, time-limited approach.* New York: Guilford Press.

Rudd, M. D., Mandrusiak, M., & Joiner, T. E. (2006). The case against no-suicide contracts: The commitment to treatment statement as a practice alternative. *Journal of Clinical Psychology, 62,* 243–251.

Rueter, M. A., Holm, K. E., McGeorge, C. R., & Conger, R. D. (2008). Adolescent suicidal ideation subgroups and their association with suicidal plans and attempts in young adulthood. *Suicide and Life-Threatening Behavior, 38,* 564–575.

Rueter, M. A., & Kwon, H. K. (2005). Developmental trends in adolescent suicidal ideation. *Journal of Research on Adolescence, 15,* 205–222.

Runyon, B. (2004). *The burn journals.* New York: Vintage.

Ruof, S., & Harris, J. (1988, May). Suicide contagion: Guilt and modeling. *NASP Communique, 18,* 8.

Rustad, R. A., Small, J. E., Jobes, D. A., Safer, M. A., & Peterson, R. J. (2003). The impact of rock music videos and music with suicidal content on thoughts and attitudes about suicide. *Suicide and Life-Threatening Behavior, 33,* 120–131.

Sanford v. Stiles, 456 F.3d 298 (3d Cir. 2006).

Satcher, D. (1998). Bringing the public health approach to the problem of suicide. *Suicide and Life-Threatening Behavior, 28,* 325–327.

Sawka-Miller, K. D., & McCurdy, B. L. (2009). Preventing antisocial behavior: Parent training in low-income urban schools. In J. K. Levine (Ed.), *Low incomes: Social, health and educational outcomes* (pp. 1–30). New York: Nova Science.

Sawka-Miller, K. D., & Miller, D. N. (2007). The third pillar: Linking positive psychology and school-wide positive behavior support. *School Psychology Forum, 2,* 26–38.

Scherff, A., Eckert, T. L., & Miller, D. N. (2005). Youth suicide prevention: A survey of public school superintendents' acceptability of school-based programs. *Suicide and Life-Threatening Behavior, 35,* 154–169.

Scott v. Montgomery County Board of Education, 1997 U.S. App. LEXIS 21258 (4th Cir. 1997).

Segal, Z. V., Williams, J. M. G., & Teasdale, J. D. (2002). *Mindfulness-based cognitive therapy for depression: A new approach to preventing relapse.* New York: Guilford Press.

Seiden, R. H. (1978). Where are they now? A follow-up study of suicide attempters from the Golden Gate Bridge. *Suicide and Life-Threatening Behavior, 8,* 1–13.

Seligman, M. E. P. (1992). *Helplessness: On depression, development, and death.* New York: Freeman.

Sewell, K. W., & Mendelsohn, M. (2000). Profiling potentially violent youth: Statistical and conceptual problems. *Children's Services: Social Policy, Research, and Practice, 3,* 147–169.

Shaffer, D., & Craft, L. (1999). Methods of adolescent suicide prevention. *Journal of Clinical Psychiatry, 60,* 70–74.

Shaffer, D., Garland, A., Gould, M., Fisher, P., & Trautman, P. (1988). Preventing teenage suicide: A critical review. *Journal of the American Academy of Child and Adolescent Psychiatry, 27,* 675–687.

Shaffer, D., Garland, A., Vieland, V., Underwood, M. M., & Busner, C. (1991). The impact of a curriculum-based suicide prevention program for teenagers. *Journal of the American Academy of Child and Adolescent Psychiatry, 30,* 588–596.

Shaffer, D., Gould, M. S., Fisher, P., Trautman, P., Moreau, D., Kleinman, M., & Flory, M. (1996). Psychiatric diagnoses in child and adolescent suicide. *Archives of General Psychiatry, 53,* 339–348.

Shaffer, D., Vieland, V., Garland, A., Rojas, M., Underwood, M., & Busner, C. (1990). Adolescent suicide attempters: Response to suicide prevention programs. *Journal of the American Medical Association, 264,* 3151–3155.

Shafii, M., & Shafii, S. L. (1982). Self-destructive, suicidal behavior, and completed suicide. In M. Shafii & S. L. Shafii (Eds.), *Pathways of human development: Normal growth and emotional disorders in infancy, childhood and adolescence* (pp. 164–180). New York: Thieme-Stratton.

Shea, S. C. (2002). *The practical art of suicide assessment.* Hoboken, NJ: Wiley.

Shinn, M. R. (2008). Best practices in using curriculum-based measurement in a problem-solving model. In A. Thomas & J. Grimes (Eds.), *Best practices in school psychology V* (pp. 243–261). Bethesda, MD: National Association of School Psychologists.

Shinn, M. R., & Walker, H. M. (Eds.). (2010). *Interventions for achievement and behavior problems in a three-tier model including RTI.* Bethesda, MD: National Association of School Psychologists.

Shipler, D. K. (2004). *The working poor: Invisible in America.* New York: Vintage.

Shneidman, E. S. (1985). *Definition of suicide.* New York: Wiley.

Shneidman, E. S. (1996). *The suicidal mind.* New York: Oxford University Press.

Shneidman, E. S. (2004). *Autopsy of a suicidal mind.* New York: Oxford University Press.

Shochet, I. M., Dadds, M. R., Ham, D., & Montague, R. (2006). School connectedness is an underemphasized parameter in adolescent mental health: Results of a community prediction study. *Journal of Clinical Child and Adolescent Psychology, 35,* 170–179.

Silenzio, V. M. B., Pena, J. B., Duberstein, P. R., Cerel, J., & Knox, K. L. (2007). Sexual orientation and risk factors for suicidal ideation and suicide attempts among adolescents and young adults. *American Journal of Public Health, 97,* 2017–2019.

Silverman, M. M., Berman, A. L., Sanddal, N. D., O'Carroll, P. W., & Joiner, T. E. (2007a). Rebuilding the tower of babel: A revised nomenclature for the study of suicide and suicidal behaviors part 1: Background, rationale, and methodology. *Suicide and Life-Threatening Behavior, 37,* 248–263.

Silverman, M. M., Berman, A. L., Sanddal, N. D., O'Carroll, P. W., & Joiner, T. E. (2007b). Rebuilding the tower of babel: A revised nomenclature for the study of suicide and suicidal behaviors part 2: Suicide-related ideations, communications, and behaviors. *Suicide and Life-Threatening Behavior, 37,* 264–277.

Simon, R. I. (2007). Gun safety management for patients at risk for suicide. *Suicide and Life-Threatening Behavior, 37,* 518–526.

Sinclair, M. F., Christenson, S. L., Hurley, C., & Evelo, D. (1998). Dropout prevention for high-risk youth with disabilities: Efficacy of a sustained school engagement procedure. *Exceptional Children, 65,* 7–21.

Smith, K., & Crawford, S. (1986). Suicidal behavior among normal high school students. *Suicide and Life-Threatening Behavior, 16,* 313–325.

Snyder, C. R., & Lopez, S. J. (2007). *Positive psychology: The scientific and practical exploration of human strengths.* Thousand Oaks, CA: Sage.

Solomon, A. (2001). *The noonday demon: An atlas of depression.* New York: Scribner.

Spirito, A., Overholser, J., Ashworth, S., Morgan, J., & Benedict-Drew, C. (1988). Evaluation of a suicide awareness curriculum for high school students. *Journal of the American Academy of Child and Adolescent Psychiatry, 27,* 705–711.

Srebnick, D., Cauce, A. M., & Baydar, N. (1996). Help-seeking pathways for children and adolescents. *Journal of Emotional and Behavioral Disorders, 4,* 210–220.

Stack, S. (2000). Suicide: A 15-year review of the sociological literature part I: Cultural and economic factors. *Suicide and Life-Threatening Behavior, 30,* 145–162.

Stack, S. (2003). Media coverage as a risk factor in suicide. *Journal of Epidemiology and Community Health, 57,* 238–240.

Stage, S. A., & Quiroz, D. R. (1997). A meta-analysis of interventions to decrease disruptive classroom behavior in public education settings. *School Psychology Review, 26,* 333–368.

Stanford, E., Goetz, R., & Bloom, J. (1994). The no-harm contract in the emergency assessment of suicidal risk. *Journal of Clinical Psychiatry, 55,* 344–348.

Steege, M. W., & Watson, T. S. (2008). Best practices in functional behavioral assessment. In A. Thomas & J. Grimes (Eds.), *Best practices in school psychology V* (pp. 337–347). Bethesda, MD: National Association of School Psychologists.

Steinhausen, H. C., Bösiger, R., & Metzke, C. W. (2006). Stability, correlates, and outcome of adolescent suicide risk. *Journal of Child Psychology and Psychiatry, 47,* 713–722.

Stengel, E. (1967). *Suicide and attempted suicide.* London, UK: Penguin.

Stoiber, K. C., & DeSmet, J. L. (2010). Guidelines for evidence-based practice in selecting interventions. In G. Gimpel Peacock, R. A. Ervin, E. J. Daly III, & K. W. Merrell (Eds.), *Practical handbook of school psychology: Effective practices for the 21st century* (pp. 213–234). New York: Guilford Press.

Stormont, M., Reinke, W. M., & Herman, K. C. (2010). Introduction to the special issue: Using prevention science to address mental health issues in schools. *Psychology in the Schools, 47,* 1–4.

Strein, W., Hoagwood, K., & Cohn, A. (2003). School psychology: A public health perspective I. Prevention, populations, and systems change. *Journal of School Psychology, 41,* 23–38.

Substance Abuse and Mental Health Services Administration, Office of Applied Studies. (September 17, 2009). *The NSDUH report: Suicidal thoughts and behaviors among adults.* Rockville, MD.

Sugai, G. (2007). Promoting behavioral competence in schools: A commentary on exemplary practices. *Psychology in the Schools, 44,* 113–118.

Sugai, G. & Horner, R. H. (2009). Defining and describing schoolwide positive behavior support. In W. Sailor, G. Dunlap, G. Sugai, & R. Horner (Eds.), *Handbook of positive behavior support* (pp. 307–326). New York: Springer.

Swearer, S. M., Espelage, D. L., Brey Love, K., & Kingsbury, W. (2008). School-wide approaches to intervention for school aggression and bullying. In B. Doll & J. A. Cummings (Eds.), *Transforming school mental health services: Population-based approaches to promoting the competency and wellness of children* (pp. 187–212). Thousand Oaks, CA: Corwin Press.

Tarasoff v. Regents of University of California, 131 Cal. Rptr. 14 (1976).

Tark, J., & Kleck, G. (2004). Resisting crime. *Criminology, 42,* 861–909.

Thompson, E. A., Mazza, J. J., Herting, J. R., Randell, B. P., & Eggert, L. L. (2005). The mediating roles of anxiety, depression, and hopelessness on adolescent suicidal behaviors. *Suicide and Life-Threatening Behavior, 35,* 14–34.

U.S. Department of Health and Human Services. (1999). *The Surgeon General's call to action to prevent suicide.* Washington, DC: Author.

U.S. Public Health Service. (2001). *National strategy for suicide prevention: Goals and objectives for action.* Rockville, MD: U.S. Department of Health and Human Services.

Van Dyke, R. B., & Schroeder, J. L. (2006). Implementation of the Dallas threat of violence risk assessment. In S. R. Jimerson & M. J. Furlong (Eds.), *Handbook of school violence and school safety: From research to practice* (pp. 603–616). Mahwah, NJ: Erlbaum.

Van Orden, K. A., Joiner, T. E., Hollar, D., Rudd, M. D., Mandrusiak, M., & Silverman, M. M. (2006). A test of the effectiveness of suicide warning signs for the public. *Suicide and Life-Threatening Behavior, 36,* 272–287.

Van Orden, K. A., Witte, T. K., Selby, E. A., Bender, T. W., & Joiner, T. E. (2008). Suicidal behavior in youth. In J. R. Z. Abela & B. L. Hankin (Eds.), *Handbook of depression in children and adolescents* (pp. 441–465). New York: Guilford Press.

Vieland, V., Whittle, B., Garland, A., Hicks, R., & Shaffer, D. (1991). The impact of curriculum-based suicide prevention programs for teenagers: An 18-month follow-up. *Journal of the American Academy of Child and Adolescent Psychiatry, 30,* 811–815.

Volpe, R. J., Heick, P. F., & Gurerasko-Moore, D. (2005). An agile behavioral model for monitoring the effects of stimulant medication in school settings. *Psychology in the Schools, 42,* 509–523.

Vossekuil, B., Fein, R. A., Reddy, M., Borum, R., & Modzeleski, W. (2002). *The final report and findings of the Safe School Initiative: Implications for the prevention of school attacks in the United States.* Washington, DC: Secret Service and U.S. Department of Education.

Wagner, B. M. (2009). *Suicidal behavior in children and adolescents.* New Haven, CT: Yale University Press.

Wagner, E. E., Rathus, J. H., & Miller, A. L. (2006). Mindfulness in dialectical behavior therapy (DBT) for adolescents. In R. A. Baer (Ed.), *Mindfulness-based treatment approaches: Clinician's guide to evidence base and applications* (pp. 167–189). San Diego, CA: Elsevier.

Walker, H. M., Horner, R. H., Sugai, G., Bullis, M., Sprague, J. R., Bricker, D., & Kaufman, M. J. (1996). Integrated approaches to preventing antisocial behavior patterns among school-age children and youth. *Journal of Emotional and Behavioral Disorders, 4,* 193–256.

Walsh, B. W. (2006). *Treating self-injury: A practical guide.* New York: Guilford Press.

Weiss, B., Catron, T., Harris, V., & Phung, T. (1999). The effectiveness of traditional child psychotherapy. *Journal of Consulting and Clinical Psychology, 67,* 82–94.

Weiss, C. H., Murphy-Graham, E., & Birkeland, S. (2005). An alternate route to policy influence: How evaluators affect D. A.R. E. *American Journal of Evaluation, 26,* 12–30.

Whitaker, R. (2010). *Mad in America: Bad science, bad medicine, and the enduring mistreatment of the mentally ill (second edition).* New York: Basic Books.

Williams, M. (2001). *Suicide and attempted suicide.* London: Penguin Books.

Witmer, L. (1907/1996). Clinical psychology. *American Psychologist, 51,* 248–251. (Reprinted from *Psychological Clinic, 1,* 1–9).

Woodbury, K. A., Roy, R., & Indik, J. (2008). Dialectical behavior therapy for adolescents with borderline features. In L. A. Greco & S. C. Hayes (Eds.), *Acceptance and mindfulness treatments for children and adolescents: A practical guide* (pp. 115–138). Oakland, CA: New Harbinger.

Woods, D. S. (2006). *Breaking point: Fighting to end America's teenage suicide epidemic!* Trafford Publications: Victoria, BC.

Woodside, M., & McClam, T. (1998). *An introduction to human services* (3rd ed.). Pacific Grove, CA: Brookes/Cole.

Wyke v. Polk County School Board, 129 F.3d 560 (11th Cir. 1997).

Ying, Y., & Chang, K. (2009). A study of suicide and socioeconomic factors. *Suicide and Life-Threatening Behavior, 39,* 214–226.

Zenere, F. J., III., & Lazarus, P. J. (1997). The decline of youth suicidal behavior in an urban multicultural school system following the introduction of a suicide prevention and intervention program. *Suicide and Life-Threatening Behavior, 16,* 360–378.

Zenere, F. J., III, & Lazarus, P. J. (2009). The sustained reduction of youth suicidal behavior in an urban multicultural school district. *School Psychology Review, 38,* 189–199.

Zirkel, P. A., & Fossey, R. (2005). Liability for student suicide. *West's Education Law Reporter, 197,* 489–497.

Zwaaswijk, M., Van der Ende, J., Verhaak, P. F., Bensing, J. M., & Vernhulst, F. C. (2003). Help seeking for emotional and behavioural problems in children and adolescents: A review of recent literature. *European Child and Adolescent Psychiatry, 12,* 153–161.

Index